CRIT

in print
for 16 50

The Rhetoric
of Romanticism

The Rhetoric
of Romanticism

Paul de Man

Columbia University Press

NEW YORK

Library of Congress Cataloging in Publication Data

Man, Paul de.
The rhetoric of romanticism.

Reprint of essays originally written 1956–1983.
Bibliography: p.
Includes index.
Contents: Intentional structure of the romantic
image—The image of Rousseau in the poetry of Hölderlin
—Wordsworth and Hölderlin—[etc.]
    1. European poetry—19th century—History and criti-
cism—Addresses, essays, lectures.   2. Romanticism—
Europe—Addresses, essays, lectures.   I. Title.
PN1261.M3 1984   809.1'9145   84-3213
ISBN 0-231-05526-9 (pbk. : alk. paper)
ISBN 0-231-05527-7   (pa.)

Columbia University Press
New York   Guildford, Surrey

Printed in the United States of America

p 10 9 8 7 6 5 4 3 2

Contents

Preface   vii

1. Intentional Structure of the Romantic Image   1
2. The Image of Rousseau in the Poetry of Hölderlin   19
3. Wordsworth and Hölderlin   47
4. Autobiography As De-Facement   67
5. Wordsworth and the Victorians   83
6. Shelley Disfigured   93
7. Symbolic Landscape in Wordsworth and Yeats   125
8. Image and Emblem in Yeats   145
9. Anthropomorphism and Trope in the Lyric   239
10. Aesthetic Formalization: Kleist's *Über das Marionettentheater*   263
Notes   291
Bibliography for Essay 8   315
Notes on Permissions   321
Index   323

Preface

THIS COLLECTION of essays on the general topic of European romantic and post-romantic literature was established at the initiative of William P. Germano, Editor-in-Chief at the Columbia University Press. It gathers articles written over a period of more than twenty-five years, between 1956 and the present. When the project was suggested to me, I agreed to write two new essays partly to indicate how I would approach such material today. With the possible addition of the essay entitled "The Rhetoric of Temporality" (now reprinted in a new edition of *Blindness and Insight*), the collection represents the main bulk of what I have written on romanticism. Except for some passing allusions, *Allegories of Reading* is in no way a book about romanticism or its heritage.

The principle of selection for this volume is clearly historical: all the essays deal with romantic poetry and its aftermath. The historical topology makes sense to the extent that the original papers were part of a project that was itself historically oriented. The choice of authors is banal enough to require no further justification, and so is the inclusion of later poets such as Baudelaire or Yeats. The chapter on Yeats, the latest poet to be considered, is also the earliest written, since it is part of a Harvard dissertation I wrote during the fifties. The reason for its inclusion is hardly sentimental: I saw no reason to resurrect other parts of the thesis, dealing with Mallarmé and other, more purely thematic, aspects of Yeats. They all now appear dated and left behind by more recent work on these authors. The Yeats chapter entitled "Image and Emblem," however, as its title suggests, was already a rhetorical analysis of figural language *avant la lettre,* anticipating a mode that would later become predominant for me. Like Monsieur Jourdain's proverbial prose, I was apparently doing rhetorical analysis before I knew that such a thing existed by name. Although I would certainly not use the same terminology and tone nowadays, the methodological trend is unmistakable. And since, as far as I know, this kind of approach has not prevailed in the critical literature on Yeats since 1960, its inclusion becomes a kind of test for the exegetic powers of figural analysis, of its capacity to help in understanding the work of a major and difficult modern poet.

I would never have by myself undertaken the task of establishing such a collection and, grateful as I am to Bill Germano for his initiative, I confess that I still look back upon it with some misgivings. Such massive evidence of the failure to make the various individual readings coalesce is a somewhat melancholy spectacle. The fragmentary aspect of the whole is made more obvious still by the hypotactic manner that prevails in each of the essays taken in isolation, by the continued attempt, however ironized, to present a closed and linear argument. This apparent coherence *within* each essay is not matched by a corresponding coherence *between* them. Laid out diachronically in a roughly chronological sequence, they do not evolve in a manner that easily allows for dialectical progression or, ultimately, for historical totalization. Rather, it seems that they always start again from scratch and that their conclusions fail to add up to anything. If some secret principle of summation is at work here, I do not feel qualified to articulate it and, as far as the general question of romanticism is concerned, I must leave the task of its historical definition to others. I have myself taken refuge in more theoretical inquiries into the problems of figural language. Not that I believe that such a historical enterprise, in the case of romanticism, is doomed from the start: one is all too easily tempted to rationalize personal shortcoming as theoretical impossibility and, especially among younger scholars, there is ample evidence that the historical study of romanticism is being successfully pursued. But it certainly has become a far from easy task. One feels at times envious of those who can continue to do literary history as if nothing had happened in the sphere of theory, but one cannot help but feel somewhat suspicious of their optimism. *The Rhetoric of Romanticism* should at least help to document some of the difficulties it fails to resolve.

Some literary historians and theoreticians have made the fragmentary nature of post-romantic literature a stylistic principle of their own critical discourse. Adorno's claim, in his *Aesthetic Theory*, for the exemplary character of parataxis—which he established interestingly enough, in connection with the poetry of Hölderlin, the obvious stumbling block of my own enterprise—is a prominent instance,[1] as are Erich Auerbach's references to the fragmentary style of his own book in the final chapter of *Mimesis*.[2] I can, of course, make no such claims. I feel myself compelled to repeated frustration in a persistent attempt to write as if a dialectical summation were possible beyond the breaks and interruptions that the readings disclose. The apparent resignation to aphorism and parataxis is often an attempt to recuperate on the level of style what is lost on the level of history. By stating the inevitability of fragmentation in a mode that is itself fragmented, one restores the aesthetic unity of manner and substance that may well be what is in question in the historical study of romanticism. Such is the cost of discursive elegance, a small price to pay, perhaps, compared to the burden of constantly falling back to nought. The only place where I come close to facing some of these questions about history and fragmentation is in the essay on Shelley's *The Triumph of Life*. How and where one goes on from there is far from clear, but certainly no longer simply a matter of syntax and diction.

All texts are reprinted as they are written, except for some minor grammatical alterations, and no attempt has been made to update the terminology or the tone.

1983   Paul de Man

The Rhetoric
of Romanticism

1
Intentional Structure of the Romantic Image

IN THE history of Western literature, the importance of the image as a dimension of poetic language does not remain constant. One could conceive of an organization of this history in terms of the relative prominence and the changing structure of metaphor. French poetry of the sixteenth century is obviously richer and more varied in images than that of the seventeenth, and medieval poetry of the fifteenth century has a different kind of imagery than that of the thirteenth. The most recent change remote enough to be part of history takes place toward the end of the eighteenth century and coincides with the advent of romanticism. In a statement of which equivalences can be found in all European literatures, Wordsworth reproaches Pope for having abandoned the imaginative use of figural diction in favor of a merely decorative allegorization. Meanwhile the term *imagination* steadily grows in importance and complexity in the critical as well as in the poetic texts of the period. This evolution in poetic terminology—of which parallel instances could easily be found in France and in Germany—corresponds to a profound change

in the texture of poetic diction. The change often takes the form
of a return to a greater concreteness, a proliferation of natural
objects that restores to the language the material substantiality
which had been partially lost. At the same time, in accordance
with a dialectic that is more paradoxical than may appear at
first sight, the structure of the language becomes increasingly
metaphorical and the image—be it under the name of symbol
or even of myth—comes to be considered as the most prominent dimension of the style. This tendency is still prevalent today, among poets as well as among critics. We find it quite
natural that theoretical studies such as, for example, those of
Gaston Bachelard in France, of Northrop Frye in America, or
of William Empson in England should take the metaphor as
their starting point for an investigation of literature in general—an approach that would have been inconceivable for
Boileau, for Pope, and even still for Diderot.

An abundant imagery coinciding with an equally abundant quantity of natural objects, the theme of imagination linked
closely to the theme of nature, such is the fundamental ambiguity that characterizes the poetics of romanticism. The tension between the two polarities never ceases to be problematic. We shall try to illustrate the structure of this latent tension
as it appears in some selected poetic passages.

In a famous poem, Hölderlin speaks of a time at which
"the gods" will again be an actual presence to man:

> . . . nun aber nennt er sein Liebstes,
> Nun, nun müssen dafür Worte, wie Blumen,
>   entstehn.
>
> ("Brot und Wein," stanza 5)

Taken by itself, this passage is not necessarily a statement
about the image: Hölderlin merely speaks of words (*"Worte"*),
not of images (*"Bilder"*). But the lines themselves contain the
image of the flower in the simplest and most explicit of all
metaphorical structures, as a straightforward simile introduced by the conjunction *wie*. That the words referred to are
not those of ordinary speech is clear from the verb: to origi-

nate (*"entstehn"*). In everyday use words are exchanged and put to a variety of tasks, but they are not supposed to originate anew; on the contrary, one wants them to be as well-known, as "common" as possible, to make certain that they will obtain for us what we want to obtain. They are used as established signs to confirm that something is recognized as being the same as before; and re-cognition excludes pure origination. But in poetic language words are not used as signs, not even as names, but in order to *name:* "Donner un sens plus pur aux mots de la tribu" (Mallarmé) or "erfand er für die Dinge eigene Namen" (Stefan George): poets know of the act of naming—"nun aber *nennt* er sein Liebstes"—as implying a return to the source, to the pure motion of experience at its beginning.

The word "entstehn" establishes another fundamental distinction. The two terms of the simile are not said to be identical with one another (the word = the flower), nor analogous in their general mode of being (the word is like the flower), but specifically in the way they originate (the word originates like the flower).[1] The similarity between the two terms does not reside in their essence (identity), or in their appearance (analogy), but in the manner in which both originate. And Hölderlin is not speaking of any poetic word taken at random, but of an authentic word that fulfills its highest function in naming being as a presence. We could infer, then, that the fundamental intent of the poetic word is to originate in the same manner as what Hölderlin here calls "flowers." The image is essentially a kinetic process: it does not dwell in a static state where the two terms could be separated and reunited by analysis; the first term of the simile (here, "words") has no independent existence, poetically speaking, prior to the metaphorical statement. It originates with the statement, in the manner suggested by the flower image, and its way of being is determined by the manner in which it originates. The metaphor requires that we begin by forgetting all we have previously known about "words"—"donner un sens plus pur aux mots de la tribu"—and then informing the term with a dynamic existence similar to that which animates the "flowers." The metaphor is not a combination of two entities or experiences more or less deliberately linked together, but one single and particular experience: that of origination.

How do flowers originate? They rise out of the earth without the assistance of imitation or analogy. They do not follow a model other than themselves which they copy or from which they derive the pattern of their growth. By calling them *natural* objects, we mean that their origin is determined by nothing but their own being. Their becoming coincides at all times with the mode of their origination: it is as flowers that their history is what it is, totally defined by their identity. There is no wavering in the status of their existence: existence and essence coincide in them at all times. Unlike words, which originate like something else ("like flowers"), flowers originate like themselves: they are literally what they are, definable without the assistance of metaphor. It would follow then, since the intent of the poetic word is to originate like the flower, that it strives to banish all metaphor, to become entirely literal.

We can understand origin only in terms of difference: the source springs up because of the need to be somewhere or something else than what is now here. The word "entstehn," with its distancing prefix, equates origin with negation and difference. But the natural object, safe in its immediate being, seems to have no beginning and no end. Its permanence is carried by the stability of its being, whereas a beginning implies a negation of permanence, the discontinuity of a death in which an entity relinquishes its specificity and leaves it behind, like an empty shell. Entities engendered by consciousness originate in this fashion, but for natural entities like the flower, the process is entirely different. They originate out of a being which does not differ from them in essence but contains the totality of their individual manifestations within itself. All particular flowers can at all times establish an immediate identity with an original Flower, of which they are as many particular emanations. The original entity, which has to contain an infinity of manifestations of a common essence, in

an infinity of places and at an infinity of moments, is necessarily transcendental. Trying to conceive of the natural object
in terms of origin leads to a transcendental concept of the Idea:
the quest for the Idea that takes the natural object for its starting point begins with the incarnated "minute particular" and
works its way upward to a transcendental essence. Beyond
the Idea, it searches for Being as the category which contains
essences in the same manner that the Idea contains particulars. Because they are natural objects, flowers originate as incarnations of a transcendental principle. "Wie Blumen entstehn" is to become present as a natural emanation of a
transcendental principle, as an epiphany.

Strictly speaking, an epiphany cannot be a beginning, since
it reveals and unveils what, by definition, could never have
ceased to be there. Rather, it is the rediscovery of a permanent
presence which has chosen to hide itself from us—unless it is
we who have the power to hide from it:

> So ist der Mensch; wenn da ist das Gut, und es sorget
>   mit Gaaben
> Selber ein Gott für ihn, kennet und sieht er es nicht.
>   ("Brot und Wein," stanza 5)

Since the presence of a transcendental principle, in fact conceived as omnipresence (parousia), can be hidden from man
by man's own volition, the epiphany appears in the guise of a
beginning rather than a discovery. Hölderlin's phrase: "Wie
Blumen entstehn" is in fact a paradox, since origination is inconceivable on the ontological level; the ease with which we
nevertheless accept it is indicative of our desire to forget. Our
eagerness to accept the statement, the "beauty" of the line,
stems from the fact that it combines the poetic seduction of
beginnings contained in the word "entstehn" with the ontological stability of the natural object—but this combination is
made possible only by a deliberate forgetting of the transcendental nature of the source.

That this forgetting, this ignorance, is also painful becomes apparent from the strategic choice of the word "flower,"

an object that seems intrinsically desirable. The effect of the line would have been thoroughly modified if Hölderlin had written, for instance, "Steinen" instead of "Blumen," although the relevance of the comparison would have remained intact as long as human language was being compared to a natural thing. The obviously desirable sensory aspects of the flower express the ambivalent aspiration toward a forgotten presence that gave rise to the image, for it is in experiencing the material presence of the particular flower that the desire arises to be reborn in the manner of a natural creation. The image is inspired by a nostalgia for the natural object, expanding to become nostalgia for the origin of this object. Such a nostalgia can only exist when the transcendental presence is forgotten, as in the "dürftiger Zeit" of Hölderlin's poem which we are all too eager to circumscribe as if it were a specific historical "time" and not Time in general. The existence of the poetic image is itself a sign of divine absence, and the conscious use of poetic imagery an admission of this absence.

It is clear that, in Hölderlin's own line, the words do *not* originate like flowers. They need to find the mode of their beginning in another entity; they originate out of nothing, in an attempt to be the first words that will arise as if they were natural objects, and, as such, they remain essentially distinct from natural entities. Hölderlin's statement is a perfect definition of what we call a natural image: the word that designates a desire for an epiphany but necessarily fails to be an epiphany, because it is pure origination. For it is in the essence of language to be capable of origination, but of never achieving the absolute identity with itself that exists in the natural object. Poetic language can do nothing but originate anew over and over again; it is always constitutive, able to posit regardless of presence but, by the same token, unable to give a foundation to what it posits except as an intent of consciousness. The word is always a free presence to the mind, the means by which the permanence of natural entities can be put into question and thus negated, time and again, in the endlessly widening spiral of the dialectic.

An image of this type is indeed the simplest and most fundamental we can conceive of, the metaphorical expression most apt to gain our immediate acquiescence. During the long development that takes place in the nineteenth century, the poetic image remains predominantly of the same kind that in the Hölderlin passage we took for our starting point—and which, be it said in passing, far from exhausts Hölderlin's own conception of the poetic image. This type of imagery is grounded in the intrinsic ontological primacy of the natural object. Poetic language seems to originate in the desire to draw closer and closer to the ontological status of the object, and its growth and development are determined by this inclination. We saw that this movement is essentially paradoxical and condemned in advance to failure. There can be flowers that "are" and poetic words that "originate," but no poetic words that "originate" as if they "were."

Nineteenth-century poetry reexperiences and represents the adventure of this failure in an infinite variety of forms and versions. It selects, for example, a variety of archetypal myths to serve as the dramatic pattern for the narration of this failure; a useful study could be made of the romantic and postromantic versions of Hellenic myths such as the stories of Narcissus, of Prometheus, of the War of the Titans, of Adonis, Eros and Psyche, Proserpine, and many others; in each case, the tension and duality inherent in the mythological situation would be found to reflect the inherent tension that resides in the metaphorical language itself. At times, romantic thought and romantic poetry seem to come so close to giving in completely to the nostalgia for the object that it becomes difficult to distinguish between object and image, between imagination and perception, between an expressive or constitutive and a mimetic or literal language. This may well be the case in some passages of Wordsworth and Goethe, of Baudelaire and Rimbaud, where the vision almost seems to become a real landscape. Poetics of "unmediated vision," such as those implicit in Bergson and explicit in Bachelard, fuse matter and imagination by amalgamating perception and reverie, sacrificing, in fact, the demands of consciousness to the realities of the object. Critics who speak of a "happy relationship" between matter and consciousness fail to realize that the very fact that the relationship has to be established within the medium of language indicates that it does not exist in actuality.

At other times, the poet's loyalty toward his language appears so strongly that the object nearly vanishes under the impact of his words, in what Mallarmé called "sa presque disparition vibratoire." But even in as extreme a case as Mallarmé's, it would be a mistake to assume that the ontological priority of the object is being challenged. Mallarmé may well be the nineteenth-century poet who went further than any other in sacrificing the stability of the object to the demands of a lucid poetic awareness. Even some of his own disciples felt they had to react against him by reasserting the positivity of live and material substances against the annihilating power of his thought. Believing themselves to be in a situation where they had to begin their work at the point where Mallarmé had finished his, they took, like Claudel, the precise counterpart of his attitudes or, like Valéry, reversed systematically the meaning of some of his key images. Yet Mallarmé himself had always remained convinced of the essential priority of the natural object. The final image of his work, in *Un Coup de Dés*, is that of the poet drowned in the ubiquitous "sea" of natural substances against which his mind can only wage a meaningless battle, "tenter une chance oiseuse." It is true that, in Mallarmé's thought, the value emphasis of this priority has been reversed and the triumph of nature is being presented as the downfall of poetic defiance. But this does not alter the fundamental situation. The alternating feeling of attraction and repulsion that the romantic poet experiences toward nature becomes in Mallarmé the conscious dialectic of a reflective poetic consciousness. This dialectic, far from challenging the supremacy of the order of nature, in fact reasserts it at all times. "Nous savons, victimes d'une formule absolue, que certes n'est que ce qui est," writes Mallarmé, and this absolute identity is rooted, for him, in "la première en date, la nature. Idée tangible pour intimer quelque réalité aux sens frustes. . . ."

Mallarmé's conception and use of imagery is entirely in agreement with this principle. His key symbols—sea, winged bird, night, the sun, constellations, and many others—are not primarily literary emblems but are taken, as he says, "au répertoire de la nature"; they receive their meaning and function from the fact that they belong initially to the natural world. In the poetry, they may seem disincarnate to the point of abstraction, generalized to the point of becoming pure ideas, yet they never entirely lose contact with the concrete reality from which they spring. The sea, the bird, and the constellation act and seduce in Mallarmé's poetry, like any earthly sea, bird, or star in nature; even the Platonic "oiseau qu'on n'ouït jamais" still has about it some of the warmth of the nest in which it was born. Mallarmé does not linger over the concrete and material details of his images, but he never ceases to interrogate, by means of a conscious poetic language, the natural world of which they are originally a part—while knowing that he could never reduce any part of this world to his own, conscious mode of being. If this is true of Mallarmé, the most self-conscious and anti-natural poet of the nineteenth century, it seems safe to assert that the priority of the natural object remains unchallenged among the inheritors of romanticism. The detailed study of Mallarmé bears this out; the same is true, with various nuances and reservations, of most Victorian and post-Victorian poets. For most of them, as for Mallarmé, the priority of nature is experienced as a feeling of failure and sterility, but nevertheless asserted. A similar feeling of threatening paralysis prevails among our own contemporaries and seems to grow with the depth of their poetic commitment. It may be that this threat could only be overcome when the status of poetic language or, more restrictively, of the poetic image, is again brought into question.

The direction that such a reconsideration might take can better be anticipated by a reading of the precursors of roman-

ticism than by the study of its inheritors. Assumptions that are
irrevocably taken for granted in the course of the nineteenth
century still appear, at an earlier date, as one among several
alternative roads. This is why an effort to understand the present predicament of the poetic imagination takes us back to
writers that belong to the earlier phases of romanticism such
as, for example, Rousseau. The affinity of later poets with
Rousseau—which can well be considered to be a valid definition of romanticism as a whole—can, in turn, be best understood in terms of their use and underlying concept of imagery. The juxtaposition of three famous passages can serve
as an illustration of this point and suggest further developments.

The three passages we have selected each represent a moment of spiritual revelation; the use of semi-religious, "sacred," or outspokenly sublime language in all three makes this
unquestionably clear. Rousseau is probably the only one to have
some awareness of the literary tradition that stands behind the
topos: his reference to Petrarch (*La Nouvelle Héloïse*, Part I, XXIII)
suggests the all-important link with the Augustinian lesson
contained in Petrarch's letter narrating his ascent of Mont
Ventoux. A similar experience, in a more Northern Alpine setting, is related in the three passages. The Rousseau text is taken
from the letter in *La Nouvelle Héloïse* in which Saint-Preux reports on his sojourn in the Valais:

Ce n'était pas seulement le travail des hommes qui rendait ces pays
étranges si bizarrement contrastés; la nature semblait encore prendre
plaisir à s'y mettre en opposition avec elle-même, tant on la trouvait
différente en un même lieu sous divers aspects. Au levant les fleurs
du printemps, au midi les fruits de l'automne, au nord les glaces de
l'hiver: elle réunissait toutes les saisons dans le même instant, tous
les climats dans le même lieu, des terrains contraires sur le même
sol, et formait l'accord inconnu partout ailleurs des productions des
plaines et de celles des Alpes. . . . J'arrivai ce jour là sur des montagnes les moins élevées, et, parcourant ensuite leurs inégalités, sur
celles des plus hautes qui étaient à ma portée. Après m'être pro-
mené dans les nuages, j'atteignis un séjour plus serein, d'où l'on voit

dans la saison le tonerre et l'orage se former au-dessous de soi; image trop vaine de l'âme du sage, dont l'exemple n'exista jamais, ou n'existe qu'aux mêmes lieux d'où l'on en a tiré l'emblême.

Ce fut là que je démêlai sensiblement dans la pureté de l'air où je me trouvais la véritable cause du changement de mon humeur, et du retour de cette paix intérieure que j'avais perdue depuis si longtemps. En effet, c'est une impression générale qu'éprouvent tous les hommes, quoiqu'ils ne l'observent pas tous, que sur les hautes montagnes, où l'air est pur et subtil, on se sent plus de facilité dans la respiration, plus de légèreté dans le corps, plus de sérénité dans l'esprit; les plaisirs y sont moins ardents, les passions plus modérées. Les méditations y prennent je ne sais quel caractère grand et sublime, proportionné aux objets qui nous frappent, je ne sais quelle volupté tranquille qui n'a rien d'âcre et de sensuel. Il semble qu'en s'élévant au-dessus du séjour des hommes on y laisse des sentiments bas et terrestres, et qu'à mesure qu'on approche des régions éthérées, l'âme contracte quelque chose de leur inaltérable pureté. On y est grave sans mélancolie, paisible sans indolence, content d'être et de penser. . . . Imaginez la variété, la grandeur, la beauté de mille étonnants spectacles; le plaisir de ne voir autour de soi que des objets tout nouveaux, des oiseaux étranges, des plantes bizarres et inconnues, d'observer en quelque sorte une autre nature, et de se trouver dans un nouveau monde. Tout cela fait aux yeux un mélange inexprimable, dont le charme augmente encore par la subtilité de l'air qui rend les couleurs plus vives, les traits plus marqués, rapproche tous les points de vue; les distances paraissent moindres que dans les plaines, où l'épaisseur de l'air couvre la terre d'un voile, l'horizon présente aux yeux plus d'objets qu'il semble n'en pouvoir contenir: enfin le spectacle a je ne sais quoi de magique, de surnaturel, qui ravit l'esprit et les sens; on oublie tout, on s'oublie soi-même, on ne sait plus où l'on est . . .

Wordsworth's text is taken from Book VI of *The Prelude* and describes the poet's impressions in crossing the Alps, after having taken part in one of the celebrations that mark the triumph of the French Revolution. Wordsworth begins by praying for the safeguard of the Convent of the Grande Chartreuse, threatened with destruction at the hands of the insurrection; his prayer is first aimed at God, then "for humbler claim" at nature:

> . . . and for humbler claim
> Of that imaginative impulse sent
> From these majestic floods, yon shining cliffs,
> The untransmuted shapes of many worlds,
> Cerulian ether's pure inhabitants,
> These forests unapproachable by death,
> That shall endure as long as man endures,
> To think, to hope, to worship, and to feel,
> To struggle, to be lost within himself
> In trepidation, from the blank abyss
> To look with bodily eyes, and be consoled.
>
> (VI.461–71)

Somewhat later in the same section, Wordsworth describes the descent of the Simplon pass:

> . . . The immeasurable height
> Of woods decaying, never to be decayed,
> The stationary blasts of waterfalls,
> And in the narrow rent at every turn
> Winds thwarting winds, bewildered and forlorn,
> The torrents shooting from the clear blue sky,
> The rocks that muttered close upon our ears,
> Black drizzling crags that spake by the way-side
> As if a voice were in them, the sick sight
> And giddy prospect of the raving stream,
> The unfettered clouds and region of the Heavens,
> Tumult and peace, the darkness and the light—
> Were all like workings of one mind, the features
> Of the same face, blossoms upon one tree;
> Characters of the great Apocalypse,
> The types and symbols of Eternity,
> Of first, and last, and midst, and without end.
>
> (VI.624–40)

Hölderlin's poem "Heimkunft" begins with a description of a sunrise in the mountains, observed by the poet on his return from Switzerland to his native Swabia:

> Drinn in den Alpen ists noch helle Nacht und die Wolke,

Freudiges dichtend, sie dekt drinnen das gähnende
Thal.
Dahin, dorthin toset und stürzt die scherzende
Bergluft,
Schroff durch Tannen herab glänzet und schwindet
ein Stral.
Langsam eilt und kämpft das freudigschauernde
Chaos,
Jung an Gestalt, doch stark, feiert es liebenden Streit
Unter den Felsen, es gährt und wankt in den ewigen
Schranken,
Denn bacchantischer zieht drinnen der Morgen
herauf.
Denn es wächst unendlicher dort das Jahr und die
heilgen
Stunden, die Tage, sie sind kühner geordnet,
gemischt.
Dennoch merket die Zeit der Gewittervogel und
zwischen
Bergen, hoch in der Luft weilt er und rufet den Tag.
. . . .
Ruhig glänzen indess die silbernen Höhen darüber,
Voll mit Rosen ist schon droben der leuchtende
Schnee.
Und noch höher hinauf wohnt über dem Lichte der
reine
Seelige Gott vom Spiel heiliger Stralen erfreut.
Stille wohnt er allein und hell erscheinet sein Antliz,
Der ätherische scheint Leben zu geben geneigt. . . .

("Heimkunft," stanzas 1 and 2)

Each of these texts describes the passage from a certain
type of nature, earthly and material, to another nature which
could be called mental and celestial, although the "Heaven"
referred to is devoid of specific theological connotations. The
common characteristic that concerns us most becomes apparent in the mixed, transitional type of landscape from which the
three poets start out. The setting of each scene is located
somewhere between the inaccessible mountain peaks and the
humanized world of the plains; it is a deeply divided and par-

adoxical nature that, in Rousseau's terms, "seems to take pleasure in self-opposition." Radical contradictions abound in each of the passages. Rousseau deliberately mixes and blurs the order of the seasons and the laws of geography. The more condensed, less narrative diction of Wordsworth transposes similar contradictions into the complexity of a language that unites irreconcilable opposites; he creates a disorder so far-reaching that the respective position of heaven and earth are reversed: ". . . woods decaying, never to be decayed . . . ," ". . . torrents shooting from the sky . . . ," ". . . the stationary blast of waterfalls. . . ." Hölderlin's text also is particularly rich in oxymorons; every word combination, every motion expresses a contradiction: "helle Nacht," "langsam eilt," "liebenden Streit," "toset und stürzt," "geordnet, gemischt," "freudigschauernde," etc. One feels everywhere the pressure of an inner tension at the core of all earthly objects, powerful enough to bring them to explosion.

The violence of this turmoil is finally appeased by the ascending movement recorded in each of the texts, the movement by means of which the poetic imagination tears itself away, as it were, from a terrestrial nature and moves toward this "other nature" mentioned by Rousseau, associated with the diaphanous, limpid, and immaterial quality of a light that dwells nearer to the skies. Gaston Bachelard has described similar images of levitation very well, but he may not have stressed sufficiently that these reveries of flight not only express a desire to escape from earth-bound matter, to be relieved for a moment from the weight of gravity, but that they uncover a fundamentally new kind of relationship between nature and consciousness; it is significant, in this respect, that Bachelard classifies images of repose with earth and not with air, contrary to what happens in the three selected texts. The transparency of air represents the perfect fluidity of a mode of being that has moved beyond the power of earthly things and now dwells, like the God in Hölderlin's "Heimkunft," higher even than light ("über dem Lichte"). Like the clouds described by Wordsworth, the poets become "Cerulian ether's

pure inhabitants." Unlike Mallarmé's "azur" or even the constellation at the end of *Un Coup de Dés* which are always seen
from the point of view of the earth by a man about to sink
away, their language has itself become a celestial entity, an in-
habitant of the sky. Instead of being, like the "flower" in
Hölderlin's "Brot und Wein," the fruit of the earth, the poetic
word has become an offspring of the sky. The ontological
priority, housed at first in the earthly and pastoral "flower,"
has been transposed into an entity that could still, if one wishes,
be called "nature," but could no longer be equated with matter, objects, earth, stones, or flowers. The nostalgia for the object has become a nostalgia for an entity that could never, by
its very nature, become a particularized presence.

   The passages describe the ascent of a consciousness trapped
within the contradictions of a half-earthly, half-heavenly nature "qui semblait prendre plaisir à (se) mettre en opposition
avec elle-même," toward another level of consciousness, that
has recovered "cette paix intérieure . . . perdue depuis si
longtemps." (It goes without saying that the sequel of the three
works from which the passages have been taken indicate that
this tranquillity is far from having been definitively recon-
quered. Yet the existence of this moment of peace in *La Nouvelle Héloïse,* in *The Prelude,* and in the poem "Heimkunft"—
"*Ruhig* glänzen indes die silbernen Höhen darüber . . ."—determines the fate of the respective authors and marks it as being
an essentially poetic destiny.) In the course of this movement,
in a passage that comes between the two descriptions we have
cited, Wordsworth praises the faculty that gives him access to
this new insight, and he calls this faculty "Imagination":

> Imagination!—lifting up itself
> Before the eye and progress of my song
> Like an unfathered vapour, . . .
> . . . In such strength
> Of usurpation, in such visitings
> Of awful promise, when the light of sense
> Goes out in flashes that have shewn to us
> The invisible world, doth Greatness make abode,

. . . .
The mind beneath such banners militant
Thinks not of spoils or trophies, nor of aught
That may attest its prowess, blest in thoughts
That are their own perfection and reward—
Strong in itself, and in the access of joy
Which hides it like the overflowing Nile.

(VI.525–48)

But this "imagination" has little in common with the faculty that produces natural images born "as flowers originate." It marks instead a possibility for consciousness to exist entirely by and for itself, independently of all relationship with the outside world, without being moved by an intent aimed at a part of this world. Rousseau stressed that there was nothing sensuous ("rien d'âcre et de sensuel") in Saint-Preux's moment of illumination; Wordsworth, who goes so far as to designate the earth by the astonishing periphrase of "blank abyss," insists that the imagination can only come into full play when "the light of sense goes out" and when thought reaches a point at which it is "its own perfection and reward"—as when Rousseau, in the Fifth *Rêverie*, declares himself "content d'être" and "ne jouissant de rien d'extérieur à soi, de rien sinon de soi-même et de sa propre existence."

We know very little about the kind of images that such an imagination would produce, except that they would have little in common with what we have come to expect from familiar metaphorical figures. The works of the early romantics give us no actual examples, for they are, at most, *underway* toward renewed insights and inhabit the mixed and self-contradictory regions that we encountered in the three passages. Nor has their attempt been rightly interpreted by those who came after them, for literary history has generally labeled "primitivist," "naturalistic," or even pantheistic the first modern writers to have put into question, in the language of poetry, the ontological priority of the sensory object. We are only beginning to understand how this oscillation in the status of the image is linked to the crisis that leaves the poetry of today under a steady threat of extinction, although, on the other hand, it remains the depository of hopes that no other activity of the mind seems able to offer.

2
The Image
of Rousseau
in the Poetry
of Hölderlin

As EARLY as 1914 Norbert von
Hellingrath, Hölderlin's most faithful editor, expressed the
necessity "of determining clearly the relationship between
Hölderlin and Rousseau. It would be one of the most important specific investigations one could undertake for the history
of ideas in general as well as for the historical definition of the
concept of 'Romanticism' in particular."[1] After fifty years of
studies which, following upon Hellingrath's edition, have im-
measurably extended our knowledge and understanding of
Hölderlin, this task remains to be done. Nearly all the general
works on Hölderlin contain some remarks on his relation to
Rousseau, but they are always of a fragmentary nature.[2] The
explicit presence of Rousseau in three poems belonging to three
different periods in Hölderlin's career[3] has more or less forced
commentators to consider the question. It is above all in regard to these poems (and most of all in regard to "The Rhine,"
the veritable keystone of Hölderlin interpretation) that useful

observations have been made. Nevertheless, the most advanced observations on the subject are contained, invisibly enough, in an excellent report on the state of Hölderlin studies, which dates from 1956.[4] We are very far, then, from the vast project that Hellingrath proposed; and we still await the tempting eventuality of a "historical definition of the concept of Romanticism" in terms of the relationship Hölderlin-Rousseau. There are good reasons for this, both superficial and those that go deeper. Precisely on account of the new wealth of our knowledge of the two figures (Rousseau studies have had a flowering almost comparable to that of Hölderlin studies), it becomes increasingly difficult to master and to coordinate the often contradictory and changing interpretations; the interpretation of Hölderlin, like that of Rousseau, has become a labor so specialized that the times do not seem favorable for comparative syntheses. Added to this, especially on the German side, is a certain persisting distrust of Rousseau, a distrust whose history extends from Schiller to Nietzsche all the way up to the present time[5] and which colors every discussion of his work in a subtly disfiguring manner. This disfiguring is far from being insignificant and would be a very rich subject for study in its own right. Here we would only point out that it has to a certain extent prevented the interpreters of Hölderlin from really grappling with the problem of the relations between the Swabian poet and the citizen of Geneva; Hölderlin's admiration for Rousseau is a bit embarrassing,[6] just as today one cannot help being a little embarrassed by signs of Hölderlin's (it is true short-lived) admiration for Ossian. But this very embarrassment hides a much more profound resistance to a problematic whose importance far exceeds questions of literary history and evaluation. Hellingrath was quite right in suspecting that the subject is so fundamental that it in fact reaches to the roots of our historical condition—and this is surely the reason one is tempted to go around it rather than facing it.

    In these few pages, then, there is no question of examining the problem in its entirety. Even reduced to its simplest form, it includes at least three distinct domains. We have first of all to undertake an exegesis of the passages in Hölderlin where Rousseau is explicitly named or at least present in the form of an allusion so transparent that there can be no doubt about the intention to designate him. But since Hölderlin's *œuvre* is made up of a tightly knit and very complex web of themes, this exegesis will have to put the theme "Rousseau" in a broader thematic context; there is, for example, an entire network that links Rousseau to the themes of festival, wine, fruit, and Dionysus—but also a more hidden network which leads to the themes of sleep and waking, forgetting and memory, water and voyage, etc. One can see that this web gradually extends to take in nearly the entire work. Having established this thematics, one would still have to compare the interpretation it leads to with the historical Rousseau before being able to speak responsibly about Rousseau's influence on Hölderlin and its import for the genesis of European Romanticism. Obviously there is enough material here for a number of chapters, indeed for a whole volume.

I will therefore make only some preliminary remarks confined to the specific references to Rousseau and without pretending to exhaustiveness even in this circumscribed domain. In addition, I will resolutely stick to the problems of local exegesis raised by previous studies, deliberately neglecting to point out others even though there are plenty of them.[7] I impose these limits not on account of methodological timidity but rather because the existing interpretations seem to converge on a central question, a kind of obstacle to thought that everyone comes up against. The aim of this essay is above all to name this obstacle in the hope of thus transforming it into a point of departure for other studies.

The enlightened but negative verdict on Rousseau—a verdict that founds a veritable school of thought in Germany—is formulated in Schiller's *On Naive and Sentimental Poetry*. Schiller here gives Rousseau qualified praise for possessing, he says, to the greatest degree the specific virtues of the poet: feeling (*"Empfindlichkeit"*) and intellect (*"Denkkraft"*). But instead of being linked in a harmonious relationship that would permit the free play of aesthetic experience, where the faculties would mesh with one another without suffering or conflict, Rousseau's two dominant faculties thwart and destroy themselves mutually without ending in a viable synthesis. It follows, then, that the work falls into two irreconcilable parts, each suffering from its own insufficiency: feeling leads to the idyll of *Julie* (which Schiller explicitly condemns in a subsequent passage on the idyll in general),[8] and the intellect to the destructive violence of the political writings. It follows, too, that Rousseau's anthropology is stunted and vitiated from the start: "his ideal of humanity insists too much on the limits and not enough on the possibilities of man. Everywhere is visible a need for repose, for physical tranquillity rather than genuine moral harmony."[9]

The most recent studies still echo this judgment[10] in the very word choice where terms like "idyll" and "repose" (in a negative sense) constantly recur. And the predominant thesis of the interpreters leads,[11] by different and sometimes even opposed paths, to the conviction that Hölderlin's final judgment on Rousseau ultimately coincides with Schiller's. One agrees with Hellingrath that the original identification with Rousseau was much more intense and deeper in Hölderlin's case than in Schiller's;[12] consequently it is as though he had to overcome a part of himself, with all the pathos such an experience implies. Hence there would be in his work a conscious and critical step beyond Rousseau in that he rejects, while referring specifically to Rousseau, the temptation of precisely the "physical repose" remarked by Schiller. Thus in discussing those strophes of "The Rhine" where Rousseau appears, Böschenstein, for example, writes: "At the core of the figure of Rousseau in 'The Rhine' is the renunciation of all activity in order to make himself the pure vessel of nature's greatest forces . . . Rousseau extinguishes all his inner aspirations, including thought, in order to perceive nothing but the regular throbbing of creation."[13] In a recent article Kurt Wais categorically rejects Böschenstein's judgment, but only to adopt the exact same point of view,[14] this time not in regard to "The Rhine" but the very late hymn "Mnemosyne"—which is quite correctly thought to allude to the same text of Rousseau as "The Rhine."[15] For our purposes it is of little importance whether the critique of Rousseau was formulated during the summer of 1801 or during the autumn of 1803; more important is whether for Hölderlin as for Schiller the juxtaposition of inwardness with historical action, of the imagination's reverie with institutionalized thought, a juxtaposition reflected in the confusing structure of Rousseau's *œuvre*, constitutes a genuine dialectic or a contradiction, the unfolding of a polarity in the temporality of thought or a break pure and simple.[16]

It is significant that in 1791 the young Hölderlin, a great admirer of Schiller, prefaced a poem dedicated to mankind ("Hymn to Humanity") with a passage from the *Social Contract* which proleptically contradicts the critique of Rousseau in *On Naive and Sentimental Poetry* (1795). Schiller will denounce the narrow limits Rousseau imposes on the ethical development of man; as though responding in advance to more than one hundred fifty years of attacks against Rousseau, Hölderlin cites: "The limits of the possible in moral affairs are less narrow than we think. It is our weaknesses, our vices, our prejudices, that constrict them. Base souls do not believe in great men: vile slaves smile mockingly at the word 'liberty.' " And throughout the competent but still impersonal rhetoric of a poetry that has yet to find its own voice, the impatient desire to reach the perfect world whose possibility Rousseau had the audacity to affirm asserts itself. Certainly there is nothing restful in the movement of this poem, where everything invites to haste, to action, to the total fulfillment of what up to now exists only in ourselves. This ultimate fulfillment of human destiny—Hölderlin speaks of "Vollendung," of "Vollkommenheit"—has to be realized by revolutionary and violent political action; the warlike images of the poem leave no doubt on that score. This may seem to us as very far removed from Jean-Jacques; nevertheless it is not at all surprising that a contemporary of Robespierre and Bonaparte should link such an activism with Rous-

seau. Hardly Rousseauistic, on the other hand, is the evocation
of this ideal state as a kind of aesthetic Elysium, eternal and
harmonious, the reign of Urania and not Mnemosyne:

> In Melodie den Geist zu wiegen,
> Ertönet nun der Saite Zauber nur;
> . . .
> Und in der Schönheit weitem Lustgefilde
> Verhöhnt das Leben knechtische Begier.

Despite the differences a contemporary would have already
recognized, this is undeniably the thought of a disciple of
Schiller, who, for the moment, no doubt under the influence
of Heinse, surpasses even his master in orthodoxy if not in
prudence.

Nevertheless, this poem contains an expression which by
its very presence suddenly opens up a much wider perspective. A line that already has an authentic Hölderlinian resonance designates the fulfillment of the human ideal thus: "Zum
Herrscher ist der Gott in uns geweih't" (l. 80). Hence the necessary externalization of the presence of being within ourselves toward a real and objective world. This poem says a great
deal about the "Herrscher" and very little about inwardness.
And yet, as though impelled by a necessity itself completely
internal, even here, in the heroic tonality of the poem, the
priority of the "God within us" over his external manifestations is affirmed. The movement goes from intimate self-consciousness ("der Gott in uns") to objective and social consciousness. And this movement, which seems not to be
perceived as problematic yet, is linked, still quite obscurely, to
the character of Rousseau. One of the next times that the
expression "the God within us" appears in the work of Hölderlin it is again associated with Rousseau.

It is in one of the most beautiful passages of the novel *Hyperion*, a book in which this initial naive unity of historical action and internalized thought is certainly no longer preserved.
Disillusioned by the experience of the revolutionary war, Hyperion invites Diotima to seek refuge in the tranquillity of an
Alpine valley or in the Pyrenees:

O komm! in den Tiefen der Gebirgswelt wird das Geheimniss unsers Herzens ruhn, wie das Edelgestein im Schacht, im Schoose der himmelragenden Wälder, da wird uns seyn, wie unter den Säulen des innersten Tempels, wo die Götterlosen nicht nahn, und wir werden sitzen am Quell, in seinem Spiegel unsre Welt betrachten, den Himmel und Haus und Garten und uns. Oft werden wir in heiterer Nacht im Schatten unsers Obstwaldes wandeln und *den Gott in uns,* den liebenden, belauschen, indess die Pflanze aus dem Mittagsschlummer ihr gesunken Haupt erhebt und deiner Blumen stilles Leben sich erfrischt, wenn sie im Thau die zarten Arme baden, und die Nachtluft kühlend sie umathmet und durchdringt, und über uns blüht die Wiese des Himmels mit all' ihren funkelnden Blumen und seitwärts ahmt das Mondlicht hinter westlichem Gewölk den Niedergang des Sonnenjünglings, wie aus Liebe schüchtern nach—. . .

(*Hyperion,* Stuttgart Edition, 3:133)[17]

This "valley of the Alps" (despite the symmetrical presence of a valley of the Pyrenees which is mentioned only to generalize the allusion) carries us into the world of the *Nouvelle Héloïse* by which Hölderlin was smitten during this period and whose traces are everywhere in *Hyperion.*[18] We are also very close to what Schiller meant, no doubt, by the "idyll" of *Julie.* It is, however, a world very different from Clarens, which is much more of a social community, but closer to the scenes from the beginning of *Julie,* or to the description of St.-Preux and Julie as "children . . . foreign . . . and solitary" in the second preface of 1761. Above all, it is already the completely inner world of the *Rêveries,* which later becomes for Hölderlin Rousseau's most revealing text. The internal landscape, where the God we carry within us dwells, appears here much more profoundly than in the poems of youth. Many of these elements were already present in the early poems "To Quiet" ("An die Ruhe") and "To Stillness" ("An die Stille"), which constitute a pendant to the active heroism of the "Hymn to Humanity" (the former poem containing an explicit allusion to Rousseau's tomb at Ermenonville).[19] As in the passage from *Hyperion,* we find there the repose (in fact sleep) in the shade of a tree linked to the drunkenness of Dionysus; the presence, still conventionally allegorical, of the wind's freshness; the regeneration of plants withered by the sun. But, especially in "An die Stille,"[20] this repose is paradoxically mixed with violence, the heroic action *("die Heldenseele")* with the calm of thought *("der Denker")*, and this is still more apparent on the level of sense perception, where the poem curiously mingles impressions of heat and cold: the shaded valley at the beginning of the poem echoed by the freshness of the shroud at the end is juxtaposed with the ardor of a cheek inflamed by enthusiasm (ll. 5–6), the heat of the desert (l. 16) mixed with the frigid snow on high mountains (l. 20). This mingling signifies the all-presence, the *parousia*, of quietude. In the passage from *Hyperion,* these oppositions, which are certainly too violent to signify repose poetically, have been drained and only peaceful images remain. Instead of being expressed in the oxymorons one finds constantly in Hölderlin (no longer to signify repose but the violence of transitional moments between two modes of being), the all-presence is now expressed by what one could call the "open" character of the landscape. It is oriented toward and opens to the totality of the elements: "sky, house, garden, and us" which together make up "our world" *("unsre Welt")*. This "us" of "God in us," the inwardness of consciousness, is like the axis on which turns the all-presence of the totality, which embraces sky and earth, men and gods.

But do we not have here a first example in Hölderlin of the going beyond Rousseau that so many interpreters point out? Let us admit, at least provisionally (we will have to return to it), that this tranquillity represents something very close to what Jean Starobinski has so well named the "transparency" in Rousseau, something richer and more conscious than the "physical repose" asserted by Schiller—although, coming from Schiller, the word "physical" should not be taken in a wholly negative sense. It is still no less true, however, that, in the skillful and deliberate structure of the novel, when Hyperion writes this, he is in error. For he does not know that at this moment Diotima—the spirit and the beauty of the Greeks born from the union of eternal plenitude and temporal poverty that is love—has already perished as a consequence of his defeat—

like the moon forced by love to follow the sun in its decline. Hence his invitation is addressed to a shadow, to the void. Does this mean that the reverie of repose is just an illusion, only a consolation after the bitterness of defeat? In that case, it would be necessary to overcome it in order to return to more concrete action, something one has reproached Rousseau for not being able to do either in his life or in his thought. For isn't it well-known that his political projects, conceived on so grand a scale, failed miserably and that he fled instead to the dreamy fiction of *Julie* and the *Rêveries?*

As Beissner has recognized, in "An die Stille" and "An die Ruhe" repose is not "inactivity, relaxation, but rather the concentration and the gathering of strength for the purpose of an accomplishment all the more effective."[21] Beissner quotes Hölderlin's letter to his brother of January 1, 1799: "In poetry man re-collects himself *(sammelt sich)*; poetry gives him repose, a living repose where all forces are at peace and appear inactive only on account of their intuitive harmony."[22] Since this tranquillity—it would be better to say "inwardness"—does not really lead to an action and moreover transcends the antinomy of life and death,[23] one can surmise that it is more than a moment of gathering strength before the battle—which would, after all, be a banal theme. But the separation as well as the interaction of these two moments (action and inwardness) is much more clearly marked in the passage from *Hyperion.* For if we situate the quoted description in the context of the novel, we see that rather than serving as the prelude to a moment of action, it is the symmetrical equivalent of the ill-fated action that has just taken place: the "error" of Hyperion's belief in the possibility of a union with Diotima in inwardness corresponds exactly to his "error" of believing in the possibility of reestablishing the grandeur of Greece on our earth by an immediate external action. In both cases the error is due not to a lack or an excess of externality or inwardness but to the illusory hope of being able to escape time. The death of Greece, in its historical and objective form as well as in its ideal and subjective form (Diotima), proves to be irremediable and irre-

versible. Nevertheless, the order in which these two moments
follow one another makes a difference, for whereas the objective defeat on the battlefield can only lead to the literal death
that Hyperion seeks in combat, the desire for repose is in fact
a turning back to the source. "Wir werden sitzen am Quell
. . . ," writes Hyperion, and the passage foreshadows in many
linguistic parallels the (otherwise quite relative) rebirth at the
end of the novel.[24] It is as though in the need and in the act
of repose one perceived anew the ground and the source of
our being, which, for a reason not yet understood, have been
lost in the din of an action that has become ineffectual. Here
it is not a question of preferring repose to action or, inversely,
of suggesting that Hyperion in giving himself up to his illusion of inward peace risks losing himself. Rather a dialectical
necessity is at work: the repose of inwardness is a way of putting oneself into a relation to being, thereby transposing the
action that preceded it and that which will follow it onto a
higher level. In the case of Hyperion, the defeat of the reverie
of repose marks the obligation to think of human destiny as
an essentially temporal unfolding, within which cyclical repetitions are no longer possible and which knows only transitory
rebirths. The grandeur to come of the German fatherland will
not revive the glory that was Greece and will not be any more
permanent. One could show (but this is obviously not the place
for it) that in the *Nouvelle Héloïse* the sacrificial death of Julie
performs a very similar function, except, of course, for the historical references. Let us simply indicate that this problematic
which integrates inwardness as a dialectical moment in history while preserving its ontological priority continues for
Hölderlin to be associated with the person and the work of
Rousseau. Although it determines the structure and tonality
of *Hyperion*, it is still implicit. To clarify this problematic fully,
it will take the considerable labor of the three versions of the
Empedocles, which lead to the theory of the historical consciousness (in the essay entitled "Das Werden im Vergehen")
and its aesthetics (in the essays entitled "Über die Verfahrungsweise des poetischen Geistes" and "Über den Unterschied der Dichtarten").

One of the stages in this raising of consciousness is the ode "Rousseau" dated convincingly by Beissner as from the final months of 1799.[25] Here we again find the distinction between Rousseau and men of action, but this time linked to the more general theme of human temporality and mortality. The ode begins with the exclamation: "Wie eng begränzt ist unsere Tageszeit . . ." and it establishes immediately the difference between those who by their heroic action are capable of going beyond the narrow limits of particular destiny, and those who, like Rousseau and no doubt like Hölderlin himself,[26] must remain standing on the shore of the future (l. 6), isolated and locked into their inaction. The poem marks considerable progress toward a deeper comprehension of this destiny and tries to name, still hesitatingly and defensively, the way in which Rousseau also participates in the historical future. For the first time, a very close association is established between Rousseau, the internalized consciousness that contains time *within itself*,[27] and language. The poem repeatedly associates Rousseau with modes of behavior that properly belong to language: he names (l. 9), he is always seen speaking, uttering the language of solitaries (*"Einsame Rede"*—l. 11), he is the one who apprehends, understands, and interprets (the most important word of the poem) the language of the gods; the word "language" (*"Sprache"*) is repeated twice in the eighth strophe which, along with the final strophe, also introduces the word "sign" (*"Wink,"* and in strophe ten *"Zeichen"*). The God within us exists in the form of language, a mediate form of contact with being and distinct from the more direct one that characterizes those who act. And now it seems that despite their apparent defeat (expressed in an image related to that in "An die Stille"), creatures of language like Rousseau and the poets possess the future perhaps more fully than others. They bear it within themselves like the tree bears its ripening fruit, that is, in a potential and mediated form for protection, a gestation—for the tree here is not the triumphant organic tree of eternal cycles but the fragile mindfulness of nascent thought. It represents distance in relation to the sacred rather than proximity: the men of action are directly and indubitably placed

into the opening of being *("ins Freie")* by the gods who themselves signal their function to them, whereas for Rousseau the
gods are strangers (l. 29) content to send signs that he must
try with great difficulty to decipher. Whereas for the men of
action, the gods signify *("zeigen")*, for the poets they are a sign
("ein Zeichen"). Nevertheless, the supreme word of the "Hymn
to Humanity"—*Vollendung*—is applied to these latter men:

> Und wunderbar, als hätte von Anbeginn
> Des Menschen Geist das Werden und Wirken all,
> Des Lebens Weise schon erfahren
> Kennt er im ersten Zeichen Vollendetes schon, . . .[28]

Here the temporal alienation that separates Hölderlin from
his time and imposes on him the solitary suffering of always
falling short of its fullness, everything that lends his thought
the tension in relation to the future expressed by verbs like *ahnen* or *sehnen*—it is all proper to his poetic nature, the fact that
he is a creature of language whose function is to interpret the
manifestations of being and not to represent them immediately.[29]

Nevertheless, one would be forcing the sense of this fragment to see in it the affirmation of the poetic man's superiority over the man of action. If the ode was to have developed
in this direction—and extending the movement that leads from
"An die Deutschen" to "Rousseau" would certainly allow one
to suppose it was—Hölderlin has not left us any more explicit
indications. In the finished part of the poem, the tone is still
apologetic, as though the poet felt inferior to those who directly take part in action and who appear to be privileged over
him. His thought is still not ready to grasp the dialectic of action and poetry in its totality or, more precisely, to include it
in its totality within the formal unity of a single poem. Most
of this thought is in fact already present in the third version
of *Empedocles* and in the theoretical essays that follow it; but it
is clear that it exceeds in all ways the ode's (including the tragic
ode's) possibilities of expression. The thought of this dialectic
has to seek refuge in the form of philosophical exposition which,

in this case, is far from being anti-poetic. It can fully unfold only in the hymns of the general Pindaric type. This is the function of one of the most finished and most definitive poems by Hölderlin that we have: "Der Rhein."

In explicating "The Rhine," the interpreters have been helped by a note in Hölderlin's own hand, miraculously preserved in the margin of the manuscript, in which he indicates the "law" regulating the structure of the poem. By using this note and by checking cross-references between recurrent terms in the poem, the interpreters have been able to construct a very convincing interpretation of the poem's first part. The work of Böschenstein has been particularly useful and could serve, for the first six strophes, as a model for Hölderlin interpretation.[30] The constant "subject" of these first six strophes is the geographical and natural reality of the river Rhine; interpretation has succeeded best in clarifying how Hölderlin, using the Rhine as a natural archetype, imagines the full and exemplary "destiny" of every earthly entity: the way this entity completely fulfills its possibilities of being yet without overstepping the temporal and spatial limits assigned to it. This helps toward an understanding of the other term closely linked to "destiny": the "demi-god" (*"Halbgott"*), mentioned a few times in the hymn. The epithet designates the three entities that appear in the first two parts of the poem: the Rhine in the first six strophes, the "hero" in the following three strophes, and finally Rousseau, explicitly designated in strophes ten, eleven, and twelve. The natures of these three entities are very different, since one is a natural thing, and the other two are conciousnesses distinguished thematically by a reference to their mythical equivalents: Prometheus (l. 100) and Dionysus (l. 145) respectively. They are nevertheless united by the common quality that makes them worthy to be called demi-gods, creatures that fulfill completely their destiny on earth. It would be a misunderstanding of Hölderlin to think of the demi-god as a mixture, a duality, or a synthesis of the human and the sacred, represented metaphorically by the half-divine, half-human birth of Dionysus, Hercules, and Christ. It would go

against the most profound characteristic of his mind, for which
the sacred is essentially parousia, an all-presence that envel-
ops and subtends all subsequent polarities. Hence the sacred
cannot be more or less present, quantitatively speaking, more
in one entity than in another, more in nature than in man. But
its mode of presence may vary considerably according to its
degree of immediacy. The presence of the sacred can be more
or less hidden, although it is always and everywhere what
grants being *(l'être)* and a destiny to a particular "being"
("étant"). For every earthly entity, the sacred exists necessarily
and irrevocably in the mode of absence or concealedness without however abdicating its all-presence for a single instant.
Demi-gods are those entities which either through their natural and objective behavior or through their internal consciousness (there is no distinction on this level) show that they con-
form to this fundamental law of the earthly creature; being is
always present for them, even if in the mediated mode of absence. Such is the source. It is a flowing, an unfolding in time
and, as such, essentially earthly; but it proceeds from the sacred because, as a beginning, it opens onto a mode of being
outside of time and deprived of existence in the earthly sense
of the term. It is the point of intersection of the sacred and the
earth, the place where time is engendered in the encounter
between the sacred—which, for Hölderlin, is sky, sun, and
fire—and the earth—which for him is, in the literal sense, the
surface of the earth which men and nature inhabit. The demi-
gods are therefore those who act in conformity with the source;
they realize themselves fully as entities whose origin is simultaneously downfall and becoming: the falling of the sacred into
time. They remember the source, not the sacred—for Hölderlin, in contrast to Plato, it is not possible for us to remember
that which we, as sons of the earth, have never known; on the
other hand, it is possible for us to recall the source and consequently also to forget it. Most entities, both men and things,
forget, but not the demi-gods:

> Denn eher muss die Wohnung vergehn,
> Und die Sazung und zum Unbild werden

Der Tag der Menschen, ehe vergessen
Ein solcher dürfte den Ursprung
Und die reine Stimme der Jugend.

(ll. 91–95)

In the first part, then, the poem names at once both the necessity and the profoundly paradoxical nature of the source:

Ein Räthsel ist Reinentsprungenes. Auch
Der Gesang kaum darf es enthüllen. . . .

(ll. 46–47)

But the poem goes further. For conformity with the source[31] is a mediate but nevertheless indubitable contact with the sacred. Thus the demi-god reaches toward an infinitely dangerous domain where the earthly entity risks going beyond its limits, raising itself to the same level as the sacred, and thereby literally destroying the earth (l. 74). In a dualistic mode of thinking which situates the sacred in certain zones of being and excludes it from others, this destruction would not be so serious because it could signify an immediate return of the sacred. But in the Hölderlinian world of parousia, the destruction is a crime against the sacred itself, against that part of the sacred entrusted to our keeping, namely the earth. The destruction of him who would remember the Father instead of remembering the source is therefore perfectly legitimate and is no cause for pity; the destiny of Semele is not a model for the poet, and when Hölderlin confides to a friend that "Apollo has struck him down" he makes the most terrible accusation possible against his poetic *I*.

In contrast, the river Rhine, a natural entity, earns the name demi-god because it was able to avoid this danger: its course shows that the Rhine has behaved in conformity with the source by first turning toward the origin (toward the sacred as a solar fire dawning in the Orient), then toward its mediate and temporal destiny (toward the sacred as a descent to the earth in the West). As Böschenstein has well shown, it is thanks to this that the Rhine can play its role as founder of civilization and history.[32]

What is the status, then, of the two entities that figure in
the second part of the poem? Here Böschenstein, like the other
commentators, does not seem to have done justice to the extreme rigor of the structural "law" imposed by the poet himself. And the question is obviously of great importance for the
meaning of the theme "Rousseau," since here the author of
the *Rêveries* appears at the most crucial point possible as he
who leads Western consciousness to the ultimate completion
anticipated in "An die Menschheit" and in "Rousseau." The
note on the structure of the poem tells us that we must understand Rousseau in contrast to the figure that precedes him
in strophes seven, eight, and nine. This figure is never designated by name; we know it only from an allusion to the myth
of the Titans and from the accusation in the menacing question:

> Wer war es, der zuerst
> Die Liebesbande verderbt
> Und Strike von ihnen gemacht hat?

(ll. 96–98)

In order to be able to respond to this question, one must
keep in mind the structural development of the poem in its
entirety. In the first part (strophes one through six) the Rhine
is a natural entity; its course determines and describes the
general law of destiny as it is fulfilled in a "being" (*"étant"*)
devoid of consciousness. In short, this part names destiny such
as it is *in itself*, or, to use the terminology of Hölderlin's theoretical writings (on the "alternation of tones"), in a "naive" tone.
In the second part, the one we are concerned with most of all,
the two entities, the Promethean hero and Rousseau, represent the destinies fulfilled by conscious and historical creatures who determine the law of this development *for themselves*, that is, from the point of view of the consciousness that
experiences it—or, in Hölderlinian terms, in a "heroic" tone.
Finally, the third part, whose final three strophes we will hardly
mention, names the knowledge derived from this experience
in its most general form, no longer on the level of particular

"beings" *("étants")* but rather on that of cognition. Hölderlin uses the term "ideal" *("idealisch")* to designate this stage. Therefore Rousseau and the figure that precedes him represent two distinct experiences of consciousness on the way to its fulfillment, which follow one another chronologically in the order indicated by the poem.

These two entities are called "hero" and "mortal man" respectively. Heroism suggests action, and Prometheus is for Hölderlin the very type of the man who acts as though he were the equal of the gods. The act of stealing the fire can only signify a direct confrontation with the sacred, which suppresses all interposed mediation. This act leads to catastrophe, both for the individual who performs it and for the nation that accepts such an individual as leader. And the historical catastrophe par excellence, associated precisely with a heroic hubris, is the decline and death of ancient Greece, which matured and perished on this "temptation of the Orient." The letter about Athens in *Hyperion* already represented Greece as a particular "destiny," like Empedocles or the Rhine later. In contrast to modern Western civilization, whose destiny is still to come and hence problematic, Greece realized herself completely and thus became semi-divine. Therefore her decline cannot be due to the forgetting of the source (as is the case, according to Hölderlin, for the majority of his German contemporaries); it is caused, on the contrary, by a too direct confrontation with being. The Greeks, inexperienced like the Rhine in its youth (l. 45), drew too near to the gods; they "mocked the heavenly fire" (l. 100), they were contemptuous of "the paths of mortals" (l. 102), and, in a sin of pride, they "strove to become the equal of the gods" (l. 104). This pride has nothing of the satanic about it; it comes from the very excess of power granted them by the sacred source they carry within themselves.[33] This power leads them at once toward the ultimate greatness and toward the greatest ultimate danger. The Greeks are those who experienced this danger in the heroic mode of historical action; the rise and fall of their civilization existed in reality and have thus concretely inscribed in human memory the absolute

law of temporality. They represent the necessary moment of
the defeat of action, precisely the moment through which Hyperion had passed just before the letter to Diotima quoted
above. But here the defeat appears in purer form: for not only
the *repetition* of the moment of plenitude is revealed to be impossible but its *continuance*, even when this moment is realized without basing itself on earlier models. This impossibility
is now clearly understood: because heroic action (that is, in
conformity with the source) makes us too much the equal of
the gods, it signifies our destruction, calls down upon us the
sacred lightning which reduces us to ashes.

But this experience is far from being in vain. In revealing
the danger to us, it makes us more experienced *(erfahren)* like
the Rhine at the end of its course. And, again like the Rhine,
the Greeks are for us who come after them precursors, pi-
oneers who, in danger, traced the first paths. The wisdom they
bequeathed us is summarized in the eighth strophe, which
contains the "ideal" lesson drawn from the "heroic" experience of the preceding strophe: that is, the understanding of
the structure of consciousness from an already semi-ontologi-
cal point of view. Ernst Müller, followed by Böschenstein, has
well shown how this strophe takes its inspiration from a contrast between the absolute "I" of Fichte and the relative "I" of
self-consciousness,[34] a philosophical problem that preoccupied
Hölderlin at least since his stay in Jena in 1795.[35] Consciousness, which is the "sentiment" of self *("fühlen"),*[36] is like an
obstacle being put in the way of the enthusiasm that draws
man toward the sacred in order to preserve him on the earth—
precisely as the banks of the Rhine, excavated by the river itself in its desire for the infinite, become the curb that keeps it
from hurling itself directly into the abyss. Self-consciousness
is therefore what preserves us on the earth and protects us from
a catastrophe like the one that destroyed Greece. This pre-on-
tology of consciousness, which is still seen in its ontic form as
an "act" of the gods, constitutes the philosophical legacy of
the Greeks. It speaks to us most of all in the negative law that
is its corollary: the impossibility of avoiding the defeat of he-

roic action and the necessity of recognizing what Goethe, in a poem we know Hölderlin profoundly understood, calls *Grenzen der Menschheit.*

It is at this moment that Rousseau appears in the poem, a "mortal man" in contrast to the "hero" of the preceding section. He is the spirit of the West enriched by the Greek legacy understood in the sense we have just defined. A demi-god, he seeks and obeys the source. But he is forbidden to find it in the Promethean act that seizes the fire directly; the wisdom of the Greeks teaches him that this means to choose death. On the contrary, he must seek the source not in the fire from heaven but on this earth which is his dwelling and his mother (l. 150).[37] What does this mean? In particular, how is the word "earth"—which names the element in which Rousseau's activity unfolds—to be understood? We have already encountered it in its literal sense,[38] but its signification has been enriched to the point of becoming one of the key words in Hölderlin's poetry. If we limit ourselves to the pastoral resonance of the word and follow the majority of the interpreters who talk about idyll, about the reverie of repose in a sense close to that of Bachelard, we miss what is essential in Hölderlin's interpretation of Rousseau. For how can one explain the absolutely central role assigned to Rousseau in the development of the hymn if it is only an idyllic interlude? That is, it is a question of him who not only in his own way goes beyond the grandeur of the Greeks but also guides the destiny of the West toward a new marriage of men and gods.[39] This is the obstacle we referred to at the beginning and on which most interpretations founder.

If we look at the passage from the Fifth Promenade that Hölderlin cites almost word for word, we find, at first sight, a problematic which seems to bear only a distant relation to what we have just outlined. The famous pages of Rousseau deal most of all—in the form of an inner experience of temporality—with the priority of what he calls "le sentiment de l'existence" over sense perception. When the senses are "fixed"[40] by the waves' steady rocking of the boat carrying Rousseau, another perception appears, one which "does not come from outside (but) arises within us." One cannot insist enough on how much these lines deepen the experience of sense perception ("sensation") to the point where one could speak of a devaluation, a going beyond sense perception. The consciousness that appears here no longer emanates from objects but rather proceeds entirely from within ourselves.[41] Formulated thus, the question is not one of those that worries Hölderlin; educated by German idealism at the moment of its greatest flowering, he did not have, like Rousseau, to make his way against the empiricist and sensualistic current of eighteenth-century thought; although one has found a translation of Hume's *Treatise on Human Understanding* in Hölderlin's library,[42] one finds almost no trace of it in his thinking. Sense perception as such does not appear either positively or negatively in the foreground of his poetry or his philosophical reflections. Nevertheless, it is Rousseau's turning away from sense perception toward the "sentiment of existence" that he sees as the crucial moment in the development of Western thought.

The passage on the structure of consciousness in the eighth strophe of the poem provides us with the necessary link. The German word *"fühlen"* in this passage (". . . weil / Die Seeligsten nichts fühlen von selbst, / Muss wohl, . . . in der Götter Nahmen / Theilnehmend fühlen ein Andrer, . . .") can mean sense perception as well as "sentiment." The fate of thought is at stake in this ambiguity. For as we have seen this double feeling (sentiment-sensation) constitutes the obstacle that restrains the earthly creature in its rush toward being. Consciousness is founded by colliding with sensuously apprehended things which keep us at a distance from being. From an ontological point of view, sensuous things are therefore those that are the farthest from being, even though they play an essential role in the dialectic that preserves the earthly entities in the mode of existence proper to them. Hence there is a temptation to grant them an ontological priority over nonsensuous entities, and to make sense perception (the immediate contact with the object) into the ontological experience par excellence. This temptation can be found at all moments in the history of thought; for Hölderlin, it manifests itself above all as a nostalgia for the world of the Greeks that we conceive (wrongly) as a world founded on the ontological priority of the sensuous object.[43] In giving in to this temptation, we commit a fundamental error, for we grant being to the entity that is the most devoid of it. We put a screen of objects which have become opaque and static between being and ourselves, and thus cut ourselves off from the source forever; it is the forgetting of the source (often called incorrectly the forgetting of Being) that characterizes our present civilization.

But if this is the case, then there has to be an entity other than the object, an experience other than sensation, in which our mediated relation to being can be established without separating us from the origin. It must be possible to apprehend things in such a way that they may appear as secondary in relation to a more fundamental entity that supports them and subtends them and which nevertheless is not being itself, which always remains inaccessible. This is precisely what happens in Rousseau's Fifth Rêverie. The sound of the water that Rousseau perceives (or, it would be better to say, of which he has the "sentiment") is the sound caused by the water which strives to plunge in the absolute depth of being but is prevented from doing so by the protective intercession of the earth; this sound of the water which Rousseau has "the sweet talent to hear" ("Süsse Gaabe zu hören"—l. 143) is the source, the power that permits us to see objects in their true dependency in relation to being and in their authentic dialectical role as a protective but nevertheless transparent obstacle.[44] Therefore this "surer sense" ("*sicherer Sinn*"—l. 142), more penetrating than sense perception because more in conformity with being, apprehends objects as contained in an entity which has a definite ontological priority over them; this entity is called the earth— "*Erde*" or, often, "*Mutter Erde.*" But one should be careful not to ascribe to this maternal earth the attributes proper to the world that engenders sense perception. On the contrary, the earth is called maternal to indicate her hierarchical dependence on being (often called "father": "*Vater Aether*," "*Vater der Zeit*," etc.)[45] and her superiority to the creature that inhabits the earth.[46] Earth is precisely the going beyond the obstacle of sense perception toward being, a going beyond which remains all the same rigorously enclosed within the limits of the mediated. The "earth" of Hölderlin is the "Being-in-the-world" ("*In-der-Welt-sein*") of Heidegger, the "sentiment of existence" ("*sentiment de l'existence*") of Rousseau; let us say, to remain within Hölderlin's own vocabulary, that it designates the ontological priority of *consciousness* over the object. In his letters and philosophical texts, Hölderlin speaks in general of consciousness ("*Bewusstsein*") as the discursive equivalent of the poetic term "earth." The earth thought of as consciousness, as mediated apprehension of being in inwardness, in opposition to the sky which is being itself. This may appear paradoxical to us, used as we are to thinking of consciousness in terms of the duality or the analogy of the subject/object relation. But it is precisely this duality founded on the ontological priority of the sensuous object that Hölderlin would go beyond. He no longer needs the apparatus of analogical thinking; for him Rousseau represents a turning point in the history of Western consciousness because he was the first to attempt a way out of this impasse.

Perhaps we can now better understand the destiny and attributes of Rousseau in "The Rhine." In contrast to the Promethean hero who is associated only with action, Rousseau, as in the ode that bears his name, appears above all as the man of language: he listens (l. 143), he speaks (l. 144), he gives language (l. 146) and song (l. 165). He also appears as the creature of temporality: the sound of the source, which his language reflects, is the fundamental rhythm, the musical measure of time. This union of language and temporality constitutes poetry. One hesitates to use the term music, for we have an almost irresistible tendency to think of sound as sense perception and identify music with the sensuous Muse of harmony. Poetic language can be called musical to the extent that it is consciousness and not object, to the extent that the word "water" is closer to the ontological essence of water than the sense perception of this element. Perhaps it would be better to use a term like "history," however corrupted by misuse it may be; it is as a creature of the earth, as a creature pivoting on language and on time, that Rousseau profoundly has an effect on history. Like Mnemosyne, he engenders history as the noematic correlative of consciousness. History becomes the music of humanity, as it were, the "still, sad music of humanity" Wordsworth speaks of in "Tintern Abbey."

What then is the historical destiny of Rousseau as narrated in the three middle strophes of "The Rhine"? Here we find again the dialectic of repose and action that we left out of the preceding analysis in order to simplify things. For in reestablishing contact with the source, Rousseau does not at all escape a temporal destiny. His pure inwardness does indeed rise above the dangerous Greek drive to action; it no longer conceives of history in the form of spectacular actions like the labors of Hercules or the Trojan War, but as a solitary meditation produced in repose. As we have seen, this was already the movement of thought from "Hymn to Humanity" on. But this initial inwardness does not at all exclude a later transposition onto the plane of reality. Only a philosophy imbued with the ontological priority of the sensuous object could confuse to this degree ideality with irreality; it is not because a thought is no longer centered on sensuous objects that it loses all possibility of practical efficacity,[47] and it is not because it emanates from inside that a thought becomes incapable of attaining universality. On the contrary, to the extent that it reestablishes an authentic relation to being, it extends itself to the entire human community, and its particular will becomes general will.[48] Hence it necessarily has an aspect not merely political but revolutionary. It is completely consistent that the author of *Julie* should also be the author of the *Social Contract.* And it is also entirely consistent that this radically revolutionary spirit should be persecuted by those who refuse to follow him on his path (ll. 148–150). But this is not the worst danger. It comes rather from an excess of truth which risks a forgetting of the mediated limits of the human. Whereas the Greeks were destroyed by an action that was all too significant, we risk being destroyed by the very success of a thought all too lucid. This danger can be seen in Rousseau when he allows himself to be carried away by the intoxication of his own lucidity and declares himself capable of being "sufficient unto himself, like God"; Böschenstein is quite right to point to this passage from the Fifth Rêverie when Hölderlin warns against this hubris of thought and accuses this language of being "mad" *("thörig")* and "lawless" *("gesezlos")*. On the political level, the equivalent of this unrestraint would be the excessive hopes aroused by the French Revolution (evoked in the violence of ll. 148 and 149), its ideological aspirations so legitimate that it risks creating a belief in the possibility of a definitive and meta-temporal political order. In the joy of this triumph, both the individual Rousseau and the revolutionary community that takes its origin from his solitary thinking experience the moment of the greatest danger: they risk destruction by a direct confrontation with the sacred. In an allusion to Hercules,[49] the poem represents this moment of peril by Rousseau's carrying the sky on his shoulders (". . . den Himmel, den / Er mit den liebenden Armen / Sich auf die Schultern gehäufft . . ."—ll. 155–157). Having thought the "earth" and self-consciousness to the limit, one finds oneself again close to reaching the sky. But Rousseau reacts like the Rhine which lets itself be brought to reason by the good will of the father (strophe 6). Instead of letting himself be carried away, he makes a movement of surprised retraction, the gesture of someone who has just incautiously touched a live flame (ll. 154–155), and then retires in the repose of a contemplative inwardness:

> Dann scheint ihm oft das Beste,
> Fast ganz vergessen da,[50]
> Wo der Stral nicht brennt,
> Im Schatten des Walds
> Am Bielersee in frischer Grüne zu seyn,
> Und sorglosarm an Tönen,
> Anfängern gleich, bei Nachtigallen zu lernen.

Is this the gesture "of 'the mortal man' taking refuge in weakness," as Böschenstein would have it?[51] Far from it. This retreat, this concentration of being in his own consciousness, this return to the originary I at the moment when this I, although saved from the temptation of the object, risks losing itself in the infinity of the divine parousia—this is Rousseau's profound fidelity to his nature as human being (for whom access to the divine is prohibited) and as demi-god (who cannot forget the presence of being in consciousness). The allusion is no longer as it was previously (ll. 145–146) to any specific passage of the Fifth Rêverie, but to this meditation in its entirety and within the context of Rousseau's life. As we know, it follows upon the stoning in Moutiers, an episode with which Hölderlin can easily identify his suffering. We have already met this alternation of violence, necessary defeat, and recovered inwardness in the passage from *Hyperion:* it is the very moment of rebirth.[52] Nothing here resembles the idyll in Schiller's sense of the term. The landscape is the same as in *Hyperion,* Hölderlin's unmistakable landscape of inwardness: the soft light of evening, the firm gentleness of the sacred presence in the evening breeze:

> Und herrlich ists, aus heiligem Schlafe dann
> Erstehen und aus Waldes Kühle
> Erwachend, Abends nun
> Dem milderen Licht entgegenzugehn,
> Wenn, der die Berge gebaut
> Und den Pfad der Ströme gezeichnet,
> Nachdem er lächelnd auch
> Der Menschen geschäfftiges Leben
> Das othemarme, wie Seegel
> Mit seinen Lüften gelenkt hat,
> Auch ruht und zu der Schülerin jetzt,
> Der Bildner, Gutes mehr
> Denn Böses findend,
> Zur heutigen Erde der Tag sich neiget.—

This moment names the aura of self-consciousness when it awakes from the retreat in which it chose to take refuge. It marks the highest experience possible for the historical man of the present day, the culmination of Western destiny. This moment is made possible by the exemplary wisdom of Rousseau who, in the confusion of suffering and ideological activity, was able to recover the tranquil, rhythmic language of inwardness. Whoever sees a critique of Rousseau in these lines has not understood this poem, never mind Rousseau. The equivalent of this moment on the level of the community, its extension to the generalized will, will naturally be the festival with which the last part of "The Rhine" begins and which post-Rousseau-ist Western thought is to prepare.

This same movement of retreat also allows the passage to the ideality which for Hölderlin is the sign of a truly complete thought, and, consequently, the only tone in which a poem like this can end. The particular consciousnesses of the second part prepare, by means of their experience, the historical moment of the festival. But at the same time they prepare the knowledge of the ephemeral character of this festival because they also lead to the comprehension of our destiny as essentially temporal. Therefore they necessarily transcend the real moment of fulfillment in order to think this moment as at the same time contained within an ideal temporality. This is why Socrates and Sinclair, who mark the beginning and the present stage of the history of the West, appear as the protagonists of the last part—not that they go beyond Rousseau as truth supersedes error or force overcomes weakness—this is Bösch-enstein's thesis—but because they represent the ideal and generalized version of Rousseau's exemplary destiny. Passages like the Socratic death of Julie attest that Rousseau himself was able to reach the serenity of this ideal knowledge. But, of course, these passages cannot figure in the autobiographical writings, for they belong to the generalized ideality of fiction.

Why, then, does Hölderlin identify the moment of retreat in Rousseau with the act of forgetting (l. 160 and n. 50)? What is it one "forgets" when consciousness bends back on itself in this way? It is not being, for it was never known in the first place; it is not the source, for it is proper to the demi-god never to leave sight of it. Rather we have to forget the fullness of our thought itself when it has been put back on the path of truth—especially in its almost uncanny understanding of the past and its concrete anticipation of the future. At the moment when the Western spirit reaches maturity (when, as the hymn "Mnemosyne" says, "Reif sind, in Feuer getaucht, gekochet / Die Frücht . . .") it permits a knowledge of its own genesis—one thinks of Hegel's *Phenomenology of Spirit*, for example—but such that the power of its clarity threatens to blind like lightning. It is against this clarity that the soul protects itself by a retreat for which the Fifth Promenade again furnishes the model:

> Vorwärts aber und rückwärts wollen wir
> Nicht sehn. Uns wiegen lassen, wie
> Auf schwankem Kahne der See.[53]
> ("Mnemosyne," Third Version, ll. 15–17)

Such is indeed divine will:

> Himmlische nemlich sind
> Unwillig, wenn einer nicht die Seele schonend sich
> Zusammengenommen, aber er muss doch; . . .
> ("Mnemosyne," ll. 48–50)

Nothing summarizes better what Rousseau signifies for Hölderlin than the conclusion that imposes itself as a result of this preparatory examination: the "one" *("einer")* designated in these lines can be none other than Rousseau. There was a man who, in reaffirming the ontological priority of consciousness over the sensuous object, put the thought and the destiny of the West back onto its authentic path; the same man had the wisdom and the patience to remain faithful to the limits that this knowledge, in accordance with its own laws, imposes upon the human spirit. He was thus able to safeguard the future of mankind. His name: Rousseau. His act: to re-collect oneself. With the reappearance of this word in "Mnemosyne" *("sich zusammennehmen")* the circle opened in the youthful poem "An die Stille" closes.

(Translated by Andrzej Warminski)

3
Wordsworth
and Hölderlin

T HE COMPARATIVE study of European romanticism is still in its beginnings. Among the great, comprehensive works that have rejuvenated the traditional perspectives and methods of literary history—I am thinking, for example, of the studies by Hazard, Vossler, Curtius, and Auerbach—the problem of romanticism has been avoided or evaded. European as well as American comparative literary history have concerned themselves a great deal with "preromanticism," that is, with the slow transition that is thought to have begun with the second half of the eighteenth century. But as much as these initial studies have contributed to modifying and enriching the stilted image that one often had of the century of enlightenment, they nonetheless have not allowed one to approach a more general interpretation of romanticism itself. To be sure, worthwhile contributions have already refined our understanding of the "period." For example, the investigations of the documents of romantic and preromantic criticism such as René Wellek or Meyer Abrams have performed have considerably deepened our knowledge of the intellectual currents of the time. But by virtue of their objects, these studies necessarily remain on the near side of the actual poetic texts. Even today, a work like Albert Béguin's *L'Âme ro-mantique et le rêve* is one of the few examples of the effort at a comprehensive understanding of romantic poetry in German as well as French. Curiously, this bold attempt has remained without successors, which is all the more surprising since methods of interpretation have made significant progress since the appearance of Béguin's book.

In no way can this lack be attributed to a decline in the influence of romanticism upon "modern" thinking. On the contrary, the problem of romanticism continues to dominate the other problems of historiography and literary criticism. The main points around which contemporary methodological and ideological arguments circle can almost always be traced directly back to the romantic heritage. This is especially striking in English-speaking countries, where because of an accident of history, romanticism represents a more clearly circumscribed phenomenon than on the Continent. The developments that have led here on the Continent to a noteworthy improvement in literary studies are to be attributed in large part to a conscious effort to think of our own historical situation in relation to the romantic movement. In this, it is of no great importance that this attempt often took the form less of a considered interpretation than of an unreflected attack upon romanticism: the reaction was only that much stronger. The enlightened formalism of the New Criticism, the history of ideas, and even the recent and highly promising rapprochement of European and American criticism can only be understood from this perspective. One of the results of this development was comparative literature itself as it is practiced today, that is, as an attempt at reflection, differentiation, and generalization that rests upon an interpretive comparison. This is the opposite of the descriptive comparison that derives from the natural sciences, and that has never allowed one to arrive at a satisfying classification or periodization in literature.

One can say without any great exaggeration that in America, comparative literary history as a whole has proceeded from the attempt to find an answer to the challenge posed by the philosopher and historian of ideas Arthur O. Lovejoy when, in 1924 in an essay "On the Discrimination of Romanticisms," he proposed quite simply to abandon the expression "romantic" since it was without meaning. The first issue of the journal *Comparative Literature*, which felt itself called upon to fill the shoes of the time-honored *Revue de la Littérature Comparée*, opened with a response to Lovejoy's challenge. That was in 1949. After many years and countless pages of bibliography, we have to concede that much remains to be done before a definitive answer to Lovejoy's objections will be possible. To be sure, the particular arguments he presented have long been refuted, and the methodological progress achieved in the course of the argument has been considerable. But a comprehensive understanding of romanticism remains essentially problematic. Something in the depth of the question seems continually to resist interpretation. All the comparative syntheses seem premature and remain on the near side of the insights one can gain from investigation of individual authors. And yet comparative literary history only makes sense if it leads to an understanding that goes beyond that which can be achieved by the investigation of individual authors. It is its task to give a word like "romanticism" a richer meaning than is possible on the basis of the study, however profound, of any one romantic writer. We have doubtless not yet arrived this far, and we will remain trapped yet longer in the labyrinth of individual interpretations.

Nonetheless, there are already certain possibilities for approaching by way of the comparative path that truth of romanticism that is beginning to be indicated by some specialized works of criticism. First of all, we must be conscious of the fact that with this task of interpretation we find ourselves in a particular position, one that is fundamentally different from the one we occupy, for example, in relation to the Middle Ages or to ancient Greece. In the case of romanticism it is a matter of the interpretation of a phenomenon that we can only consider from the temporal perspective of a period of time that we have ourselves experienced. The proximity of the event on the historical plane is such that we are not yet able to view it in the form of a clarified and purified memory, such as Greece presents itself to us. We carry it within ourselves as the experience of an *act* in which, up to a certain point, we ourselves have participated. Perhaps this obtains for every attempt at understanding the past, but it nonetheless remains the case that with romanticism we are not separated from the past by that layer of forgetfulness and that temporal opacity that could awaken in us the illusion of detachment. To interpret romanticism means quite literally to interpret the past as such, *our* past precisely to the extent that we are beings who want to be defined and, as such, interpreted in relation to a totality of experiences that slip into the past. The content of this experience is perhaps less important than the fact that we have experienced it in its passing away, and that it thereby has contributed in an unmediated way (that is, in the form of an act) to the constitution of our own consciousness of temporality. Now it is precisely this experience of the temporal relation between the act and its interpretation that is one of the main themes of romantic poetry, and it appears with such frequency that one can treat it comparatively—not in order to demonstrate the secondary fact that certain poets have said more or less the same thing about this question; but rather because at this level of truth, the discourse *(das Sprechen)* of all the poets in that which constitutes their irreducibly personal character strives toward one and the same thing. Thus we want to direct our attention to what two of the greatest poets of this time, Wordsworth and Hölderlin, have said about this problem. This will perhaps help us better understand why the interpretation of romanticism remains for us the most difficult and at the same time the most necessary of tasks.

There is a short poem by Wordsworth that was written toward the end of 1798 during his stay in Goslar, and that the poet always granted a particular significance. He sent it to his friend Coleridge, collected it in the 1800 volume of the *Lyrical Ballads,* put it at the head of the "Poems of the Imagination"— the most important section of his poetic works—and finally

made a place for it in the fifth book of his great autobiographical poem *The Prelude*, the first version of which dates from 1805
but which was published only posthumously in a version that
was considerably—and infelicitously—revised by the author.
These thirty-three lines suffice for Wordsworth to provide us
with a first approach to the problem that we seek to understand.

The poem leads us at first into an apparently idyllic world
in which nature and consciousness correspond with the reassuring symmetry of voice and echo:

> There was a Boy, ye knew him well, ye Cliffs
> And Islands of Winander! many a time
> At evening, when the stars had just begun
> To move along the edges of the hills,
> Rising or setting, would he stand alone
> Beneath the trees, or by the glimmering Lake,
> And there, with fingers interwoven, both hands
> Press'd closely, palm to palm, and to his mouth
> Uplifted, he, as through an instrument,
> Blew mimic hootings to the silent owls
> That they might answer him. —And they would
>   shout
> Across the watery Vale, and shout again,
> Responsive to his call, with quivering peals,
> And long halloos, and screams, and echoes loud
> Redoubled and redoubled; concourse wild
> Of mirth and jocund din! . . .
>
>   (V.389–404)[1]

Readers of Wordsworth know the charm of this world, the
gentle constancy of which is expressed in words like "responsive" or "interwoven." The analogical correspondence between man and nature is so perfect that one passes from one
to the other without difficulty or conflict, in a dialogue full of
echo and joyful exchange. The significance in Wordsworth's
thought of this unity filled with analogy is well-known; one
finds frequent evidence of it in his poetic as well as his critical
works, as, for example, in the oft-cited explanation in the 1800

Preface to the *Lyrical Ballads:* "[the poet] considers man and
nature as essentially adapted to each other, and the mind of
man as naturally the mirror of the fairest and most interesting
properties of nature."² Criticism, meanwhile, has especially
emphasized this somewhat pantheistic and Schellingesque aspect of Wordsworth, so much so that even the most recent investigations hesitate to go beyond it. And yet we sense, even
in this poem, how another dimension opens up and replaces
this illusory analogy. For when, in the continuation of the
poem, the voice of the birds becomes silent and that of the
mountain streams takes its place, the reassuring stability of the
beginning disappears and gives way to the precarious adjective "uncertain" that is added to the key word "Heaven":

> . . . the visible scene
> Would enter unawares into his mind
> With all its solemn imagery, its rocks,
> Its woods, and that *uncertain* Heaven, receiv'd
> Into the bosom of the steady Lake.
>
> (V.409–13)

This tone of uncertainty may already be noted in an earlier passage of the poem where, in lines 18 and 19, one finds
the unusual expression ". . . *hung* / Listening . . ." when one
would have expected ". . . *stood* / Listening . . .":

> Then sometimes, in that silence, while he *hung*
> Listening, a gentle shock of mild surprise
> Has carried far into his heart the voice
> Of mountain torrents; . . .
>
> (V.406–9)

It is as if at the very moment that the corresponding echo
is lost, the solid ground of a world in which nature and consciousness are "interwoven" slips out from under one's feet
and leaves us hovering between heaven and earth. But the word
"hung" in ". . . *hung* / Listening . . ." concerns us for other
reasons as well. Wordsworth chose it in the second, 1815,
Preface to the *Lyrical Ballads* (in examples that he borrowed from
Virgil and Milton) in order to illustrate the moment in which

the lower form of poetic imagination—"fancy"—transforms it-self into true visionary "imagination."[3] While "fancy" de-pends upon a relationship between mind and nature, "imagi-nation" is defined by the power of its language precisely not to remain imitatively and repetitively true to sense perception. This language is empowered to produce appearances "for the gratification of the mind in contemplating the image itself." The transition from perception to imagination implies a growing boldness of language which distances itself more and more from the norm. In contrast to the language of imagination, the "jo-cund din" and "mimic hootings" of the beginning appear flat and mechanical. But at the same time an element of anxiety is introduced into the poem.

We may better understand the essence of this anxiety if we observe that the same verb "to hang" reappears in the sec-ond part of the poem (typographically separated from the first by a space), and that it represents the thematic connection be-tween the two apparently free-standing halves. When Words-worth tells us in the most unadorned manner that the boy died, we expect the discreet lament of an elegy or the formal reserve of an epitaph. Instead we note the ardent and—for Words-worth—typical poetry of an ode to a specific and privileged place, a poetry the earnestness of which stands in profound contrast to the overflowing joy of the earlier world of echoes:

> This Boy was taken from his Mates, and died
> In childhood, ere he was full ten years old.
> —Fair are the woods, and beauteous is the spot,
> The Vale where he was born; the Churchyard *hangs*
> Upon a Slope above the Village School,
> And there, along that bank, when I have pass'd
> At evening, I believe that oftentimes
> A full half-hour together I have stood
> Mute—looking at the Grave in which he lies.
>
> (V.414–22)

With this, the origin of the anxiety is disclosed to us. There is a hidden but indubitable connection between the loss of the sense of correspondence and the experience of death. The boy's surprise at standing perplexed before the sudden silence of nature was an anticipatory announcement of his death, a movement of his consciousness passing beyond the deceptive constancy of a world of correspondences into a world in which our mind knows itself to be in an endlessly precarious state of suspension: above an earth, the stability of which it cannot participate in, and beneath a heaven that has rejected it. The only hope is that the precariousness will be fully and wholly understood through the mediation of poetic language, and that thereby the fall into death will be every bit as gentle as that of the "uncertain Heaven, receiv'd / Into the bosom of the steady Lake."

Thus, in Wordsworth's poetic world there seem to be two tendencies that are separated by the instant of transition from the one to the other. This sequence—the transformation of an echo language into a language of the imagination by way of the mediation of a poetic understanding of mutability—is a reappearing theme in this poet. In the second book of *The Prelude*, in a passage that probably dates from shortly after "There was a boy . . . ," there is a similar scene that plays itself out in a related setting. In a somewhat too conspicuous inn, built on the site of a simple hut "more worthy of a poet's love," the young Wordsworth and his friends play in the noisy manner of children, and their voices echo back from the hills. As in "There was a boy . . . ," this noisy pleasure suddenly gives way to the delicate melody of a solitary flute:

> But ere the fall
> Of night, when in our pinnace we return'd
> Over the dusky Lake, and to the beach
> Of some small Island steer'd our course with one,
> The Minstrel of our troop, and left him there,
> And row'd off gently, while he blew his flute
> Alone upon the rock; Oh! then the calm
> And dead still water lay upon my mind
> Even with a weight of pleasure, and the sky
> Never before so beautiful, sank down
> Into my heart, and held me like a dream.

(II.170–80)

Even more strongly than the ending of "There was a boy . . . ," these lines testify to the fine mixture of anxiety and consenting submission with which consciousness admits mortality. The contrast between the two worlds is always the same: a lively, pleasurably entertaining but destructive world strikes up against a reflective and silent world that stands nearer to an authentic understanding of our situation, the threatened beauty of which, however, is necessarily brittle. The essential moment above all other poetic moments is that of the transition from one world to the other. The poet's language takes its impetus from this meeting place: it illuminates this midpoint from which it glimpses its inauthentic past in the light of the precarious knowledge of its future.

These first two examples stem from the private sphere of personal memory. The third example will open the way to the world of history. In the sixth book of *The Prelude* Wordsworth records a journey that he took on foot on the continent in July 1790, a short time after the outbreak of the French Revolution. On their way to Simplon through the French provinces, Wordsworth and his companion meet a group of delegates to the *états généraux* who are returning from the federation festivities of July 14, 1790, at the Champ de Mars. Journeying together with this merry company, the two Englishmen are taken with the revolutionary spirit and feel themselves carried away by the joy of a rejuvenating historical act. This joy is spontaneous and sincere, as had been the corresponding joy of the boy who stood in evening conversation with the invisible birds. It is the joy in an active world in which the movement of our wishes appears to correspond to that of the age. But despite its doubtless healthy character, this joy conceals a danger which the continuation of the poem embodies in the threat posed to the cloister of the Grande Chartreuse in the wake of the revolutionary enthusiasm. In 1802, when Wordsworth wrote these lines, it was in no way a matter (as it often was later) of protecting the ruling religion against a social reform in which he had fully believed. The cloister represents something much more worthy of consideration than a particular religious symbol. It signifies a thing that is so capacious as to take in faith and reason, but also nature in its most universal form. This is not that nature which docilely fits our will and puts itself at the disposal of the play of our faculty of understanding. Rather, it is nature as the principle in which time finds itself preserved, without losing the movement of passing away which makes it real *(eignet)* for those who are submitted to it. Wordsworth's language tries to grasp this apparently contradictory nature in paradoxes in which the movement of passing away curiously joins with a condition of remaining, and a unity arises that lies at the very limit of comprehensible language. Wordsworth describes this nature as:

> . . . these majestic floods—these shining cliffs
> The untransmuted shapes of many worlds,
> Cerulian ether's pure inhabitants,
> These forests unapproachable by death
> That shall endure as long as man endures,
>
> (MS. A²: VI.67–71)

and somewhat later in the same episode:

> The immeasurable height
> Of woods decaying, never to be decay'd,
> The stationary blasts of water-falls, . . .
> Were all like workings of one mind, the features
> Of the same face, blossoms upon one tree,
> Characters of the great Apocalypse,
> The types and symbols of Eternity,
> Of first and last, and midst, and without end.
>
> (VI.556–72)

Thus, what the insurgents threaten to destroy in their enthusiasm is the temporal nature of our existence. Their joy expresses itself with such self-assurance and lack of measure that it believes itself capable of reconciling the moment with eternity. They mean to possess something that endures which they fashion according to the intoxication of the act, and yet this thing that endures exists only in a nature that endures precisely because it negates the instant, just as reflection must negate the act that nonetheless constitutes its origin. Thus history is, to the extent that it is an act, a dangerous and destructive act, a kind of hubris of the will that rebels against the grasp of time. But on the other hand it is also temporally productive, since it allows for the language of reflection to constitute itself. In order to demonstrate this complex comprehension of history, Wordsworth makes use of a symbolic narrative, a kind of rhetoric that has caused a good deal of confusion among the interpreters of his work. After the two travelers have left Vallombre and the threatened cloister, they begin the ascent toward Simplon. But in the maze of climbing and falling paths, they miss the exact moment at which they cross the Alps and attain the goal of their long hike. They are actually beyond their goal and must climb back to the top of the pass. At this rather sad point in the poem—a missed high point!—Wordsworth interrupts what had at first appeared as a simple, realistic report, and without any transition writes twenty-four lines that are a hymn to the imagination as the poet's highest faculty. Then he resumes the course of the narrative with the dizzying description of the descent from which we took the passage cited above.

The twenty-four lines inserted in this context summarize the relationship between poetry and history in Wordsworth. The imagination appears there as the faculty which allows us to think of our striving for action as a need for a future, as a *maladie d'idéalité* (as Mallarmé put it) that projects us out of the everyday present into the future:

> Our destiny, our nature, and our home
> Is with infinitude, and only there;
> With hope it is, hope that can never die,
> Effort, and expectation, and desire,
> And something evermore about to be.
>
> (VI.538–42)

When the travelers unsuspectingly set to climbing a mountain that already lies beyond their goal, or when the insurgents head toward destroying the cloister of the Grande Chartreuse with the same naive enthusiasm, there is no doubt that they are driven by the same, almost divine wish and stand under the influence of the poetic faculty. This gives them the power to direct themselves decisively toward the future. But it is just as certain that in this same instant, this faculty is conscious of neither its power nor its limits, and that it errs through excess. The interpretive reflection begins in the experience of this excess in the moment when the travelers come to recognize that they are in error, or in the corresponding moment when Wordsworth feels himself compelled to warn the insurgents of their transgressions. The transition of imagination from the active to the interpretive stage results in a feeling of disorder and confusion:

> Imagination! . . . here that Power,
> In all the might of its endowments, came
> Athwart me; I was lost as in a cloud,
> Halted, without a struggle to break through.

(VI.525–30)

The moment of active projection into the future (which is also the moment of the loss of self in the intoxication of the instant) lies for the imagination in a past from which it is separated by the experience of a failure (Scheitern). The interpretation is possible only from a standpoint that lies on the far side of this failure, and that has escaped destruction thanks to an effort of consciousness to make sure of itself once again. But this consciousness can be had only by one who has very extensively partaken of the danger and failure. Act and interpretation are thus connected in a complex and often contradictory manner. For the interpreter of history, it is never a simple and uniform movement like the ascent of a peak or the installation of a definitive social order. Rather, it appears much more in that twilight in which for Wordsworth the crossing of the Alps was bathed, in which the coming-to-consciousness is in arrears vis-à-vis the actual act, and consequently is to be understood not as a conquest but rather as a rectification or even a reproach. The future is present in history only as the remembering of a failed project that has become a menace. For Wordsworth there is no historical eschatology, but rather only a never-ending reflection upon an eschatological moment that has failed through the excess of its interiority. The poetry partakes of the interiority as well as the reflection: it is an act of the mind which allows it to turn from one to the other.

With these observations and this terminology, we have moved from Wordsworth to Hölderlin, along a path that lies no less hidden than the one that the English poet walked during his Alpine journey. In truth, we have already been for some time in the poetic world of Hölderlin as well as of Wordsworth, and perhaps without being clear about this ourselves. We abandoned Wordsworth as soon as the concept of a correspondence between nature and consciousness seemed to be definitely surpassed. This overcoming—which in Wordsworth ensues at a highly advanced point in his thinking—belongs to Hölderlin's knowledge almost from the beginning. We are therefore not surprised to find in him nothing corresponding to the analogical echo, the overcoming of which is a major theme of Wordsworth's work. The echo that appears in Hölderlin, for example, in the ode "Ermunterung," in "Chiron," or in the elegy "Heimkunft" is closer to the "longs échos" of Baudelaire's "Correspondances": it is the opening onto the divine, the way by which man and the gods encounter one another along a purely mental path. When Hölderlin, in the second version of the hymn "Mnemosyne," writes "Also wendet es sich, das Echo, / Mit diesen" ("Thus the echo turns, / With these [i.e., the mortals]"),[4] this instant is only distantly comparable with that other one in which Wordsworth's boy similarly "turns round" when the echo no longer answers him. Nonetheless, we must turn to this late hymn if we want to pursue our investigation to its end, even though the difficulty of the text is so great that only a few general remarks will be possible here. The relationship between poetry and history in "Mnemosyne" is so closely related to the one we found in Wordsworth that we can make the transition from one poet to the other without abandoning the core of one and the same problematic. At precisely this moment, the comparison stops being an exercise and becomes truly illuminating.

"Mnemosyne" is often interpreted as an eschatological poem in which Hölderlin, inspired by the memory of ancient heroism, decides to actively prepare the fulfillment of history. The temporal perspective of the poem demands that we considerably refine this interpretation. For the poem does not stand in a period of interregnum between two ages of divine presence on earth. Rather, it takes place—like the sixth book of Wordsworth's *Prelude*—after this presence has visibly presented itself in the historical action of mankind. The first version of the opening strophe leaves no doubt about this: the nearly chaotic state of violence and confusion in which the earth finds itself at the beginning of the poem is to be ascribed not to the absence of the gods, but rather to the covetous excess with which gods and men unite:

> Denn schön ist
> Der Brauttag, bange sind wir aber
> Der Ehre wegen. Denn furchtbar gehet
> Es ungestalt, wenn Eines uns
> Zu gierig genommen . . .
>
> (p. 193, ll. 4–8)

(where "the One" [*Eines, das Eine*] signifies the union of men and gods).

This state of too intimate a proximity between men and gods is described with the greatest precision in the second version of the hymn. (I am intentionally ignoring the third version, the reconstruction of which by Beissner does not seem convincing to me, and which poses a particular philological problem.) It is a state that distinguishes itself through the necessity of history to succeed anew in unmediated action, to strike a new path for itself: "Ströme müssen / Den Pfad sich suchen" (p. 195, ll. 7–8). Viewed positively, it is therefore a state in which a feeling for the future once again becomes possible, but expressed negatively, it is a time span of uncertainty and the greatest danger. In "Der Rhein" Hölderlin speaks in similar terms of the particularly precarious situation of beings (or ages) that are permeated by the divine. It is said there of the sons of gods:

> . . . doch jenen ist
> Der Fehl, dass sie nicht wissen wohin
> In die unerfahrne Seele gegeben.
>
> (pp. 143, ll. 42–45)

This confusion, similar to the one that in Wordsworth characterizes the moment when imagination springs forth, appears in Hölderlin in the form of a loss of language. In such moments the omnipresent god allows his voice to be heard (". . . so redet / Das Meer . . . ," p. 195, ll. 6–7), but we run the risk of losing the power of language in our contact with him. Without consciousness, and caught in the confusion of non-knowing, we are incapable of understanding our own existence: "Deutungslos" ("Without interpretation"). In this most extreme self-negation, man is thrown beyond the ultimate horizon of his destiny toward death. This theme of an excess issuing from a fullness which causes us to transgress our own limits takes on an increasing significance in Hölderlin's late work, above all in the hymns and fragments that are written from the fall of 1803 onward. The theme of the Titans, present from the beginning, unfolds here in its full breadth.

Hölderlin's Titanism has been well worked over by many scholars. The poem "Mnemosyne," and the comparison with Wordsworth, nonetheless allow one to dispute the direct opposition between Titanism and poetry that has been maintained, explicitly or implicitly, by so many interpreters that it has become a commonplace of Hölderlin criticism. Such a dichotomy would lend a Manichaean streak, as it were, to Hölderlin's thought that would be profoundly alien to his pietistic heritage. Furthermore, it leads to glorifying the power of Titanism, which would thereby be raised to an autonomous force capable of withdrawing from the control of the will. In reality, there is in Hölderlin not an oppositional relationship between

the activity of the Titans and that of the poet, but rather one
of prematurity. The Titanic moment precedes an inversion that
reestablishes a true relation between the human and the divine, and that can be the result of a human as well as a divine
action:

> Denn nicht vermögen
> Die Himmlischen alles. Nemlich es reichen
> Die Sterblichen eh' an den Abgrund. Also wendet es
>   sich, das Echo
> Mit diesen.
>
> (p. 195, ll. 12–15)

The manner in which this inversion accomplishes itself
through human action is the object of "Mnemosyne"'s second strophe. As with Wordsworth, we find ourselves at a level
of experience that is far removed from the everyday and that
is oriented toward the divine (in the context of the imagery, it
is a mountain path); and as with Wordsworth, this path does
not lead to the conquest of a precisely described peak or an
unequivocal crossing of a pass. Especially striking in this scene
is the lack of unity in an experience that nonetheless indicates
the return to a more exact self-understanding. The landscape
is not a whole, but rather the contrast of two different and
successive worlds: the eternal snow and the meadow grass, the
mountain pine and the valley oak. This world is, as Hölderlin
says, "hälftig" ("half-like"), an expression that reappears in the
key concept "Halbgott" ("half-god") and denotes the lawful
degree of divine presence in the human. And the traveler is
not alone in this state, but is accompanied by someone else
(" . . . da ging . . . Ein Wandersmann mit / Dem andern
. . . ," p. 196, ll. 29–34). We understand Hölderlin poorly if
we believe we have to identify this other with a particular divine or human being. He completes a pair that always reappears in the work: it is the pair Hyperion-Alabanda, Empe-
dokles-Hermokrates (later, in greatly altered form, the pair
Empedokles and his opponent), the pair Rousseau and his Ti-

tanic counterpart in the second part of the hymn "Der Rhein." This pair always combines a Titanic element with a reflexive one, and represents the doubled aspect of the poetic act between the two modes of being. This double structure is like that of the Rhine, which has to bend back upon itself, but also like the necessary presence of two different kinds of tone in the poetry—the heroic and idealistic—which spring from the common ground of a naive and still-undifferentiated harmony. It also shows that a dimension similar to Titanism can reside within the poetic act, although it represents at the same time a turning back through which consciousness transforms the excess into language. The divine world then becomes every bit as earthly as the May flowers to which the poet compares the eternal snow, and it signifies (in contrast to the nonsignifying unity of the beginning) a human characteristic—"Das Edelmüthige," the magnanimous one—which the Titan and the poet can have in common:

> Und Schnee, wie Majenblumen
> Das Edelmüthige, wo
> Es seie, bedeutend, glänzet mit
> Der grünen Wiese
> Der Alpen, hälftig, . . .
>
> (p. 195, ll. 25–29)

It is thus possible for a certain poetry to achieve the transition from the Titans to the interiority of interpretation, and to preserve in itself the traces of both these elements. The heroic and the prophetic elements that are found in many romantic poets derive from this Titanic origin. But poetry never allows this power to rush blindly to meet the unknown future of death. It turns back upon itself and becomes part of a temporal dimension that strives to remain bound to the earth, and that replaces the violent temporality (*reissende Zeit*) of action with the sheltering temporality (*schützende Zeit*) of interpretation. The ending of "Mnemosyne" names this protecting act of the logos through which the soul preserves itself safe in folding back upon itself:

Unwillig nemlich
Sind Himmlische, wenn einer nicht die Seele
schonend sich
Zusammengenommen . . .

(p. 196, ll. 48–50)

But the protective act is possible only after the Titanic heroism has run its course. Both are necessary, and the phrase
that follows immediately upon the preceding quotation ("aber
er muss doch," "but he must nonetheless")—and that apparently refers to the heroic death of the Greek heroes who went
"divinely compelled" onto death—holds just as well for the
necessity of the turning back upon oneself. The poet, meanwhile, must affirm the death of the hero in the form of a memory, the mournfulness of which almost draws him on to a similar dying. For him, this death would be only a failure: the
mournful ones (the Greek heroes) must nonetheless (die) but
the mourning (of the poet) is in error.

The Titanism of Hölderlin and Wordsworth is therefore in
no way to be equated with the Satanism that, for example,
Milton faces in *Paradise Lost*. It is one of the modes of the past
on which poetry relies to be able to originate, and it characterizes above all that poetry that is grounded less in a personal
than in a historical experience. One of the possible correspondences for historical Titanism on a more personal level would
be, as we saw in the first of our examples borrowed from
Wordsworth, the inner absorption of mortality. This temporal
doubling of the act and its interpretation, which Hölderlin
symbolizes through the double image of the poet, Wordsworth through the gap that separates the completion of an action from its understanding—this separation discloses a general structure of poetic temporality: it lends duration to a past
that otherwise would immediately sink into the nonbeing of a
future that withdraws itself from consciousness. It is thus an
act through which a memory threatened with its own loss succeeds in sustaining itself. Mnemosyne's death, affirmed at the
end of the third version of Hölderlin's hymn, would also be
the end of poetry. The poet finally distinguishes himself from

the hero through his care for preserving memory, even the memory of the heroic act that throws itself into the future and destroys itself in this project. The poet and the historian converge in this essential point to the extent that they both speak of an action that precedes them but that exists for consciousness only because of their intervention.

In precisely this way one can also understand the difficulties that the literary historians experience vis-à-vis romanticism. As a nearer and particularly more active moment in the history of consciousness, romanticism necessarily appears to us in a Titanic light which no amount of demythologizing can entirely dissolve. Whence issues our bifurcated attitude toward a phenomenon that always unduly attracts or repels us, depending on whether we accent the aspect of renewal or of danger. But Wordsworth's and Hölderlin's reflection upon the relationship between act and interpretation allows us to conclude that we cannot avoid the interpretive task left us by our romantic precursors if, for our part, we would achieve a historical significance. We cannot allow the poetic magnanimity to which our own consciousness owes tribute to sink into forgetfulness.

(Translated by Timothy Bahti)

4
Autobiography As De-Facement

THE THEORY of autobiography is plagued by a recurrent series of questions and approaches that are not simply false, in the sense that they are farfetched or aberrant, but that are confining, in that they take for granted assumptions about autobiographical discourse that are in fact highly problematic. They keep therefore being stymied, with predictable monotony, by sets of problems that are inherent in their own use. One of these problems is the attempt to define and to treat autobiography as if it were a literary genre among others. Since the concept of genre designates an aesthetic as well as a historical function, what is at stake is not only the distance that shelters the author of autobiography from his experience but the possible convergence of aesthetics and of history. The investment in such a convergence, especially when autobiography is concerned, is considerable. By making autobiography into a genre, one elevates it above the literary status of mere reportage, chronicle, or memoir and gives it a place, albeit a modest one, among the canonical hierarchies of the major literary genres. This does not go without some embarrassment, since compared to tragedy, or epic, or lyric poetry, autobiography always looks slightly disreputable and self-in-

dulgent in a way that may be symptomatic of its incompatibility with the monumental dignity of aesthetic values. Whatever
the reason may be, autobiography makes matters worse by responding poorly to this elevation in status. Attempts at generic definition seem to founder in questions that are both
pointless and unanswerable. Can there be autobiography before the eighteenth century or is it a specifically preromantic
and romantic phenomenon? Generic historians tend to think
so, which raises at once the question of the autobiographical
element in Augustine's *Confessions,* a question which, despite
some valiant recent efforts, is far from resolved. Can autobiography be written in verse? Even some of the most recent theoreticians of autobiography categorically deny the possibility
though without giving reasons why this is so. Thus it becomes irrelevant to consider Wordsworth's *The Prelude* within
the context of a study of autobiography, an exclusion that
anyone working in the English tradition will find hard to con-
done. Empirically as well as theoretically, autobiography lends
itself poorly to generic definition; each specific instance seems
to be an exception to the norm; the works themselves always
seem to shade off into neighboring or even incompatible genres and, perhaps most revealing of all, generic discussions,
which can have such powerful heuristic value in the case of
tragedy or of the novel, remain distressingly sterile when autobiography is at stake.

Another recurrent attempt at specific circumscription, certainly more fruitful than generic classification though equally
undecisive, confronts the distinction between autobiography
and fiction. Autobiography seems to depend on actual and
potentially verifiable events in a less ambivalent way than fiction does. It seems to belong to a simpler mode of referentiality, of representation, and of diegesis. It may contain lots of
phantasms and dreams, but these deviations from reality remain rooted in a single subject whose identity is defined by
the uncontested readability of his proper name: the narrator of
Rousseau's *Confessions* seems to be defined by the name and
by the signature of Rousseau in a more universal manner than

is the case, by Rousseau's own avowal, for *Julie*. But are we so certain that autobiography depends on reference, as a photograph depends on its subject or a (realistic) picture on its model? We assume that life *produces* the autobiography as an act produces its consequences, but can we not suggest, with equal justice, that the autobiographical project may itself produce and determine the life and that whatever the writer *does* is in fact governed by the technical demands of self-portraiture and thus determined, in all its aspects, by the resources of his medium? And since the mimesis here assumed to be operative is one mode of figuration among others, does the referent determine the figure, or is it the other way round: is the illusion of reference not a correlation of the structure of the figure, that is to say no longer clearly and simply a referent at all but something more akin to a fiction which then, however, in its own turn, acquires a degree of referential productivity? Gérard Genette puts the question very correctly in a footnote to his discussion of figuration in Proust. He comments on a particularly apt articulation between two patterns of figuration—the example being the image of flowers and of insects used in describing the encounter between Charlus and Jupien. This is an effect of what Genette calls a "concommitance" (right *timing*) of which it is impossible to say whether it is fact or fiction. For, says Genette, "it suffices to locate oneself [as reader] outside the text (*before* it) to be able to say that the timing has been manipulated in order to produce the *metaphor*. Only a situation supposed to have been forced upon the author from the outside, by history, or by the tradition, and thus (for him) not fictional . . . imposes upon the reader the hypothesis of a *genetic* causality in which the metonymy functions as cause and the metaphor as effect, and *not* the *teleological* causality in which the metaphor is the end (*fin*) and the metonymy the means toward this end, a structure which is always possible within a hypothetically pure fiction. It goes without saying, in the case of Proust, that each example taken from the *Recherche* can produce, on this level, an endless discussion between a reading of the novel as fiction and a reading of the same novel as autobiography. We should perhaps remain *within* this whirligig *(tourniquet)*."[1]

It appears, then, that the distinction between fiction and autobiography is not an either/or polarity but that it is undecidable. But is it possible to remain, as Genette would have it, *within* an undecidable situation? As anyone who has ever been caught in a revolving door or on a revolving wheel can testify, it is certainly most uncomfortable, and all the more so in this case since this whirligig is capable of infinite acceleration and is, in fact, not successive but simultaneous. A system of differentiation based on two elements that, in Wordsworth's phrase, "of these [are] neither, and [are] both at once" is not likely to be sound.

Autobiography, then, is not a genre or a mode, but a figure of reading or of understanding that occurs, to some degree, in all texts. The autobiographical moment happens as an alignment between the two subjects involved in the process of reading in which they determine each other by mutual reflexive substitution. The structure implies differentiation as well as similarity, since both depend on a substitutive exchange that constitutes the subject. This specular structure is interiorized in a text in which the author declares himself the subject of his own understanding, but this merely makes explicit the wider claim to authorship that takes place whenever a text is stated to be *by* someone and assumed to be understandable to the extent that this is the case. Which amounts to saying that any book with a readable title page is, to some extent, autobiographical.

But just as we seem to assert that all texts are autobiographical, we should say that, by the same token, none of them is or can be. The difficulties of generic definition that affect the study of autobiography repeat an inherent instability that undoes the model as soon as it is established. Genette's metaphor of the revolving door helps us to understand why this is so: it aptly connotes the turning motion of tropes and confirms that the specular moment is not primarily a situation or an event that can be located in a history, but that it is the manifestation, on the level of the referent, of a linguistic structure. The specular moment that is part of all understanding reveals the tropological structure that underlies all cognitions, including knowledge of self. The interest of autobiography, then, is not that it reveals reliable self-knowledge—it does not—but that it demonstrates in a striking way the impossibility of closure and of totalization (that is the impossibility of coming into being) of all textual systems made up of tropological substitutions.

For just as autobiographies, by their thematic insistence on the subject, on the proper name, on memory, on birth, eros, and death, and on the doubleness of specularity, openly declare their cognitive and tropological constitution, they are equally eager to escape from the coercions of this system. Writers *of* autobiographies as well as writers *on* autobiography are obsessed by the need to move from cognition to resolution and to action, from speculative to political and legal authority. Philippe Lejeune, for example, whose works deploy all approaches to autobiography with such thoroughness that it becomes exemplary, stubbornly insists—and I call his insistence stubborn because it does not seem to be founded in argument or evidence—that the identity of autobiography is not only representational and cognitive but contractual, grounded not in tropes but in speech acts. The name on the title page is not the proper name of a subject capable of self-knowledge and understanding, but the signature that gives the contract legal, though by no means epistemological, authority. The fact that Lejeune uses "proper name" and "signature" interchangeably signals both the confusion and the complexity of the problem. For just as it is impossible for him to stay within the tropological system of the name and just as he has to move from ontological identity to contractual promise, as soon as the performative function is asserted, it is at once reinscribed within cognitive constraints. From specular figure of the author, the reader becomes the judge, the policing power in charge of verifying the *authenticity* of the signature and the consistency of the signer's behavior, the extent to which he respects or fails to honor the contractual agreement he has signed. The transcendental authority had at first to be decided between author and reader, or (what amounts to the same), between the author *of* the text and the author *in* the text who bears his name. This specular pair has been replaced by the signature of a single subject no longer folded back upon itself in mirror-like self-understanding. But Lejeune's way of reading, as well as his theoretical elaborations, show that the reader's attitude toward this contractual "subject" (which is in fact no longer a subject at all) is again one of transcendental authority that allows him to pass judgment. The specular structure has been displaced but not overcome, and we reenter a system of tropes at the very moment we claim to escape from it. The study of autobiography is caught in this double motion, the necessity to escape from the tropology of the subject and the equally inevitable reinscription of this necessity within a specular model of cognition. I propose to illustrate this abstraction by reading an exemplary autobiographical text, Wordsworth's *Essays upon Epitaphs*.[2]

We are not only considering the first of these three essays, which Wordsworth also included as a footnote to Book VII of the *Excursion*, but the sequence of three consecutive essays written presumably in 1810, which appeared in *The Friend*. It requires no lengthy argument to stress the autobiographical components in a text which turns compulsively from an essay *upon* epitaphs to being itself an epitaph and, more specifically, the author's own monumental inscription or autobiography. The essays quote numerous epitaphs taken from a variety of sources, commonplace books such as John Weever's *Ancient Funerall Monuments*, which dates from 1631, as well as high literary instances composed by Gray or by Pope. But Wordsworth ends up with a quotation from his own works, a passage from the *Excursion* inspired by the epitaph and the life of one Thomas Holme. It tells, in the starkest of languages, the story of a deaf man who compensates for his infirmity by substituting the reading of books for the sounds of nature.

The general plot of the story, strategically placed as the exemplary conclusion of an exemplary text, is very familiar to readers of *The Prelude*. It tells of a discourse that is *sustained* beyond and in spite of *deprivation* which, as in this case, may be an accident of birth or which can occur as a sudden shock, at times catastrophical, at times apparently trivial. The shock interrupts a state of affairs that was relatively stable. One thinks of such famous passages in *The Prelude* as the hymn to the new-born child in Book II ("Bless'd the infant babe . . .") that tells how "the first / Poetic spirit of our human life" manifests itself. A condition of mutual exchange and dialogue is first established, then interrupted without warning when "the props of my affections were remov'd" and restored when it is said that ". . . the building stood, as if sustain'd / By its own spirit!" (II.294–96). Or one thinks of the drowned man in Book V who " 'mid that beauteous scene / Of trees and hills and water, bolt upright / Rose, with his ghastly face, a spectre shape / Of terror even" (V.470–73); Wordsworth reports that the nine-year-old boy he was at the time found solace in the thought that he had previously encountered such scenes in books. And one thinks most of all of the equally famous episode that almost immediately precedes this scene, the Boy of Winander. Numerous verbal echoes link the passage from the *Excursion* quoted at the end of the *Essays upon Epitaphs* to the story of the boy whose mimic mirth is interrupted by a sudden silence prefigurative of his own death and subsequent restoration. As is well known, it is this episode which furnishes, in an early variant, the textual evidence for the assumption that these figures of deprivation, maimed men, drowned corpses, blind beggars, children about to die, that appear throughout *The Prelude* are figures of Wordsworth's own poetic self. They reveal the autobiographical dimension that all these texts have in common. But the question remains how this near-obsessive concern with mutilation, often in the form of a loss of one of the senses, as blindness, deafness, or, as in the key word of the Boy of Winander, *muteness*, is to be understood and, consequently, how trustworthy the ensuing claim

of compensation and restoration can be. The question has further bearing on the relationship of these tales to other episodes in *The Prelude* which also involve shocks and interruptions, but occur in a mood of sublimity in which the condition
of deprivation is no longer clearly apparent. This takes us, of
course, beyond the scope of this paper; I must limit myself to
suggesting the relevance of the *Essays upon Epitaphs* for the larger
question of autobiographical discourse as a discourse of self-
restoration.

Wordsworth's claim for restoration in the face of death, in
the *Essays upon Epitaphs,* is grounded in a consistent system of
thought, of metaphors, and of diction that is announced at the
beginning of the first essay and developed throughout. It is a
system of mediations that converts the radical distance of an
either/or opposition in a process allowing movement from one
extreme to the other by a series of transformations that leave
the negativity of the initial relationship (or lack of relationship) intact. One moves, without compromise, from death *or*
life to life *and* death. The existential poignancy of the text stems
from the full acquiescence to the power of mortality; no sim-
plification in the form of a negation of the negation can be said
to take place in Wordsworth. The text constructs a sequence
of mediations between incompatibles: city and nature, pagan
and Christian, particularity and generality, body and grave,
brought together under the general principle according to which
"origin and tendency are notions inseparably co-relative."
Nietzsche will say the exactly symmetrical opposite in the *Genealogy of Morals*—"origin and tendency *(Zweck)* [are] two
problems that are not and should not be linked"—and historians of romanticism and of post-romanticism have had little
difficulty using the system of this symmetry to unite this origin (Wordsworth) with this tendency (Nietzsche) in a single
historical itinerary. The same itinerary, the same image of the
road, appears in the text as "the lively and affecting analogies
of life as a journey" interrupted, but not ended, by death. The
large, overarching metaphor for this entire system is that of
the sun in motion: "As, in sailing upon the orb of this planet,

a voyage towards the regions where the sun sets, conducts gradually to the quarter where we have been accustomed to behold it come forth at its rising; and, in like manner, a voyage toward the east, the birth-place in our imagination of the morning, leads finally to the quarter where the sun is last seen when he departs from our eyes; so the contemplative Soul, travelling in the direction of mortality, advances to the country of everlasting life; and, in like manner, may she continue to explore those cheerful tracts, till she is brought back, for her advantage and benefit, to the land of transitory things—of sorrow and of tears." In this system of metaphors, the sun is more than a mere natural object, although it is powerful enough, as such, to command a chain of images that can see a man's work as a tree, made of trunks and branches, and language as akin to "the power of gravitation or the air we breathe" (p. 154), the parousia of light. Relayed by the trope of light, the sun becomes a figure of knowledge as well as of nature, the emblem of what the third essay refers to as "the mind with absolute sovereignty upon itself." Knowledge and mind imply language and account for the relationship set up between the sun and the text of the epitaph: the epitaph, says Wordsworth, "is open to the day; the sun looks down upon the stone, and the rains of heaven beat against it." The sun becomes the eye that *reads* the text of the epitaph. And the essay tells us what this text consists of, by way of a quotation from Milton that deals with Shakespeare: "What need'st thou such weak witness of thy *name?*" In the case of poets such as Shakespeare, Milton, or Wordsworth himself, the epitaph can consist only of what he calls "the naked name" (p. 133), as it is read by the eye of the sun. At this point, it can be said of "the language of the senseless stone" that it acquires a "voice," the *speaking* stone counterbalancing the *seeing* sun. The system passes from sun to eye to language as name and as voice. We can identify the figure that completes the central metaphor of the sun and thus completes the tropological spectrum that the sun engenders: it is the figure of prosopopeia, the fiction of an apostrophe to an absent, deceased, or voiceless entity, which posits the possibility of the latter's reply and confers upon it the power of speech. Voice assumes mouth, eye, and finally face, a chain that is manifest in the etymology of the trope's name, *prosopon poien,* to confer a mask or a face *(prosopon).* Prosopopeia is the trope of autobiography, by which one's name, as in the Milton poem, is made as intelligible and memorable as a face. Our topic deals with the giving and taking away of faces, with face and deface, *figure,* figuration and disfiguration.

From a rhetorical point of view, the *Essays upon Epitaphs* are a treatise on the superiority of prosopopeia (associated with the names of Milton and of Shakespeare) over antithesis (associated with the name of Pope). In terms of style and narrative diction, prosopopeia is also the art of delicate transition (a feat easier to perform in autobiography than in epic narrative). The gradual transformations occur in such a way that "feelings [that] seem opposite to each other have another and finer connection than that of contrast." The stylistics of epitaph are very remote from the "unmeaning antitheses" of satire; they proceed instead by gliding displacements, by, says Wordsworth, "smooth gradation or gentle transition, to some other kindred quality," "kept within the circle of qualities which range themselves quietly by each other's sides." Metaphor and prosopopeia bring together a thematic pathos with a subtly differentiated diction. It reaches, in Wordsworth, the triumph of an autobiographical narrative grounded in a genuine dialectic, which is also the most encompassing system of tropes conceivable.

Yet, despite the perfect closure of the system, the text contains elements that not only disrupt its balance but its principle of production. We saw that the name, be it the proper name of the author or of a place, is an essential link in the chain. But in the striking passage that illustrates the unity of origin and of destination through the metaphor of a flowing river, Wordsworth insists that, whereas the literal sense of the dead figure may indeed be, as in Milton's poem on Shakespeare, a name, "an image gathered from a map, or from the real object in nature," "the spirit . . . [on the other hand] must have been *as* inevitably,—a receptacle without bounds or dimensions;—nothing less than infinity." The opposition between literal and figural functions here by analogy with the opposition between the name and the nameless, although it is the burden of the entire argument to overcome this very opposition.

The quotation from Milton is remarkable in still another respect. It omits six lines from the original, which is certainly legitimate enough, yet revealing with regard to another, more puzzling, anomaly in the text. The dominant figure of the epitaphic or autobiographical discourse is, as we saw, the prosopopeia, the fiction of the voice-from-beyond-the-grave; an unlettered stone would leave the sun suspended in nothingness. Yet at several points throughout the three essays, Wordsworth cautions consistently against the use of prosopopeia, against the convention of having the "Sta Viator" addressed to the traveler on the road of life by the voice of the departed person. Such chiasmic figures, crossing the conditions of death and of life with the attributes of speech and of silence are, says Wordsworth, "too poignant and too transitory"—a curiously phrased criticism, since the very movement of the consolation is that of the transitory and since it is the poignancy of the weeping "silent marble," as in Gray's epitaph on Mrs. Clark, for which the essays strive. Whenever prosopopeia is discussed, and it recurs at least three times, the argument becomes singularly inconclusive. "Representing [the deceased] as speaking from his own tomb-stone" is said to be a "tender fiction," a "shadowy interposition [which] harmoniously unites the two worlds of the living and the dead . . . ," everything, in other words, that the thematics and the stylistics of the autobiographical theme set out to accomplish. Yet, in the next paragraph, it is said that "the latter mode, namely, that in which the survivors speak in *their own* persons, seems to me upon the whole greatly preferable" because "it excludes the fiction which is the groundwork of the other" (p. 132). Gray and Milton are chided for what are in fact figurations derived from prosopopeia. The text counsels against the use of its own main figure. Whenever this happens, it indicates the threat of a deeper logical disturbance.

The omissions from the Milton sonnet offer one way to account for the threat. In the elided six lines Milton speaks of the burden that Shakespeare's "easy numbers" represent for those who are, like all of us, capable only of "slow-endeavoring art." He then goes on to say

> Then thou our fancy of itself bereaving
> Dost make us marble with too much conceiving.

Isabel MacCaffrey paraphrases the two difficult lines as follows: "our imaginations are rapt 'out of ourselves' leaving behind our soulless bodies like statues." "Doth make us marble," in the *Essays upon Epitaphs,* cannot fail to evoke the latent threat that inhabits prosopopeia, namely that by making the death speak, the symmetrical structure of the trope implies, by the same token, that the living are struck dumb, frozen in their own death. The surmise of the "Pause, Traveller!" thus acquires a sinister connotation that is not only the prefiguration of one's own mortality but our actual entry into the frozen world of the dead. It could be argued that Wordsworth's awareness of this threat is clear-eyed enough to allow for its inscription within the cognitive, solar system of specular self-knowledge that underlies the essays, and that the warnings against the use of prosopopeia are strategic and didactic rather than actual. He knows that the advocated "exclusion" of the fictional voice and its replacement by the actual voice of the living in fact reintroduces the prosopopeia in the fiction of *address.* Nevertheless, the fact that this statement is made by ways of omissions and contradictions rightly awakens one's suspicions.

The main inconsistency of the text, which is also the source of its considerable theoretical importance, occurs in a related but different pattern. The *Essays* speak out forcefully against the antithetical language of satire and invective and plead eloquently for a lucid language of repose, tranquillity, and serenity. Yet, if we ask the legitimate question which of the two prevail in this text, the mode of aggression or of repose, it is clear that the essays contain large portions that are most openly antithetical and aggressive. "I cannot suffer any Individual, however highly and deservedly honoured by my Countrymen, to stand in my way"; this reference to Pope, together with many others addressed to the same, are anything but gentle. Wordsworth is sufficiently bothered by the discrepancy—it *is* a discrepancy, for there is no reason in the world why Pope could not have been handled with the same dialectical generosity accorded to death—to generate an abundant discourse of self-justification that spills over into a redundantly insistent Appendix. The most violent language is saved however, not for Alexander Pope, but for language itself. A certain misuse of language is denounced in the strongest of terms: "Words are too awful an instrument for good and evil to be trifled with: they hold above all other external powers a dominion over thoughts. If words be not . . . an incarnation of the thought but only a clothing for it, then surely they will prove an ill gift; such a one as those poisoned vestments, read of in the stories of superstitious times, which had power to consume and to alienate from his right mind the victim who put them on. Language, if it do not uphold, and feed, and leave in quiet, like the power of gravitation or the air we breathe, is a counter-spirit . . ." (p. 154). What is the characteristic of the language so severely condemned? The distinction between total good and radical evil rests on the distinction between incarnate thought and "a clothing for thought," two notions which seem indeed to "have another and a finer connection than that of contrast." De Quincey singled out this distinction and read it as a way to oppose compelling figures to arbitrary ones. But incarnate flesh and clothing have at least one property in common, in opposition to the thoughts they both represent, namely their visibility, their accessibility to the senses. A little earlier in the passage, Wordsworth has similarly characterized the *right* kind of language as being "not what the garb is to the body but what the body is to the soul" (p. 154). The sequence garb—

body—soul is in fact a perfectly consistent metaphorical chain: garment is the visible outside of the body as the body is the visible outside of the soul. The language so violently denounced is in fact the language of metaphor, of prosopopeia and of tropes, the solar language of cognition that makes the unknown accessible to the mind and to the senses. The language of tropes (which is the specular language of autobiography) is indeed like the body, which is like its garments, the veil of the soul as the garment is the sheltering veil of the body. How can this harmless veil then suddenly become as deadly and violent as the poisoned coat of Jason or of Nessus?

The coat of Nessus, which caused the violent death of Hercules, as narrated in Sophocles' *Trachiniae*, was given to his wife Deianeira, in the hope of regaining the affections from which she would soon be deprived. It was supposed to restore the love which she lost, but the restoration turned out to be a worse deprivation, a loss of life and of sense. The passage from the *Excursion* that concludes the *Essays* tells a similar story, though not to the end. The deafness of the "gentle Dalesman" who is the protagonist of the tale finds its outside equivalent, by a consistent enough crossing, in the muteness of a nature of which it is said that, even at the height of the storm, it is "silent as a picture." To the extent that language is figure (or metaphor, or prosopopeia) it is indeed not the thing itself but the representation, the picture of the thing and, as such, it is silent, mute as pictures are mute. Language, as trope, is always privative. Wordsworth says of evil language, which is in fact all language including his own language of restoration, that it works "unremittingly and *noiselessly*" (p. 154). To the extent that, in writing, we are dependent on this language we all are, like the Dalesman in the *Excursion*, deaf and mute— not silent, which implies the possible manifestation of sound at our own will, but silent as a picture, that is to say eternally deprived of voice and condemned to muteness. No wonder that the Dalesman takes so readily to books and finds such solace in them, since for him the outside world has in fact always been a book, a succession of voiceless tropes. As soon as we understand the rhetorical function of prosopopeia as positing voice or face by means of language, we also understand that what we are deprived of is not life but the shape and the sense of a world accessible only in the privative way of understanding. Death is a displaced name for a linguistic predicament, and the restoration of mortality by autobiography (the prosopopeia of the voice and the name) deprives and disfigures to the precise extent that it restores. Autobiography veils a defacement of the mind of which it is itself the cause.

5
Wordsworth
and the Victorians

I‍T IS all too tempting to condescend
to the Victorian critics of Wordsworth, as if the later eighteen
hundreds, after the intuitive engagement of younger contemporaries such as Keats or De Quincey and before the reasoned
complexity of twentieth-century critics, represented a low point
of obfuscation in the understanding of England's major romantic poet. True enough, the predominant stress, in these
Victorian texts, on ethical as well as aesthetic judgment, at the
expense of even the slightest trace of analytic "reading," now
appears all the more dated since many of the resulting opinions must strike us as rather odd. Frederick Myers,[1] a by no
means conventional Victorian who, in 1881, wrote the "English Men of Letters" volume on Wordsworth, is nevertheless
conventional enough to identify Wordsworth so strongly with
"the county-seat of the English squire or nobleman"[2] that he
discusses the issues raised in "Two letters on the Kendal and
Windermere Railway" (1844) in much greater detail than those
raised in *The Excursion*. And Matthew Arnold, locked in the
ever recurring and never resolved battle between the defend-
ers of Wordsworth-the-poet and those of Wordsworth-the-
philosopher, has no qualms dismissing the entire *Prelude* in one

casual sentence. Since then, so many lifted interdicts and so much refinement of linguistic perception should make those earnest attempts to explain Wordsworth seem entirely obsolete, all the more since few of our contemporaries would still share Arnold's concern that Tennyson might supplant Wordsworth in the canon of English poetry. Even though Wordsworth's reputation beyond the limits of the English-speaking world has remained as dim as ever—a fact already noted and worried over by Arnold—the challenge of understanding his work remains almost urgently felt. The passion of his interpreters, up to the latest, bears witness to this in a manner of which the German involvement with Hölderlin or the French concern with Rousseau are the only comparable instances.

And yet, when all due allowances are made, the question remains whether a certain enigmatic aspect of Wordsworth, obliquely noted by the Victorians as well as by contemporary commentators, has in any way come closer to being identified nowadays than in the days of Arnold and Pater. Take the sexual taboo for instance, the usual criterion by which we measure the progress of our emancipation since pre-Freudian times. It took until 1915 to reveal the secret of Wordsworth's liaison with Annette Vallon and, at the time, the purveyor of this information feels called upon to excuse "this strange lover" by pointing out that he had been an orphan since early boyhood and that the end of the eighteenth century was lax in its views on sexual morality.[3] We have come a long way since. F. W. Bateson, with robust literalism, is obviously impatient with the conventional views of those "who find Annette lurking behind every rock, stone and tree" and delighted with the gamier task of giving Dorothy her proper libidinal due.[4] Nowadays, an infinitely more subtle and tactful critic does not even have to heighten his tone to suggest the "unutterable blessing" of incestuous phantasms involving father and daughter rather than brother and sister.[5] What is perhaps most striking about this rapid metamorphosis of a taboo into a commonplace is the lack of a proportionate liberation from the nineteenth-century standards by which Wordsworth is to be understood and evaluated. These standards were moral and religious and so, for all their refinement, they have remained, with very few and local exceptions, till today.

The place where the truly puzzling element in Wordsworth makes its presence felt can be located by ways of the somewhat irrelevant but insistent question which has shaped Wordsworth criticism for generations: is he a poet or a philosopher—or, somewhat less naively put, what is it in his work that forces upon us, for reasons that philosophy itself may not be able to master, this question of the compatibility between philosophy and poetry? Common sense tells us that poetry and philosophy are modes of discourse that should be kept distinct: to couple such power of seduction with such authority is to tempt fate itself. Hence the urge to protect, as the most pressing of moral imperatives, this borderline between both modes of discourse. Many poets can easily be enlisted in the service of this cause but others are more recalcitrant, though not necessarily because they are formally involved with philosophical systems. Wordsworth, rather than Coleridge, is a case in point. It is as if his language came from a region in which the most carefully drawn distinctions between analytic rigor and poetic persuasion are no longer preserved, at no small risk to either. Trying to state why this is so is to suggest an alternative to the canonical reading which has dominated the interpretation of Wordsworth from Victorian to modern times. Some contemporary writing on Wordsworth begins to break with this tradition or, to be more precise, begins to reveal the break that has always been hidden in it.

When Leslie Stephen, in 1876, made the claim that Wordsworth was to be considered a philosopher,[6] he meant by philosopher something very different from what the term may conjure up today. He meant *moral* philosophy, the fact that Wordsworth's poetry was not just "a thing of beauty," an object of aesthetic pleasure, but that it also had the power to console, to edify, and to protect from anxieties that threaten life and reason. Stephen's tone, of course, is one of moral piety, so much so that one now has some difficulty, at more than

one hundred years' distance, in seeing why Arnold felt impelled to react so strongly against an ethical emphasis not all
that different from his own.[7] Yet he did react and protested,
at the cost of considerable critical aberration, against the attempt to take Wordsworth seriously as a thinker, seriously
enough to be led by him beyond the realm of decorous aesthetic delight into a more barren area forbiddingly called "philosophy." Arnold's instinct was not unsound, especially in
making it apparent that Stephen's claim for Wordsworth's
consoling power was less convincing than his awareness of the
threat which these powers were supposed to console one from.
The strategy of denegation which calls a threat a shelter in the
hope of thus laying it to rest is all too familiar; Arnold was·
reacting in his own defensive manner to Stephen's defensive
attempts at reassurance. "Philosophy" is supposed to shelter
us from something to which Wordsworth's poetry, unlike any
other romantic poetry, gives access, although it remains un-
named and undefined. The effort of all subsequent Wordsworth interpreters has been, often with the poet's own assistance, to domesticate it by giving it at least a recognizable
content.

Thus, in parallel with the development of phenomenological and existential modes of thought, Wordsworth becomes,
in the twentieth century, a poet of the self-reflecting consciousness rather than a moralist. Hazlitt, Keats (who spoke,
by implication, of Wordsworth as "thinking into the human
heart"), and De Quincey had anticipated this responsiveness
to the lucid interiorization so much in evidence from "The Ruined Cottage" on. The measure of this lucidity lies in the absolute refusal to cope with the powers of negation otherwise
than by the rigorous acknowledgment of their manifestation,
be it as phenomenal, natural event or as affect. The precise
shade of recorded affectivity, in Wordsworth, is so delicate in
its refusal to make any concession to notions of sensory experience that it acquires an amazing power of recuperation in
the face of the most unadorned destructions that the mind can
imagine. The pathos of stoical eloquence is replaced by the

matter-of-factness for which Wordsworth became famous. It attracted a distinguished rostrum of parodists that includes Byron and Lewis Carroll and it produced some of the flattest lines of which the English language is capable,[8] the reverse side, as it were, of passages that are so radically unpredictable, so audacious in the sparseness of their means, that any attempt to link them to the high tradition of English verse is out of order. At those moments, the triumph of consciousness over its ever-threatening undoing is entire, and all the more unquestionable since Wordsworth never has to stoop to its explicit celebration. All remains implicit, inward, sheltered in the unsuspected nuances of common speech. No equivalence of this most distinctive Wordsworthian manner can be found, least of all in the Spenserian and Miltonic lineage of the romantic tradition. The best contemporary criticism is attuned to this inner voice that Victorian didacticism could only perceive at a muted distance, and it has been able to convey the resilience of the Wordsworthian sublime as a power of pure mind.

Leslie Stephen's "philosophy" is thus displaced from moral philosophy to a phenomenology of mind, a move to which Wordsworth's texts respond with almost suspicious docility. The threat from which we were to be sheltered and consoled is now identified as a condition of consciousness. Maiming, death, the wear and tear of mutability are the predicaments of "the unimaginable touch of time" and time, in this version of Wordsworth, is the very substance of the self-reflecting, recollecting mind. Time and language can then unite in metaphors of consciousness, the "rising," "sinking," "hanging," and "lying" motions of the intellectual, temporal light able to engender a complete solar world. By acquiescing to the shock, mild or violent, of the threat, the mind recovers its empire over itself and over the world. For the miracle of Wordsworth's figural diction is that, by stating its own precariousness so to speak face to face, without aesthetic evasion, it recovers the totality of the phenomenal world of sky and earth and thus, in a deeper sense than any color or melody could achieve, recovers the aesthetic in the process of its refusal. This is the aspect of Wordsworth which surfaces, though in less austere surroundings, among his poetic descendants: in Hardy, in unexplored corners of Yeats, evasively and with divergent strategies in Stevens and Frost. It is this same aspect which has shaped some of the best American literary criticism of the century, sometimes in direct encounter with Wordsworth, more often perhaps in dealing with other, not even necessarily romantic poets.

And yet, the very alacrity with which Wordsworth's major texts respond to this approach should make one wary. Are there no elements in the work that refuse to fit within the uncompromising order of Wordsworth's philosophy of the experience of consciousness? The suspicion is based, in part, on lexicological considerations. One essay stands out from the fundamentally harmonious consensus that unites, for all apparent disagreement, all contemporary writers on Wordsworth:[9] William Empson's essay entitled "Sense in the Prelude."[10] Empson shows that, if one follows the trace of a recurrent word in a given corpus, the emerging confusion cannot be reduced to any known model of trope that would control an identifiable semantic field; it is impossible, in other words, to make sense out of Wordsworth's "sense." This can hardly be an entirely trivial matter, and commentators have had to forget Empson's inquiry in order to carry on. One wonders if similar misadventures would befall other key terms in Wordsworth's lexicon. In his study, Empson set very respectable standards for the tact with which such a potentially mischievous task should be carried out in order to have any significance, at the furthest remove, that is, of statistical quantification, neglect of context, or clumsiness in the deciphering of figuration. One suspects that the results of such a study would be as complex as the procedure would have to be. Wordsworth himself has shown the way when, in a remarkably unthematic and technical rhetorical analysis, he singled out for examination the word "hangs" as it occurs in passages from Vergil and Milton.[11] His own use of "hangs" (or other verb forms such as "hung") in many key passages reveals, contrary to Empson's findings on "sense," a remarkably consistent pattern. A full-fledged theory of metaphor as suspended meaning, as loss and restoration of the principle of analogy beyond sensory experience, can be elaborated on the basis of Wordsworth's use of "hangs." In this case, there can be no doubt that the lexical choice is entirely meaningful, accessible to understanding on an advanced level of existential and rhetorical awareness. But then "hangs" is, by Wordsworth's own avowal, *the* exemplary metaphor for metaphor, for figuration in general. It is possibly the case that, whereas "hangs" makes sense but "sense" does not, meaning, in Wordsworth, cannot be reduced to the figural scheme that a philosophy of consciousness allows one to reach.

Consider for instance another key word in the corpus of *The Prelude* (1805),[12] the word "face" as it appears in the opening section of Book V (entitled "Books"):

> Hitherto
> In progress through this Verse, my mind hath look'd
> Upon the speaking face of earth and heaven
> As her prime Teacher . . .
>
> (V.10–13)

"Face" is, first of all, a *"speaking* face," the locus of speech, the necessary condition for the existence of articulated language. The lines are not simply an anthropomorphism, a conceit by which human consciousness is projected or transferred into the natural world. They assume the recognition of an entity or agency that bridges the distinction between mind and world by allowing them to exist in the proximity, in the dialogue of this distinction. Hence that, unlike other moments in Wordsworth (such as the *Essays upon Epitaphs*), "face" does not appear here in the context of an apostrophic stance in which nature is *addressed* by man. The passage from which these lines are taken is indeed apostrophic, but the apostrophe, the voiced eloquence within which it is encased, is addressed, not by or to the "face of earth and heaven," but to man: "O Man, / Thou paramount Creature . . ." (ll. 3–4) or "Thou also, Man, hast wrought . . ." (l. 17). Man can address and face other men, within life or beyond the grave, because he has a face, but he has a face only because he partakes of a mode of discourse that is neither entirely natural nor entirely human. The encounter between mind and earth (or heaven) is therefore not itself a dialogue or even, as in an earlier section, a listening (as in II.327–28 for example), but a mute scene of looking, the mind gazing upon a speaking face.[13] Compared to "speaking," "looking" may indeed appear as a loss or a deprivation. Yet, in this passage, it designates a prior encounter of which the other, later exchanges between men are derived. One can speak only because one can look upon a mode of speech which is not quite our own. A link is created between face and speech, but it remains obscure why this implies a seeing, an eye. The burden of the passage, which sets up a system that coordinates face, speech, man, and eye is to understand the connection between face and eye, two notions that are always co-present in the *Prelude*, also and perhaps most emphatically when one or the other of the two remains implicit.

The link between "face" and "eye" is clarified in the famous section in Book II beginning with the line "Bless'd be the infant Babe . . ." in which Wordsworth sets out "with my best conjectures" to ". . . trace / The progress of our being" (ll. 237–341). It can be considered Wordsworth's essay on the origins of language as poetic language, containing his most explicit description of the beginnings and workings of the "Poetic spirit of our human life" (l. 276). "Face" does not explicitly appear, yet the possibility and the status of its existence is at stake throughout the narration. "Eye," on the other hand, is prominent enough to displace "breast" where one would most naturally expect it:

> the Babe,
> Nurs'd in his Mother's arms, the Babe who sleeps
> Upon his mother's breast, who, when his soul
> Claims manifest kindred with an earthly soul,
> Doth gather passion from his Mother's *eye*![14]

What is later called a "mute dialogue with my Mother's heart" begins here in the exchange of a gaze, a meeting of "eyes." But this encounter is not a recognition, a shared awareness of common humanity. It occurs as an active verbal deed, a *claim* of "manifest kindred" which is not given in the nature of things. The power and the structure of this act are described in sufficient detail to give meaning to the by itself enigmatic phrase: to "gather passion." This "gathering" is a process of exchange by which the eye is "combin[d] / In one appearance . . ." with "all the elements / And parts of the same object, else detach'd / And both to coalesce . . ." Without having to evoke the technical vocabulary of associationist psychology which is here used, it is clear that what is being described is the possibility of inscribing the eye, which is nothing by itself, into a larger, total entity, the "same object" which, in the internal logic of the text, can only be the face, the face as the combination of parts which the mind, working like a synecdochical trope, can lay claim to—thus opening the way to a process of totalization which, in the span of a few lines, can grow to encompass everything, "*All* objects through *all* intercourse of sense." Language originates with the ability of the eye to establish the contour, the borderline, the surface which allows things to exist in the identity of the kinship of their distinction from other things.

"Face" then, in this passage, not unlike the earlier "hangs," designates the dependence of any perception or "eye" on the totalizing power of language. It heralds this dependency as "the first / Poetic spirit of our human life." The possibility of any contact between mind and nature depends on this spirit manifested by and in language. Just before this passage, Wordsworth has cautioned against the false distinctions which literal-minded psychologists (such as, presumably, Hartley) tend to make in their false claims to "analyse a soul" (II.232). He then offers his own theory of mind as the counterprocedure to the coarseness of what he calls the "outward shows" of science. Yet in a somewhat later passage, in Book III of the *Pre-*

lude, this same face-making, totalizing power is shown at work in a process of endless differentiation correctly called perpetual "logic," of which it is said that it "Could find no surface where its power might sleep" (l. 164). The face, which is the power to surface from the sea of infinite distinctions in which we risk to drown, can find no surface. How are we to reconcile the *meaning* of face, with its promise of sense and of filial preservation, with its *function* as the relentless undoer of its own claims?

This all too hasty reading shows that one can find, in Wordsworth's text, lexical continuities which are perfectly coherent; despite the somewhat ominous overtones of the literal predicament it invokes, the word "hangs" is a case in point. Other words, such as "sense" in Empson's essay, lead instead to near-total chaos. Somewhere in between, at the interface of these contradictory directions, words such as "face" can be said to embody this very incompatibility. They do not master or certainly do not resolve it, but they allow for some mode of discourse, however precarious, to take place within the tension of a conflict that can longer be reduced to existential or psychological causes. The work of Wordsworth is moral or religious only on the level of a surface which it prohibits us from finding. This would become even more manifest if, instead of considering such obviously figural terms as "face" or "hangs," we considered the syntactical and grammatical backbones of Wordsworth's diction, words such as "even" or "but" or the ever-recurring "not" and its many cognates. Victorian as well as contemporary Wordsworth criticism have in fact always responded to linguistic complexities of this kind and, as is inevitable, they built their defenses against them in ethical and aesthetic terms. It would be naive to believe that we could ever face Wordsworth, a poet of sheer language, outright. But it would be more naive still to think we can take shelter from what he knew by means of the very evasions which this knowledge renders impossible.

6
Shelley Disfigured

> . . . while digging in the grounds for the new
> foundations, the broken fragments of a mar-
> ble statue were unearthed. They were sub-
> mitted to various antiquaries, who said that,
> so far as the damaged pieces would allow
> them to form an opinion, the statue seemed
> to be that of a mutilated Roman satyr; or, if
> not, an allegorical figure of Death. Only one
> or two old inhabitants guessed whose statue
> those fragments had composed.
>
> Thomas Hardy,
> *"Barbara of the House of Grebe"*

LIKE SEVERAL of the English ro-
mantics' major works *The Triumph of Life,* Shelley's last poem,
is, as is well-known, a fragment that has been unearthed, edited, reconstructed, and much discussed. All this archeological labor can be considered a response to the questions that
articulate one of the text's main structures: ". . . 'And what
is this? / Whose shape is that within the car? and why—' " (ll.
177–78);[1] later repeated in a more subject-oriented, second-
person mode: " 'Whence camest thou? and whither goest thou?
/ How did thy course begin,' I said, 'and why?' " (ll. 296–97);
finally repeated again, now in the first person: " 'Shew whence

I came, and where I am, and why— . . .' " (l. 398). These
questions can easily be referred back to the enigmatic text they
punctuate and they are characteristic of the interpretive labor
associated with romanticism. In the case of this movement, they
acquire an edge of urgency which is often lacking when they
are addressed to earlier periods, except when these periods are
themselves mediated by the neo-hellenism, the neo-medieval-
ism, or the neo-baroque of the late eighteenth and the early
nineteenth century. This is not surprising, since they are precisely the archeological questions that prompt us to deduce the
present from the identification of the more or less immediately
anterior past, as well as from the process that leads from then
to now. Such an attitude coincides with the use of history as
a way to new beginnings, as "digging in the grounds for the
new foundations." Much is invested in these metaphors of ar-
chitecture and of statuary on which seems to hinge our ability
to inhabit the world. But if this curiosity about antecedents has
produced admirable philological results and allowed, as in the
case of *The Triumph of Life*, for the establishment of texts whose
unreliability is at least controlled by more reliable means, the
questions which triggered all this industry remain more than
ever in suspense: What is the meaning of *The Triumph of Life*,
of Shelley, and of romanticism? What shape does it have, how
did its course begin and why? Perhaps the difficulty of the answers is prefigured in the asking of the questions. The status
of all these where's and what's and how's and why's is at stake,
as well as the system that links these interrogative pronouns,
on the one hand, to questions of definition and of temporal
situation and, on the other hand, to questions of shape and of
figure. Such questions allow one to conclude that *The Triumph
of Life* is a fragment of something whole, or romanticism a
fragment, or a moment, in a process that now includes us
within its horizon. What relationship do we have to such a text
that allows us to call it a fragment that we are then entitled to
reconstruct, to identify, and implicitly to complete? This supposes, among other things, that Shelley or romanticism are
themselves entities which, like a statue, can be broken into

pieces, mutilated, or allegorized (to use Hardy's alternatives) after having been stiffened, frozen, erected, or whatever one wants to call the particular rigidity of statues. Is the status of a text like the status of a statue? Yeats, one of Shelley's closest readers and disciples, wrote a fine poem about history and form called *The Statues*, which it would be rewarding to read in conjunction with *The Triumph of Life*. But there are more economic ways to approach this text and to question the possibility of establishing a relationship to Shelley and to romanticism in general. After all, the link between the present I and its antecedents is itself dramatized in the poem, most explicitly and at greatest length in the encounter between the narrator and the figure designated by the proper name Rousseau, who has himself much to say about his own predecessors.

The unearthed fragments of this fragment, the discarded earlier versions, disclose that the relationship between Shelley and Rousseau, or between Rousseau and his ancestors, underwent considerable changes as the composition of the poem progressed. Consider, for instance, the passage in which the poet, guided at this moment by Rousseau, passes judgment upon his contemporaries and immediate predecessors, including the openly alluded to Wordsworth, with such vehemence that he condemns them all to oblivion.[2] He is reproached for this by Rousseau who intervenes to assert that he himself, as well as Voltaire, would have ascended to "the fane / Where truth and its inventors sit enshrined," if they had not been so fainthearted as to lack faith in their own intellectual labor as well as, by implication, that of their ancestors. Those encrypted statues of Truth are identified as "Plato and his pupil" (presumably Aristotle) who "Reigned from the center to the circumference" and prepared the way for Bacon and modern science. Rousseau's and Voltaire's capitulation is not a sheer loss however, since Rousseau has gained insight that he is able to communicate in turn to the young Shelley. Donald Reiman, the editor of *The Triumph of Life*, glosses the passage as follows:

Rousseau . . . tries to impress on the Poet that it was exactly this attitude toward the past struggle of great men that led him and Voltaire to abandon their reforming zeal and succumb to life. Thus the poet's contemptuous allusion to Wordsworth turns against him as Rousseau endeavors to show the Poet how the mistakes of those who have preceded him, especially idealists like himself, can serve as a warning to him: Rousseau and Voltaire fell because they adopted the contemptuous attitude toward history that the poet now displays; the child *is* father of the man, and Shelley's generation, representing the full mastery of the age that dawned in the French Revolution, can learn from the mistakes of that age's earlier generations (those of Rousseau and Voltaire and of Wordsworth).

Although this is certainly not presented as an interpretation of the entire text, but only of this discarded passage, it remains typical of the readings generally given of *The Triumph of Life*, even when they are a great deal more complicated than this straightforward statement. It is a clear example of the recuperation of a failing energy by means of an increased awareness: Rousseau lacked power, but because he can consciously articulate the causes of his weakness in words, the energy is preserved and recovered in the following generation. And this reconversion extends back to its originators, since the elders, at first condemned, are now reinstated in the name of their negative but exemplary knowledge. The child *is* father of the man, just as Wordsworth lucidly said, both humbling and saving himself in the eyes of his followers. This simple motion can take on considerable dialectical intricacy without altering its fundamental scheme. The entire debate as to whether *The Triumph of Life* represents or heralds a movement of growth or of degradation is part of this same genetic and historical metaphor.[3] The unquestioned authority of this metaphor is much more important than the positive or negative valorization of the movement it generates.

The initial situation of Rousseau—allied with Voltaire and Wordsworth in a shared failure, as opposed to Plato, Aristotle, and Bacon, and as opposed, by implication, to Shelley himself—changes in later versions. In the last available text, itself frozen into place by Shelley's accidental death, the hier-archy is quite different: Rousseau is now set apart quite sharply from the representatives of the Enlightenment (which include Voltaire next to Kant and Frederick the Great) who are con-demned with some of the original severity, without Rousseau reproving him for it. No allusion to Wordsworth is included at this point, though Wordsworth is certainly present in other regions of the poem. Rousseau is now classified with Plato and Aristotle, but whereas these philosophers were held up as un-tarnished images of Truth in the earlier version, they are now fallen and, in the imagery of the poem, chained to the chariot of Life, together with "the great bards of old" (l. 247). The rea-sons for their fall, as well as the elements in their works and in their lives that both unite and distinguish them from Rous-seau, are developed in passages that are not difficult to inter-pret from a thematic point of view. The resulting hierarchies have become more complex: we first have a class of entirely condemned historical personages, which includes representa-tives of the Enlightenment as well as the emperors and popes of Christianity (ll. 281 ff.); on a distinctly higher level, but nevertheless defeated, we find Rousseau, Plato, Aristotle, and Homer. As possibly exonerated from this defeat, the poem mentions only Bacon, a remnant from the earlier passage who now has lost much of his function, as well as "the sacred few" (l. 128) who, unlike Adonais in the earlier poem, had no earthly destiny whatsoever, either because, by choice or destiny, they died too early or because, like Christ or Socrates, they are mere fictions in the writings of others. As for Shelley himself, his close proximity to Rousseau is now more strongly marked than in the earlier passage; the possibility of his escape from Rous-seau's destiny has now become problematic and depends on one's reading of Rousseau's own story, which constitutes the main narrative sequence of the poem.[4]

Lengthy and complex as it is, Rousseau's self-narrated history provides no answer to his true identity, although he is himself shown in quest of such an answer. Questions of ori-gin, of direction, and of identity punctuate the text without ever receiving a clear answer. They always lead back to a new scene of questioning which merely repeats the quest and recedes in infinite regress: the narrator asks himself " 'And what is this? . . .' " (l. 177) and receives an enigmatic answer (" 'Life!' ") from an enigmatic shape; once identified as Rousseau, the shape can indeed reveal some other names in the pageant of history but is soon asked, by the poet, to identify itself in a deeper sense than by a mere name: " 'How did thy course begin . . . and why?' " Complying with this request, Rousseau narrates the history of his existence, also culminating in an encounter with a mysterious entity, " 'A shape all light . . .' " (l. 352) to whom, in his turn, he puts the question " 'whence I came, and where I am, and why—.' " As an answer, he is granted a vision of the same spectacle that prompted the poet-narrator's questioning in the first place; we have to imagine the same sequence of events repeating themselves for Shelley, for Rousseau, and for whomever Rousseau chose to question in his turn as Shelley questioned him. The structure of the text is not one of question and answer, but of a question whose meaning, as question, is effaced from the moment it is asked. The answer to the question is another question, asking what and why one asked, and thus receding ever further from the original query. This movement of effacing and of forgetting becomes prominent in the text and dispels any illusion of dialectical progress or regress. The articulation in terms of the questions is displaced by a very differently structured process that pervades all levels of the narrative and that repeats itself in the main sequences as well as in what seem to be lateral episodes. It finally engulfs and dissolves what started out to be, like *Alastor, Epipsychidion,* or even *Prometheus Unbound,* a quest (or, like *Adonais,* an elegy), to replace it by something quite different for which we have no name readily available among the familiar props of literary history.

Whenever this self-receding scene occurs, the syntax and the imagery of the poem tie themselves into a knot which arrests the process of understanding. The resistance of these passages is such that the reader soon forgets the dramatic situation and is left with only these unresolved riddles to haunt him: the text becomes the successive and cumulative experience of these tangles of meaning and of figuration. One of these tangles occurs near the end of Rousseau's narration of his encounter with the "shape all light" assumed to possess the key to his destiny:

> ". . . as one between desire and shame
> Suspended, I said . . .
> . . . .
> 'Shew whence I came, and where I am, and why—
> Pass not away upon the passing stream.'
>
> " 'Arise and quench thy thirst' was her reply.
> And as a shut lily, stricken by the wand
> Of dewy morning's vital alchemy,
>
> "I rose; and bending at her sweet command,
> Touched with faint lips the cup she raised,
> And suddenly my brain became as sand
>
> "Where the first wave had more than half erased
> The track of deer on desert Labrador,
> Whilst the fierce wolf from which they fled amazed
>
> "Leaves his stamp visibly upon the shore
> Until the second bursts—so on my sight
> Burst a new Vision never seen before.—"
>
> (ll. 394–410)

The scene dramatizes the failure to satisfy a desire for self-knowledge and can therefore indeed be considered as something of a key passage. Rousseau is not given a satisfactory answer, for the ensuing vision is a vision of continued delusion that includes him. He undergoes instead a metamorphosis in which his brain, the center of his consciousness, is transformed. The transformation is also said to be the erasure of an imprinted track, a passive, mechanical operation that is no longer within the brain's own control: both the production and the erasure of the track are not an act performed by the brain, but the brain being acted upon by something else. The resulting "sand" is not, as some commentators imply, an image of drought and sterility (this is no desert, but a shore washed by abundant waters).[5] "My brain became as sand" suggests the modification of a knowledge into the surface on which this knowledge ought to be recorded. Ought to be, for instead of being clearly imprinted it is "more than half erased" and covered over. The process is a replacement, a substitution, continuing the substitution of "brain" by "sand," of one kind of track, said to be like that of a deer, by another, said to be like that of a wolf "from which [the deer] fled amazed." They mark a stage in the metamorphosis of Rousseau into his present state or shape; when we first meet him, he is

> . . . what I thought was an old root which grew
> To strange distortion out of the hill side . . .
>
> And . . . the grass which methought hung so wide
> And white, was but his thin discoloured hair,
> And . . . the holes he vainly sought to hide
>
> Were or had been eyes.
>
> (ll. 182–88)[6]

The erasure or effacement is indeed the loss of a face, in French *figure*. Rousseau no longer, or hardly (as the tracks are not all gone, but more than half erased), has a face. Like the protagonist in the Hardy story, he is disfigured, *défiguré*, defaced. And also as in the Hardy story, to be disfigured means primarily the loss of the eyes, turned to "stony orbs" or to empty holes. This trajectory from erased self-knowledge to disfiguration is the trajectory of *The Triumph of Life*.

The connotations of the pair deer/wolf, marking a change in the inscriptions made upon Rousseau's mind, go some way in explaining the presence of Rousseau in the poem, a choice that has puzzled several interpreters.[7] The first and obvious contrast is between a gentle and idyllic peace pursued by violent aggression. Shelley, an assiduous reader of Rousseau at a time when he was being read more closely than he has been since, evokes an ambivalence of structure and of mood that is indeed specifically Rousseau's rather than anyone else's, including Wordsworth's. Rousseau's work is characterized in part by an introspective, self-reflexive mode which uses literary models of Augustinian and pietistic origin, illustrated, for instance, by such literary allusions as Petrarch and the *Astrée* and, in general, by the elements that prompted Schiller to discuss him under the heading of the contemporary idyll. But to this are juxtaposed elements that are closer to Machiavelli than to Petrarch, concerned with political power as well as with economic and legal realities. The first register is one of delicacy of feeling, whereas a curious brand of cunning and violence pervades the other. The uneasy mixture is both a commonplace and a crux of Rousseau interpretation. It appears in the larger as well as the finer dimensions of his writings, most obviously in such broad contrasts as separate the tone and import of a text such as *The Social Contract* from that of *Julie*. That the compatibility between inner states of consciousness and acts of power is a thematic concern of *The Triumph of Life* is clear from the political passages in the poem. In the wake of the in itself banal passage on Bonaparte, the conflict is openly stated:

> . . . much I grieved to think how power and will
> In opposition rule our mortal day—
>
> And why God made irreconcilable
> Good and the means of good; . . .
>
> (ll. 228–31)

Rousseau is unique among Shelley's predecessors not only in that this question of the discrepancy between the power of words as acts and their power to produce other words is inscribed within the thematics and the structure of his writings, but also in the particular form that it takes there. For the tension passes, in Rousseau, through a self which is itself experienced as a complex interplay between drives and the conscious reflection on these drives; Shelley's understanding of this configuration is apparent in this description of Rousseau as "between desire and shame / Suspended. . . ."

The opposition between will and power, the intellectual goal and the practical means, reappears when it is said, by and of Rousseau, that ". . . my words were seeds of misery—/ Even

as the deeds of others . . ." (ll. 280–81). The divergence between words and deeds (by way of "seeds") seems to be suspended in Rousseau's work, albeit at the cost of, or rather because of, considerable suffering: "I / Am one of those who have
created, even / If it be but a world of agony" (ll. 293–95). For
what sets Rousseau apart from the representatives of the Enlightenment is the pathos of what is here called the "heart"
("I was overcome / By my own heart alone. . . ."). The contrast between the cold and skeptical Voltaire and the sensitive
Rousseau is another commonplace of popular intellectual history. But Shelley's intuition of the "heart" in Rousseau is more
than merely sentimental. Its impact becomes clearer in the
contrast that sets Rousseau apart from "the great bards of old,"
Homer and Vergil, said to have ". . . inly quelled / The passions which they sung . . ." (ll. 274–75), whereas Rousseau
has ". . . suffered what [he] wrote, or viler pain!" Unlike the
epic narrators who wrote about events in which they did not
take part, Rousseau speaks out of his own self-knowledge, not
only in his *Confessions* (which Shelley did not like) but in all
his works, regardless of whether they are fictions or political
treatises. In the tradition of Augustine, Descartes, and Malebranche, the self is for him not merely the seat of the affections but the primary center of cognition. Shelley is certainly
not alone in thus characterizing and praising Rousseau, but the
configuration between self, heart, and action is given even
wider significance when Rousseau compares himself to the
Greek philosophers. Aristotle turns out to be, like Rousseau,
a double structure held together by the connivance of words
and deeds; if he is now enslaved to the eroding process of "life,"
it is because he does not exist singly, as pure mind, but cannot be separated from the "woes and wars" his pupil Alexander the Great inflicted upon the world. Words cannot be
isolated from the deeds they perform; the tutor necessarily
performs the deeds his pupil derives from his mastery. And
just as "deeds" cause the undoing of Aristotle, it is the "heart"
that brought down Plato who, like Rousseau, was a theoretician of statecraft and a legislator. Like Aristotle and like Rous-

seau (who is like a deer but also like a wolf) Plato is at least
double; life "conquered [his] heart" as Rousseau was "overcome by [his] own heart alone." The reference to the apocry-
phal story of Aster makes clear that "heart" here means more
than mere affectivity; Plato's heart was conquered by "love"
and, in this context, love is like the intellectual eros that links
Socrates to his pupils. Rousseau is placed within a configuration, brought about by "words," of knowledge, action, and
erotic desire. The elements are present in the symbolic scene
from which we started out, since the pursuit of the deer by
the wolf, in this context of Ovidian and Dantesque metamorphoses, is bound to suggest Apollo's pursuit of the nymphs
as well as scenes of inscription and effacement.

The scene is one of violence and grief, and the distress
reappears in the historical description of Rousseau with its repeated emphasis on suffering and agony, as well as in the
dramatic action of defeat and enslavement. But this defeat is
paradoxical: in a sense, Rousseau has overcome the discrepancy of action and intention that tears apart the historical world,
and he has done so because his words have acquired the power
of actions as well as of the will. Not only because they represent or reflect on actions but because they themselves, literally, are actions. Their power to act exists independently of their
power to know: Aristotle's or Plato's mastery of mind did not
give them any control over the deeds of the world, also and
especially the deeds that ensued as a consequence of their
words and with which they were directly involved. The power
that arms their words also makes them lose their power over
them. Rousseau gains shape, face, or figure only to lose it as
he acquires it. The enigma of this power, the burden of whatever understanding Shelley's poem permits, depends primarily on the reading of Rousseau's recapitulative narrative of his
encounter with the "Shape all light" (ll. 308–433).

Rousseau's history, as he looks back upon his existence from
the "April prime" of his young years to the present, tells of a
specific experience that is certainly not a simple one but that

can be designated by a single verb: the experience is that of forgetting. The term appears literally (l. 318) and in various periphrases (such as "oblivious spell," l. 331), or in metaphors with a clear analogical vehicle such as "quell" (l. 329), "blot [from memory]" (l. 330), "trample" (l. 388), "tread out" (l. 390), "erase" (l. 406), etc. It combines with another, more familiar metaphorical strain that is present throughout the entire poem: images of rising and waning light and of the sun.

The structure of "forgetting," in this text, is not clarified by echoes of a Platonic recollection and recognition (anamnesis) that enter the poem, partly by way of Shelley's own Platonic and Neoplatonic readings,[8] partly by way of Wordsworth's *Immortality Ode* whose manifest presence, in this part of the poem, has misled even the most attentive readers of *The Triumph of Life*. In the *Phaedo* (73) and, with qualifications too numerous to develop here, in Wordsworth's *Ode*, what one forgets is a former state which Yeats, who used the same set of emblems, compares to the Unity of Being evoked in Aristophanes' *Symposium* speech as the mainspring of erotic desire. Within a Neoplatonic Christian tradition, this easily becomes a fitting symbol for the Incarnation, for a birth out of a transcendental realm into a finite world. But this is precisely what the experience of forgetting, in *The Triumph of Life*, is not. What one forgets here is not some previous condition, for the line of demarcation between the two conditions is so unclear, the distinction between the forgotten and the remembered so unlike the distinction between two well-defined areas, that we have no assurance whatever that the forgotten ever existed:

> "Whether my life had been before that sleep
> The Heaven which I imagine, or a Hell
>
> Like this harsh world in which I wake to weep
> I know not."
>
> (ll. 332–35)

The polarities of waking and sleeping (or remembering and forgetting) are curiously scrambled, in this passage, with those of past and present, of the imagined and the real, of knowing and not knowing. For if, as is clear from the previous scene,[9] to be born into life is to fall asleep, thus associating life with sleep, then to "wake" from an earlier condition of non-sleeping into "this harsh world" of life can only be to become aware of one's persistent condition of slumber, to be more than ever asleep, a deeper sleep replacing a lighter one, a deeper forgetting being achieved by an act of memory which remembers one's forgetting. And since Heaven and Hell are not here two transcendental realms but the mere opposition between the imagined and the real, what we do not know is whether we are awake or asleep, dead or alive, forgetting or remembering. We cannot tell the difference between sameness and difference, and this inability to know takes on the form of a pseudo-knowledge which is called a forgetting. Not just because it is an unbearable condition of indetermination which has to be repressed, but because the condition itself, regardless of how it affects us, necessarily hovers between a state of knowing and not-knowing, like the symptom of a disease which recurs at the precise moment that one remembers its absence. What is forgotten is absent in the mode of a possible delusion, which is another way of saying that it does not fit within a symmetrical structure of presence and absence.

In conformity with the consistent system of sun imagery, this hovering motion is evoked throughout the poem by scenes of glimmering light. This very "glimmer" unites the poet-narrator to Rousseau, as the movement of the opening sunrise is repeated in Rousseau's encounter with the feminine shape, just as it unites the theme of forgetting with the motions of the light. The verb appears in the opening scene:

> . . . a strange trance over my fancy grew
> Which was not slumber, for the shade it spread
>
> Was so transparent that the scene came through
> As clear as when a veil of light is drawn
> O'er the evening hills they *glimmer*; . . .
> (ll. 29–33, emphasis added)[10]

and then again, later on, now with Rousseau on stage:

The presence of that shape which on the stream
Moved, as I moved along the wilderness,

More dimly than a day appearing dream,
The ghost of a forgotten form of sleep,
A light from Heaven whose half extinguished beam

Through the sick day in which we wake to weep
Glimmers, forever sought, forever lost.—
So did that shape its obscure tenour keep. . . .

(ll. 425–32, emphasis added)

It is impossible to say, in either passage, how the polarities of light and dark are matched with those of waking and sleep; the confusion is the same as in the previously quoted passage on forgetting and remembering. The light, in the second passage, is said to be like a dream, or like sleep ("the ghost of a forgotten form of sleep"), yet it shines, however distantly, upon a condition which is one of awakening ("the sad day in which we wake to weep"); in this light, to be awake is to be as if one were asleep. In the first passage, it is explicitly stated that since the poet perceives so clearly, he cannot be asleep, but the clarity is then said to be like that of a veil drawn over a darkening surface, a description which necessarily connotes covering and hiding, even if the veil is said to be "of light." Light covers light, trance covers slumber and creates conditions of optical confusion that resemble nothing as much as the experience of trying to read *The Triumph of Life*, as its meaning glimmers, hovers, and wavers, but refuses to yield the clarity it keeps announcing.

This play of veiling and unveiling is, of course, altogether tantalizing. Forgetting is a highly erotic experience; it is like glimmering light because it cannot be decided whether it reveals or hides; it is like desire because, like the wolf pursuing the deer, it does violence to what sustains it; it is like a trance or a dream because it is asleep to the very extent that it is conscious and awake, and dead to the extent that it is alive. The passage that concerns us makes this knot, by which knowledge, oblivion, and desire hang suspended, into an articulated sequence of events that demands interpretation.

The chain that leads Rousseau from the birth of his consciousness to his present state of impending death passes through a well-marked succession of relays. Plato and Wordsworth provide the initial linking of birth with forgetting, but this forgetting has, in Shelley's poem, the glimmering ambivalence which makes it impossible to consider it as an act of closure or of beginning and which makes any further comparison with Wordsworth irrelevant. The metaphor for this process is that of "a gentle rivulet . . . [which] filled the grove / With sound which all who hear must needs forget / All pleasure and all pain . . ." (ll. 314–19). Unlike Yeats', Shelley's river does not function as the "generated soul," as the descent of the transcendental soul into earthly time and space. As the passage develops, it enters into a system of relationships that are natural rather than esoteric. The property of the river that the poem singles out is its sound; the oblivious spell emanates from the repetitive rhythm of the water, which articulates a random noise into a definite pattern. Water, which has no shape of itself, is molded into shape by its contact with the earth, just as in the scene of the water washing away the tracks, it generates the very possibility of structure, pattern, form, or shape by way of the disappearance of shape into shapelessness. The repetition of the erasures rhythmically articulates what is in fact a disarticulation, and the poem seems to be shaped by the undoing of shapes. But since this pattern does not fully correspond to what it covers up, it leaves the trace which allows one to call this ambivalent shaping a forgetting. The birth of what an earlier Shelley poem such as *Mont Blanc* would still have called the mind occurs as the distortion which allows one to make the random regular by "forgetting" differences.

As soon as the water's noise becomes articulated sound it can enter into contact with the light. The birth of form as the interference of light and water passes, in the semi-synaesthesia of the passage, through the mediation of sound; it is however only a semi-synaesthesia, for the optical and auditory perceptions, though simultaneous, nevertheless remain treated in asymmetrical opposition:

> A shape all light, which with one hand did fling
> Dew on the earth, as if she were the Dawn
> Whose invisible rain forever seemed to sing
>
> A silver music on the mossy lawn,
> *And still* before her on the dusky grass
> Iris her many coloured scarf had drawn.
>
> > (ll. 352–57, emphasis added)[11]

The water of the original river here fulfills a double and not necessarily complementary action, as it combines with the light to form, on the one hand, Iris's scarf or rainbow and, on the other hand, the "silver music" of oblivion. A traditional symbol of the integration of the phenomenal with the transcendental world, the natural synthesis of water and light in the rainbow is, in Shelley, the familiar "dome of many coloured glass" whose "stain" is the earthly trace and promise of an Eternity in which Adonais' soul is said to dwell "like a star." As such, it irradiates all the textures and forms of the natural world with the veil of the sun's *farbiger Abglanz*, just as it provides the analogical light and heat that will make it possible to refer to the poet's mind as "embers." The metaphorical chain which links the sun to water, to color, to heat, to nature, to mind, and to consciousness, is certainly at work in the poem and can be summarized in this image of the rainbow. But this symbol is said to exist here in the tenuous mode of insistence, as something that *still* prevails (l. 356) despite the encroachment of something else, also emanating from water and sun and associated with them from the start, called music and forgetting. This something else, of which it could be said that it wrenches the final statement of *Adonais* into a different shape, appears in some degree of tension with the symbol of the rainbow.

The entire scene of the shape's apparition and subsequent waning (l. 412) is structured as a near-miraculous suspension between these two different forces whose interaction gives to the figure the hovering motion which may well be the mode of being of all figures. This glimmering figure takes on the form of the unreachable reflection of Narcissus, the manifestation of shape at the expense of its possession. The suspended fascination of the Narcissus stance is caught in the moment when the shape is said to move

> . . . with palms so tender
> Their tread broke not the mirror of its billow, . . .
>
> (ll. 361–62)

The scene is self-reflexive: the closure of the shape's contours is brought about by self-duplication. The light generates its own shape by means of a mirror, a surface that articulates it without setting up a clear separation that differentiates inside from outside as self is differentiated from other. The self that comes into being in the moment of reflection is, in spatial terms, optical symmetry as the ground of structure, optical repetition as the structural principle that engenders entities as shapes. "Shape all light" is referentially meaningless since light, the necessary condition for shape, is itself, like water, without shape, and acquires shape only when split in the illusion of a doubleness which is not that of self and other. The sun, in this text, is from the start the figure of this self-contained specularity. But the double of the sun can only be the eye conceived as the mirror of light. "Shape" and "mirror" are inseparable in this scene, just as the sun is inseparable from the shapes it generates and which are, in fact, the eye,[12] and just as the sun is inseparable from itself since it produces the illusion of the self as shape. The sun can be said "to stand," a figure which assumes the existence of an entire spatial organization, because it stands personified

> amid the blaze
> Of his own glory, . . .
>
> (ll. 349–50)

The sun "sees" its own light reflected, like Narcissus, in a well that is a mirror and also an eye:

> . . . the Sun's image radiantly intense
> Burned on the waters of the well that glowed
> Like gold, . . .
>
> (ll. 345–47)

Because the sun is itself a specular structure, the eye can be said to generate a world of natural forms. The otherness of a world that is in fact without order now becomes, for the eye, a maze made accessible to solar paths, as the eye turns from the blank radiance of the sun to its green and blue reflection in the world, and allows us to be in this world as in a landscape of roads and intents. The sun

> threaded all the forest maze
> With winding paths of emerald fire. . . .
>
> (ll. 347–48)

The boldest, but also the most traditional, image in this passage is that of the sunray as a thread that stitches the texture of the world, the necessary and complementary background for the eye of Narcissus. The water and pupil of the eye generate the rainbow of natural forms among which it dwells in sensory self-fulfillment. The figure of the sun, present from the beginning of the poem, repeats itself in the figure of the eye's self-erotic contact with its own surface, which is also the mirror of the natural world. The erotic element is marked from the start, in the polarity of a male sun and a feminine shape, eye or well, which is said to

> bend her
> Head under the dark boughs, till like a willow
> Her fair hair swept the bosom of the stream
> That whispered with delight to be their pillow.—
>
> (ll. 363–66)

   Shelley's imagery, often assumed to be incoherent and erratic, is instead extraordinarily systematic whenever light is being thematized. The passage condenses all that earlier and later poets (one can think of Valéry and Gide's Narcissus, as well as of the *Roman de la Rose* or of Spenser) ever did with light, water, and mirrors. It also bears witness to the affinity of his imagination with that of Rousseau, who allowed the phantasm of language born rhapsodically out of an erotic well to tell its story before he took it all away. Shelley's treatment of the birth of light reveals all that is invested in the emblem of the rainbow. It represents the very possibility of cognition, even for processes of articulation so elementary that it would be impossible to conceive of any principle of organization, however primitive, that would not be entirely dependent on its power. To efface it would be to take away the sun which, if it were to happen to this text, for example, would leave little else. *And still,* this light is allowed to exist in *The Triumph of Life* only under the most tenuous of conditions.

The frailty of the stance is represented in the supernatural delicacy which gives the shape "palms so tender / Their tread broke not the mirror of [the river's] billow" and which allows it to "glide along the river." The entire scene is set up as a barely imaginable balance between this gliding motion, which remains on one side of the watery surface and thus allows the specular image to come into being, and the contrary motion which, like Narcissus at the end of the mythical story, breaks through the surface of the mirror and disrupts the suspended fall of its own existence. As the passage develops, the story must run its course. The contradictory motions of "gliding" and "treading" which suspended gravity between rising and falling finally capsize. The "threading" sunrays become the "treading" of feet upon a surface which, in this text, does not stiffen into solidity.[13] Shelley's poem insists on the hyperbolic lightness of the reflexive contact, since the reflecting surface is never allowed the smooth stasis that is necessary to the duplication of the image. The water is kept in constant motion: it is called a "billow" and the surface, although compared to a crystal, is roughened by the winds that give some degree of verisimilitude to the shape's gliding motion. By the end of the section, we have moved from "thread" to "tread" to "trample," in a movement of increased violence that erases the initial tenderness. There is no doubt that, when we again meet the shape (ll. 425 ff.) it is no longer gliding along the river but drowned, Ophelia-like, below the surface of the water. The violence is confirmed in the return of the rainbow, in the ensuing vision, as a rigid, stony arch said "fiercely [to extoll] the fortune" of the shape's defeat by what the poem calls "life."

This chain of metaphorical transformations can be understood, up to this point, without transposition into a vocabulary that would not be that of their own referents, not unlike the movement of the figure itself as it endeavors to glide incessantly along a surface which it tries to keep intact. Specifically, the figure of the rainbow is a figure of the unity of perception and cognition undisturbed by the possibly disruptive mediation of its own figuration. This is not surprising, since the underlying assumption of such a paraphrastic reading is itself one of specular understanding in which the text serves as a mirror of our own knowledge and our knowledge mirrors in its turn the text's signification. But we can only inadequately understand in this fashion why the shaped light of understanding is itself allowed to wane away, layer by layer, until it is entirely forgotten and remains present only in the guise of an edifice that serves to celebrate and to perpetuate its oblivion. Nor can we understand the power that weighs down the seductive grace of figuration until it destroys itself. The figure of the sun, with all its chain of correlatives, should also be read in a non-phenomenal way, a necessity which is itself phenomenally represented in the dramatic tension of the text.

The transition from "gliding" to "trampling" passes, in the action that is being narrated, through the intermediate relay of "measure." The term actively reintroduces music which, after having been stressed in the previous scene (ll. 354–55), is at first only present by analogy in this phase of the action (ll. 359–74).[14] Measure is articulated sound, that is to say language. Language rather than music, in the traditional sense of harmony and melody. As melody, the "song" of the water and, by extension, the various sounds of nature, only provide a background that easily blends with the seduction of the natural world:

> . . . all the place
> Was filled with many sounds woven into one
> Oblivious melody, confusing sense
> Amid the gliding waves and shadows dun; . . .
>
> (ll. 339–42)

As melody and harmony, song belongs to the same gliding motion that is interrupted only when the shape's feet

> to the ceaseless song
> Of leaves and winds and waves and birds and bees
> And falling drops moved in a measure new. . . .
>
> (ll. 375–77)

The "tread" of this dancer, which needs a ground to the extent that it carries the weight of gravity, is no longer melodious, but reduces music to the mere measure of repeated articulations. It singles out from music the accentual or tonal punctuation which is also present in spoken diction. The scene could be said to narrate the birth of music out of the spirit of language, since the determining property is an articulation distinctive of verbal sound prior to its signifying function. The thematization of language in *The Triumph of Life* occurs at this point, when "measure" separates from the phenomenal aspects of signification as a specular *representation*, and stresses instead the literal and material aspects of language. In the dramatic action of the narrative, measure disrupts the symmetry of cognition as representation (the figure of the rainbow, of the eye and of the sun). But since measure is any principle of linguistic organization, not only as rhyme and meter but as any syntactical or grammatical scansion, one can read "feet" not just as the poetic meter that is so conspicuously evident in the *terza rima* of the poem, but as any principle of signification. Yet it is precisely these "feet" which extinguish and bury the poetic and philosophical light.

It is tempting to interpret this event, the shape's "trampling" the fires of thought "into the dust of death" (l. 388), certainly the most enigmatic moment in the poem, as the bifurcation between the semantic and the non-signifying, material properties of language. The various devices of articulation, from word to sentence formation (by means of grammar, syntax, accentuation, tone, etc.), which are made to convey meaning, and these same articulations left to themselves, independently of their signifying constraints, do not necessarily determine each other. The latent polarity implied in all classical theories of the sign allows for the relative independence of the signifier and for its free play in relation to its signifying function. If, for instance, compelling rhyme schemes such as "billow," "willow," "pillow" or transformations such as "thread" to "tread" or "seed" to "deed" occur at crucial moments in the text, then the question arises whether these particularly meaningful movements or events are not being generated by random and superficial properties of the signifier rather than by the constraints of meaning. The obliteration of thought by "measure" would then have to be interpreted as the loss of semantic depth and its replacement by what Mallarmé calls "le hasard infini des conjonctions" (*Igitur*).

But this is not the story, or not the entire story, told by *The Triumph of Life*. For the arbitrary element in the alignment between meaning and linguistic articulation does not by itself have the power to break down the specular structure which the text erects and then claims to dissolve. It does not account for the final phase of the Narcissus story, as the shape traverses the mirror and goes under, just as the stars are conquered by the sun at the beginning of the poem and the sun then conquered in its turn by the light of the Chariot of Life. The undoing of the representational and iconic function of figuration by the play of the signifier does not suffice to bring about the disfiguration which *The Triumph of Life* acts out or represents. For it is the alignment of a signification with any principle of linguistic articulation whatsoever, sensory or not, which constitutes the figure. The iconic, sensory or, if one wishes, the aesthetic moment is not constitutive of figuration. Figuration is the element in language that allows for the reiteration of meaning by substitution; the process is at least twofold and this plurality is naturally illustrated by optical icons of specularity. But the particular seduction of the figure is not necessarily that it creates an illusion of sensory pleasure, but that it creates an illusion of meaning. In Shelley's poem, the shape is a figure regardless of whether it appears as a figure of light (the rainbow) or of articulation in general (music as measure and language). The transition from pleasure to signification, from the aesthetic to the semiological dimension, is clearly marked in the passage, as one moves from the figure of the rainbow to that of the dance, from sight to measure. It marks the identification of the shape as the model of figuration in general. By taking this step beyond the traditional conceptions of figuration as modes of representation, as polarities of subject and object, of part and whole, of necessity and chance or of sun and eye, the way is prepared for the subsequent undoing and erasure of the figure. But the extension, which coincides with the passage from tropological models such as metaphor, synecdoche, metalepsis, or prosopopoeia (in which a phenomenal element, spatial or temporal, is necessarily involved) to tropes such as grammar and syntax (which function on the level of the letter without the intervention of an iconic factor) is not by itself capable of erasing the figure or, in the representational code of the text, of drowning the shape or trampling out thought. Another intervention, another aspect of language has to come into play.

The narrative sequence of Rousseau's encounter, as it unfolds from the apparition of the shape (l. 343) to its replacement (l. 434) by a "new vision," follows a motion framed by two events that are acts of power: the sun overcoming the light of the stars, the light of life overcoming the sun. The movement from a punctual action, determined in time by a violent act of power, to the gliding, suspended motion "of that shape which on the stream/ Moved, as I moved along the wilderness" (ll. 425–26) is the same motion inherent in the title of the poem. As has been pointed out by several commentators, "triumph" designates the actual victory as well as the *trionfo,* the pageant that celebrates the outcome of the battle. The reading of the scene should allow for a more general interpretation of this contradictory motion.

We now understand the shape to be the figure for the figurality of all signification. The specular structure of the scene as a visual plot of light and water is not the determining factor but merely an illustration (*hypotyposis*) of a plural structure that involves natural entities only as principles of articulation among others. It follows that the figure is not naturally given or produced but that it is posited by an arbitrary act of language. The appearance and the waning of the light-shape, in spite of the solar analogon, is not a natural event resulting from the mediated interaction of several powers, but a single, and therefore violent, act of power achieved by the positional power of language considered by and in itself: the sun masters the stars because it *posits* forms, just as "life" subsequently masters the sun because it posits, by inscription, the "track" of historical events. The positing power does not reside in Rousseau as subject; the mastery of the shape over Rousseau is never in question. He rises and bends at her command and his mind is passively trampled into dust without resistance. The positing power of language is both entirely arbitrary, in having a strength that cannot be reduced to necessity, and entirely inexorable in that there is no alternative to it. It stands beyond the polarities of chance and determination and can therefore not be part of a temporal sequence of events. The sequence has to be punctured by acts that cannot be made a part of it. It cannot begin, for example, by telling us of the waning of the stars under the growing impact of the sun, a natural motion which is the outcome of a mediation, but it must evoke the violent "springing forth" of a sun detached from all antecedents. Only retrospectively can this event be seen and misunderstood as a substitution and a beginning, as a dialectical relationship between day and night, or between two transcendental orders of being. The sun does not appear in conjunction with or in reaction to the night and the stars, but of its own unrelated power. *The Triumph of Life* differs entirely from such Promethean or titanic

myths as Keats's *Hyperion* or even *Paradise Lost* which thrive
on the agonistic pathos of dialectical battle. It is unimaginable
that Shelley's non-epic, non-religious poem would begin by
elegiacally or rebelliously evoking the tragic defeat of the former gods, the stars, at the hands of the sun. The text has no
room for the tragedy of defeat or of victory among next-of-kin,
or among gods and men. The previous occupants of the narrative space are expelled by decree, by the sheer power of utterance, and consequently at once forgotten. In the vocabulary
of the poem, it occurs by *imposition* (l. 20), the emphatic mode
of positing. This compresses the prosopopoeia of the personified sun, in the first lines of the poem, into a curiously absurd
pseudo-description. The most continuous and gradual event
in nature, the subtle gradations of the dawn, is collapsed into
the brusque swiftness of a single moment:

> Swift as a spirit hastening to his task
> . . . the Sun sprang forth
> . . . and the mask
> Of darkness fell from the awakened Earth.
>
> (ll. 1–4)[15]

The appearances, later in the poem, of the Chariot of Life are
equally brusque and unmotivated. When they occur, they are
not "descendants" of the sun, not the natural continuation of
the original, positing gesture but positings in their own right.
Unlike night following day, they always again have to be posited, which explains why they are repetitions and not beginnings.

How can a positional act, which relates to nothing that
comes before or after, become inscribed in a sequential narrative? How does a speech act become a trope, a catachresis which
then engenders in its turn the narrative sequence of an allegory? It can only be because we impose, in our turn, on the
senseless power of positional language the authority of sense
and of meaning. But this is radically inconsistent: language
posits and language means (since it articulates) but language
cannot posit meaning; it can only reiterate (or reflect) it in its

reconfirmed falsehood. Nor does the knowledge of this impossibility make it less impossible. This impossible position is
precisely the figure, the trope, metaphor as a violent—and not
as a dark—light, a deadly Apollo.

The imposition of meaning occurs in The Triumph of Life in
the form of the questions that served as point of departure for
the reading. It is as a questioning entity, standing within the
pathos of its own indetermination, that the human subject appears in the text, in the figures of the narrator who interrogates Rousseau and of Rousseau who interrogates the shape.
But these figures do not coincide with the voice that narrates
the poem in which they are represented; this voice does not
question and does not share in their predicament. We can
therefore not ask why it is that we, as subjects, choose to impose meaning, since we are ourselves defined by this very
question. From the moment the subject thus asks, it has already foreclosed any alternative and has become the figural
token of meaning, "Ein Zeichen sind wir / Deutungslos . . ."
(Hölderlin). To question is to forget. Considered performa-
tively, figuration (as question) performs the erasure of the
positing power of language. In The Triumph of Life, this happens when a positional speech act is represented as what it
resembles least of all, a sunrise.

To forget, in this poem, is by no means a passive process.
In the Rousseau episode, things happen because the subject
Rousseau keeps forgetting. In his earliest stages, he forgets the
incoherence of a world in which events occur by sheer dint of
a blind force, in the same way that the sun, in the opening
lines, occurs by sheer imposition. The episode describes the
emergence of an articulated language of cognition by the erasure, the forgetting of the events this language in fact performed. It culminates in the appearance of the shape, which
is both a figure of specular self-knowledge, the figure of
thought, but also a figure of "thought's empire over thought,"
of the element in thought that destroys thought in its attempt
to forget its duplicity. For the initial violence of position can
only be half erased, since the erasure is accomplished by a de-

vice of language that never ceases to partake of the very violence against which it is directed. It seems to extend the instantaneousness of the act of positing over a series of transformations, but this duration is a fictitious state, in which "all . . . seemed as if it had been not" (l. 385). The trampling gesture enacts the necessary recurrence of the initial violence: a figure of thought, the very light of cognition, obliterates thought. At its apparent beginning as well as at its apparent end, thought (i.e., figuration) forgets what it thinks and cannot do otherwise if it is to maintain itself. Each of the episodes forgets the knowledge achieved by the forgetting that precedes it, just as the instantaneous sunrise of the opening scene is at once covered over by a "strange trance" which allows the narrator to imagine the scene as something remembered even before it could take place.[16] Positing "glimmers" into a glimmering knowledge that acts out the aporias of signification and of performance.

The repetitive erasures by which language performs the erasure of its own positions can be called disfiguration. The disfiguration of Rousseau is enacted in the text, in the scene of the root, and repeats itself in a more general mode in the disfiguration of the shape:

> . . . The fair shape waned in the coming
> light
> As veil by veil the silent splendour drops
> From Lucifer, amid the chrysolite
>
> Of sunrise ere it strike the mountain tops—
>
> (ll. 412–15)

Lucifer, or metaphor, the bearer of light which carries over the light of the senses and of cognition from events and entities to their meaning, irrevocably loses the contour of its own face or shape. We see it happen when the figure first appears as water music, then as rainbow, then as measure, to finally sink away "below the watery floor" trampled to death by its own power. Unlike Lycidas, it is not resurrected in the guise of a star, but repeated on a level of literality which is not that of meaning but of actual events, called "Life" in Shelley's poem. But "Life" is as little the end of figuration as the sunrise was its beginning. For just as language is misrepresented as a natural event, life is just as falsely represented by the same light that emanates from the sun and that will have to engender its own rainbow and measure. Only that this light destroys its previous representation as the wolf destroys the deer. The process is endless, since the knowledge of the language's performative power is itself a figure in its own right and, as such, bound to repeat the disfiguration of metaphor as Shelley is bound to repeat the aberration of Rousseau in what appears to be a more violent mode. Which also implies, by the same token, that he is bound to forget him, just as, in all rigor, *The Social Contract* can be said to erase *Julie* from the canon of Rousseau's works, or *The Triumph of Life* can be said to reduce all of Shelley's previous work to nought.

The persistence of light imagery, in the description of the Chariot of Life as well as in the inaugural sunrise, creates the illusion of a continuity and makes the knowledge of its interruption serve as a ruse to efface its actual occurrence. The poem is sheltered from the performance of disfiguration by the power of its negative knowledge. But this knowledge is powerless to prevent what now functions as the decisive textual articulation: its reduction to the status of a fragment brought about by the actual death and subsequent disfigurement of Shelley's body, burned after his boat capsized and he drowned off the coast of Lerici. This defaced body is present in the margin of the last manuscript page and has become an inseparable part of the poem. At this point, figuration and cognition are actually interrupted by an event which shapes the text but which is not present in its represented or articulated meaning. It may seem a freak of chance to have a text thus molded by an actual occurrence, yet the reading of *The Triumph of Life* establishes that this mutilated textual model exposes the wound of a fracture that lies hidden in all texts. If anything, this text is more rather than less typical than texts that have not been thus truncated. The rhythmical interruptions that mark off the successive episodes of the narrative are not new moments of cognition but literal events textually reinscribed by a delusive act of figuration or of forgetting.

In Shelley's absence, the task of thus reinscribing the disfiguration now devolves entirely on the reader. The final test of reading, in *The Triumph of Life*, depends on how one reads the textuality of this event, how one disposes of Shelley's body. The challenge that is in fact present in all texts and that *The Triumph of Life* identifies, thematizes, and thus tries to avoid in the most effective way possible, is here actually carried out as the sequence of symbolic interruptions is in its turn interrupted by an event that is no longer simply imaginary or symbolic. The apparent ease with which readers of *The Triumph of Life* have been able to dispose of this challenge demonstrates the inadequacy of our understanding of Shelley and, beyond him, of romanticism in general.

For what we have done with the dead Shelley, and with all the other dead bodies that appear in romantic literature— one thinks, among many others, of the "dead man" that " 'mid that beauteous scene / Of trees, and hills and water, bolt upright / Rose with his ghastly face; . . ." in Wordsworth's *Prelude* (V.470–72)—is simply to bury them, to bury them in their own texts made into epitaphs and monumental graves. They have been made into statues for the benefit of future archeologists "digging in the grounds for the new foundations" of their own monuments. They have been transformed into historical and aesthetic objects. There are various and subtle strategies, much too numerous to enumerate, to accomplish this.

Such monumentalization is by no means necessarily a naive or evasive gesture, and it certainly is not a gesture that anyone can pretend to avoid making. It does not have to be naive, since it does not have to be the repression of a self-threatening knowledge. Like *The Triumph of Life*, it can state the full power of this threat in all its negativity; the poem demonstrates that this rigor does not prevent Shelley from allegorizing his own negative assurance, thus awakening the suspicion that the negation is a *Verneinung*, an intended exorcism. And it is not avoidable, since the failure to exorcize the threat, even in the face of such evidence as the radical blockage that befalls this poem, becomes precisely the challenge to understanding that always again demands to be read. And to read is to understand, to question, to know, to forget, to erase, to deface, to repeat—that is to say, the endless prosopopoeia by which the dead are made to have a face and a voice which tells the allegory of their demise and allows us to apostrophize them in our turn. No degree of knowledge can ever stop this madness, for it is the madness of words. What *would* be naive is to believe that this strategy, which is not *our* strategy as subjects, since we are its product rather than its agent, can be a source of value and has to be celebrated or denounced accordingly.

Whenever this belief occurs—and it occurs all the time—it leads to a misreading that can and should be discarded, unlike the coercive "forgetting" that Shelley's poem analytically thematizes and that stands beyond good and evil. It would be of little use to enumerate and categorize the various forms and names which this belief takes on in our present critical and literary scene. It functions along monotonously predictable lines, by the historicization and the aesthetification of texts, as well as by their use, as in this essay, for the assertion of methodological claims made all the more pious by their denial of piety. Attempts to define, to understand, or to circumscribe romanticism in relation to ourselves and in relation to other literary movements are all part of this naive belief. *The Triumph of Life* warns us that nothing, whether deed, word, thought, or text, ever happens in relation, positive or negative, to anything that precedes, follows, or exists elsewhere, but only as a random event whose power, like the power of death, is due to the randomness of its occurrence. It also warns us why and how these events then have to be reintegrated in a historical and aesthetic system of recuperation that repeats itself regardless of the exposure of its fallacy. This process differs entirely from the recuperative and nihilistic allegories of historicism. If it is true and unavoidable that any reading is a monumentalization of sorts, the way in which Rousseau is read and disfigured in *The Triumph of Life* puts Shelley among the few readers who "guessed whose statue those fragments had composed." Reading as disfiguration, to the very extent that it resists historicism, turns out to be historically more reliable than the products of historical archeology. To monumentalize this observation into a *method* of reading would be to regress from the rigor exhibited by Shelley which is exemplary precisely because it refuses to be generalized into a system.

7
Symbolic Landscape in Wordsworth and Yeats

Wordsworth's NARRATIVE poem *The Prelude* opens with an invocation to a "gentle breeze" blowing "from the green fields and from yon azure sky" and shows the poet guided in his work by ". . . nothing better than a wandering cloud." Very early in Book I—by line 60—one moves from general nature to a specific and "known Vale," the first in a series of landscapes that will recur to mark the main articulations of the narrative. Keats's epic *Hyperion* begins by introducing the fallen Titan Saturn with more attention given to the setting than to the figure—a setting that captures beautifully the sheltered quiet of a summer landscape. In both cases, where we would traditionally, in works of epic tonality, have expected an invocation to the muse, we are given a landscape instead. As so often in romantic poetry, the landscape replaces the muse; and just as the relationship between poet and muse can take on a variety of shades, the dramatic interaction between poet and landscape acquires a rich diversity in romantic writing.

In the case of a "natural" romantic like Wordsworth, who

urged "at all times, to look steadily at the subject," one might be tempted to think of the poet as a painter, whose language merely records and imitates sense perceptions. It is well-known, however, that this urge to keep the eye on the subject is only Wordsworth's starting point and that, perhaps more than any poet, he appreciates the complexity of what happens when eye and object meet. The delicate interplay between perception and imagination could nowhere be more intricate than in the representation of a natural scene, transmuted and recollected in the ordering form of Wordsworth's poetic language. The sonnet I have chosen for illustration is a typical instance: in the short span of its fourteen lines, one can observe the juxtaposition of two very different attitudes toward a landscape, held together by a dramatic progression which constitutes the key to the interpretation. Similar tensions can be shown to underlie the entire work.

Wide as the scope of Wordsworth's vision extends, it would never encompass Yeats's occasional claim of rejecting natural reality altogether, to ". . . scorn aloud / In glory of changeless metal / Common bird or petal." A considerable distance separates Wordsworth's involved but persistently reverent "look(ing) at the subject" from Yeats's intermittent contempt for "natural thing(s)"; one is not surprised to find Yeats much more reserved in his praise of Wordsworth than in his laudatory references to Blake and Shelley. Before venturing any speculation, historical or other, on the significance of this fundamental discrepancy between two poets both labeled "romantic," the nature of the difference needs to be clarified; one way of attempting this is by comparing a characteristic use of landscape in one of the later Yeats poems with an equally representative example from Wordsworth.

Our first example will be the sonnet by Wordsworth, "Composed by the Side of Grasmere Lake":

> Clouds, lingering yet, extend in solid bars
> Through the grey West; and lo! these waters, steeled
> By breezeless air to smoothest polish, yield

A vivid repetition of the stars;
Jove, Venus, and the ruddy crest of Mars
Amid his fellows beauteously revealed
At happy distance from earth's groaning field,
Where ruthless mortals wage incessant wars.
Is it a mirror?—or the nether Sphere
Opening to view the abyss in which she feeds
Her own calm fires?—But list! a voice is near;
Great Pan himself low-whispering through the reeds.
"Be thankful, thou; for, if unholy deeds
Ravage the world, tranquillity is here!"

As so often in Wordsworth, the statement, the message of the poem is made explicit in the concluding lines. The poem names "tranquillity," and this alone would be a sufficient reason to single it out from the other words, since it is to convey a feeling that recurs in numberless places throughout the work of this writer, including his most famous definition of poetry as "taking its origin from emotion recollected in tranquillity." Of the three terms of that definition, "tranquillity" is perhaps the most subjective, and any text that conveys Wordsworth's particular feeling of tranquillity deserves full attention.

Although suggestion partly yields to assertion in the last two lines of the sonnet, the term "tranquillity" still appears in a dramatic setting, in the form of an appeasing promise spoken by "great Pan" himself. But the immediate context does not suffice for a full understanding of the feeling; it could even be misleading. That Pan, as the voice of nature echoed in the poet's own voice, should be the speaker here is no doubt important, but Pan can take on many forms, and the traditional connotations of the myth are perhaps more a hindrance than a help in this case. Wordsworth's "tranquillity" is not a pantheistic oneness with nature, not even the subtler adjustment between mind and object referred to in the "Preface" to the *Lyrical Ballads*. One should perhaps forget the traditional Pan for the moment and ask instead what makes this landscape the place in which he would choose to appear.

Another element of indetermination keeps the final lines

in a state of suggestive suspense. Pan affirms that ". . . tranquillity is *here*," but such a complex set of spatial ambiguities have preceded this concluding assertion that one may well wonder where this "here" is located. The landscape makes us experience various kinds of quietness in various places, and the full impact of the final "here" depends entirely on the changing relationship between poet and landscape that develops in the main body of the sonnet.

We receive a first and literal impression of tranquillity from the near absence of wind in the "breezeless air," just enough stirred to allow for the slight motion and rustling of the reeds at the end. This absence of movement allows for the reflection, at sundown, of the brighter planets in the still surface of the lake. That this reflection will eventually convey the true meaning of "tranquillity" will become increasingly evident as the poem progresses, but not until we have been first led to believe in another, more obvious kind of peace. For in the lines

> Jove, Venus, and the ruddy crest of Mars
> Amid his fellows beauteously revealed
> At happy distance from earth's groaning field,
> Where ruthless mortals wage incessant wars

the poet's eye rests not on the reflection, but on the actual planets in the sky. The word "field," in the singular, transforms the pastoral earth into the one huge battlefield of the Napoleonic wars, and in contrast to this turmoil, the order of the heavens exists in a peaceful serenity, at a safe and "happy distance" from all this strife. But this kind of tranquillity is certainly not to be found *here*, on this earth, but emphatically *there*, away from it and among the stars. It is not from "there," however, that Pan's voice finally reaches the poet's ear. Wordsworth's "tranquillity" does not dwell in the detached serenity of the stars.

In the temporal development of the poem, we first encounter the stars in line 4 as a "vivid repetition," a reflected presence on this earth. They are no random constellation, but three specific planets with obvious and commonly known mythological associations, so obvious that the least esoterically inclined of readers cannot fail to notice them. This simplicity of mythological allusion is important, especially in comparison with what we shall have to say later about Yeats, and also because it serves Wordsworth's overriding desire for simple concreteness, his genuine aversion for an elaborate use of mythology as a rhetorical device. Here Jupiter, Venus, and Mars are first and foremost the actual planets, observed by the poet at a definite time and place and participating in the poem as real, nonsymbolic presences. Yet as he looks, still with his outer eye, at their reflection, the mythological meaning begins to partake more and more in the action. The traditional couple of Love and War (Venus and Mars) plays an important part in the stormy destiny (Jupiter) of human passions and human history, and the relatively strong emphasis on the personified Mars with his ruddy crest "Amid his fellows beauteously revealed" establishes a mirrorlike correspondence between the order of the heavens and the realities of earth, where war also occupies a most untranquil prominence. The "happy distance" between earth and the stars is perhaps not so difficult to bridge as physical observation would tend to suggest. For if the opaque surface of the lake is indeed a mirror of celestial order, then this order is present on earth, albeit in a mediate, reflected form. It follows that the agitation of our loves and our wars mirrors in fact a turbulence that exists on a cosmic scale among heavenly bodies as well as on a human scale on this earth. There is a slight suggestion, perhaps more intuitive than conscious, of a correspondence between macrocosm and microcosm, but the harmony of the spheres is jarred by "incessant wars" and Mars's persistent presence on earth would seem to ban tranquillity not only from this earth but from heaven as well. How then can Pan nevertheless make his final promise that "tranquillity is here"?

Up to the phrase "Is it a mirror?" in line 9, which marks the turning point of the poem, we have been using the outward eye of direct perception. The relationship between landscape and poet has been that of observer and thing observed, and consequently language has been mimetically descriptive throughout. After an entirely objective beginning:

> Clouds, lingering yet, extend in sold bars
> Through the grey West . . .

a slight intensification of tone stresses the joyful surprise of discovery as the eye catches sight of the reflected stars:

> . . . and lo! these waters, steeled
> By breezeless air to smoothest polish, yield
> A vivid repetition of the stars . . .

The increased liveliness of description, apparent in the somewhat unexpected verb "yield" and in the willed abstraction of "repetition," indicates the more active role played by the imagination in the visual description. This imaginative activity, however, is not yet strong enough to break through the surface of things. It could go so far as to conceive of human order as a reflection of cosmic order, and to make the connection between the planet Mars and Mars the God of War. But it remains firmly rooted in observation. It could never seriously ask the question in line 9: "Is it a mirror?" To a rational mind, fed by the observation of outward things, the question could not make sense; it knows without doubt that the light in the lake reflects the light of the stars above and that the lake acts like a mirror. The poem, however, suggests an alternative:

> Is it a mirror?—or the nether Sphere
> Opening to view the abyss in which she feeds
> Her own calm fires?

"Nether Sphere" has an unmistakably Miltonic ring, and the presence of Miltonic diction in Wordsworth generally indicates a rise in the pitch of imaginative intensity. Up till now, the surface of the lake ". . . steeled / By breezeless air to smoothest polish" has been as opaque as a sheet of metal, its depth hidden from the poet's eye. But by suddenly allowing that the light may very well not emanate from the stars at all, but from fires burning in another sphere buried deep under the surface, a radical change of perspective has taken place. We have moved far beyond the borders of empirical observation. The careful observer is now able to reach beyond the surface and to penetrate into a realm that lies hidden from the light of day, well beyond the reach of earthly vision. The lake becomes a kind of gate to the underworld, mysterious and unfathomable enough to be called an "abyss." And it is difficult to escape the implication that the "fires" have some infernal quality, a slight hint of a passing beyond a line which it is unsafe to cross—although one must hasten to add that these fires nowise imply the moral torment and punishment of Hell. Wordsworth's "nether Sphere" seems to be a curious synthesis between a pagan Hades and a Christian Inferno, a world of fire that lies beyond life but which, strangely enough, brings calmness rather than turmoil to the soul. Whereas the poem has first taken us upward into the distant sky, it now discovers a corresponding "nether Sphere" and, paradoxically enough, it is in that realm that the final "tranquillity" seems to originate. As we have seen, the peace of the heavens was a mere illusion to a mind that refuses to separate human destiny from cosmic order. The word "calm" appears for the first time explicitly in association with the "nether Sphere," who feeds her "own *calm* fires" in contrast with the natural fires of earth. The latter are seen as the disquieting fires of love and war, and are not granted the attribute of calmness. There is tranquillity on this earth, the poem seems to be saying, but only for those who are *also* able to see, with the inward eye, beyond the surface, and discover the quiet that inhabits depths where no natural light could reach.

Is this calmness then the tranquillity of death, to which the victims of "incessant wars" are destined? It certainly contains elements of this kind of peace, but only as it also contains elements of the harmonious peace of planetary movements, or the natural peace of a breezeless evening. For the final tranquillity is to be found neither in the "nether Sphere" nor upward "at happy distance from earth's groaning field"— although the particular strategy of the poem stresses the elusive peacefulness of the underworld over the more obvious quiet of the heavens. Still, the dominant movement stems from the return to earth, enriched by discoveries made in far-flung excursions; although the eye covers a very large scope, it finally comes to rest by the reeds at the side of the lake. Tranquillity is in *this* place on *this* earth, and it exists for the poet who can hear its voice, not because he is endowed with supernatural wisdom, or because he can dwell beyond the boundaries of space or of life, but because he possesses the kind of double vision that allows him to see landscapes as objects, as well as entrance gates to a world lying beyond visible nature. "Tranquillity," it seems, is the right balance between the literal and the symbolic vision, a balance reflected in a harmonious proportion between mimetic and symbolic language in the diction of the poem.

Perhaps we can now understand why the landscape should be as it appears in the opening lines:

> Clouds, lingering yet, extend in solid bars
> Through the grey West . . .

The delicate balance between direct and imagined vision demands precisely this degree of twilight grayness—so different from the sunlit noonday landscape of Mediterranean poets—with just enough light to perceive shapes and contours but not so much that the brilliance of the surfaces would prevent the eye from penetrating beyond them. Nor should the sky be cloudless; in that case the eye would be irresistibly drawn upward, whereas the clouds force it to turn inward, from an open to an enclosed space, and thus prepare for the necessary descent into the underworld. And the emphasis on "solid bars" draws, at the beginning of the poem, the strong horizontal line which, in spite of subsequent ascents and descents, becomes the final level on which the resolved poem comes to rest. Finally, the reflected light in the lake reminds us that this rest does not exclude the awareness of a cosmic realm above and a supernatural realm beyond. Both have to be present in the final vision; Wordsworth's Pan—since this is how he chooses to call his god here—is by no means devoid of transcendental dimensions. But even those transcendental elements are first revealed to sight before they can become an audible voice. All the action in the poem stems from visual events and obeys the logic of the eye. Wordsworth's landscape of tranquillity symbolizes in fact the complex act of pure vision.

During his later years, Yeats wrote several poems of tribute to the aged or deceased friends and companions of his literary life, in which he officiates somewhat like the Poet Laureate of a small court ruled over by Lady Gregory. In those "official" poems, he frequently bewails the passing of a gracious world of aristocratic refinement, brought to ruin by "this filthy modern tide." Because these poems appeal to a very public and readily comprehensible kind of emotion, and are bound to provoke a very direct response in the reader (favorable or unfavorable, depending on the strength of his own conservative leanings), they have contributed greatly to the picture of Yeats as the courtier of a bygone age—although numerous unsettling poems of the same period create a very different impression.

One of the most successful poems in this manner is "Coole Park and Ballylee, 1931" (a text which has been recorded in part as read by Yeats himself):

> 1 Under my window-ledge the waters race,
> Otters below and moor-hens on the top,
> Run for a mile undimmed in Heaven's face
> Then darkening through 'dark' Raftery's 'cellar'
> drop,
> 5 Run underground, rise in a rocky place
> In Coole demesne, and there to finish up
> Spread to a lake and drop into a hole.
> What's water but the generated soul?
>
> Upon the border of that lake's a wood
> 10 Now all dry sticks under a wintry sun,
> And in a copse of beeches there I stood,
> For Nature's pulled her tragic buskin on
> And all the rant's a mirror of my mood:
> At sudden thunder of the mounting swan

15 I turned about and looked where branches break
The glittering reaches of the flooded lake.

Another emblem there! That stormy white
But seems a concentration of the sky;
And, like the soul, it sails into the sight
20 And in the morning's gone, no man knows why;
And is so lovely that it sets to right
What knowledge or its lack had set awry,
So arrogantly pure, a child might think
It can be murdered with a spot of ink.

25 Sound of a stick upon the floor, a sound
From somebody that toils from chair to chair;
Beloved books that famous hands have bound,
Old marble heads, old pictures everywhere;
Great rooms where travelled men and children
found
30 Content or joy; a last inheritor
Where none has reigned that lacked a name and
fame
Or out of folly into folly came.

A spot whereon the founders lived and died
Seemed once more dear than life; ancestral trees,
35 Or gardens rich in memory glorified
Marriages, alliances and families,
And every bride's ambition satisfied.
Where fashion or mere fantasy decrees
We shift about—all that great glory spent—
40 Like some poor Arab tribesman and his tent.

We were the last romantics—chose for theme
Traditional sanctity and loveliness;
Whatever's written in what poets name
The book of the people; whatever most can bless
45 The mind of man or elevate a rhyme;
But all is changed, that high horse riderless,
Though mounted in that saddle Homer rode
Where the swan drifts upon a darkening flood.

Several of Yeats's poems, at all periods, contain or sometimes begin with landscapes, and it has often been observed

that, as the style gains in maturity and control, they become more and more concrete and specific. The river at the beginning of "Coole Park and Ballylee, 1931," certainly seems as "real" as can be, its course described in circumstantial and matter-of-fact detail, with almost geographical precision. And the general unity of the poem is brought about by equally natural means: the single locale of the lake in Coole Park, to which Yeats takes us in the first stanza, following the course of the river that connects his house, at Thoor Ballylee, with Lady Gregory's estate at Coole.

Beyond this first unifying principle, the question remains as to the experience conveyed by the juxtaposition of the three scenes: the stream, the swan in the woods, and finally Lady Gregory, her house, and all they have come to stand for in Yeats's life. At first sight, the poem seems to be built on a broad system of analogies between a natural, a semimythical, and a personal event, the last having overtones of a more general historical significance. The pattern is most concretely shown by the movements of the river in stanza 1: after running alternately through phases of light and darkness, it loses itself in the shapeless anonymity of the lake and "drops into a hole" (l. 7). The presence of realistic detail (the otters and the moorhens) and of specific place names helps to make this description as literal as possible; one is not tempted to read it as still another version of the recurrent romantic metaphor likening the course of human existence to that of a river. It merely defines a pattern of motion, from a charted and controlled course to the final "drop" into nothingness. The landscape seems as "natural" as Wordsworth's, and although we may be somewhat taken aback by the sudden leap into total generality in line 8,

What's water but the generated soul?

we could still interpret this as a transition to the next scene.

Within another analogical setting—the autumnal landscape suggestive of old age and decay—the swan suddenly appears. It is still a natural, real swan; the reader can well imagine such swans inhabiting Coole Park, and he may remember having met them before in an earlier poem, "The Wild Swans at Coole." But this time Yeats's language makes it clear that the swan is more than a mere natural bird: it is called an "emblem" in line 17; in line 19 it is explicitly likened to the soul, and although the terms "loveliness" and "purity" fit the physical characteristics of the swan, it is clear from the development in stanza 4 that they are primarily intended as attributes of the "soul." The reference is without doubt to the passage in the *Phaedo* where Plato likens the human soul to a swan. The general effect of the stanza, however, remains pictorial and concrete rather than speculative—and this is due, in large measure, to the analogy between the movement of the swan and that of the stream of stanza 1, both departing from this earth irresistibly drawn into another realm, the river "drop(ping) into a hole," the swan disappearing "no man knows why."

In this reading of the poem, the two first episodes are a preparation for the second half: the homage to Lady Gregory's world, in sharp contrast to the homeless, uprooted condition of modern man. The more general considerations in the final stanza lead to the picture of Lady Gregory and Yeats, allied in a vast historical perspective as the last representatives of a tradition about to disappear into chaos—as the swan and the river both disappeared into a void. The swan and the lake recur in the recapitulating last line to mark Coole Park as the place where no lesser poetic spirit than Homer's was for the last time manifest:

> Though mounted in that saddle Homer rode
> Where the swan drifts upon a darkening flood.

It is well-known that Yeats compared Lady Gregory's rather pedestrian collection of folk tales to Homer, and called it the "greatest book to come out of Ireland in our times"—a fact that James Joyce was all too eager to record for posterity by making it the object of one of his relatively few open allusions to Yeats in *Ulysses.*

Read in this manner, the poem's main theme becomes the

decadence "of a time / Half dead at the top," treated not "In mockery . . ." (as, for instance, in "Blood and the Moon") but in an elegiac confrontation between the splendors of the past and the uncertainties of a shapeless future. The landscapes in the first two stanzas function as natural images, enriching by their concreteness the abstract analogous movement of history evoked in the concluding part. Although the relationship between landscape and statement is no doubt less intimate and more rhetorical than in Wordsworth's sonnet, it does not seem to be essentially different; the symbolic action springs naturally from a perceived scene, the starting point for the imagination as it grows from natural to historical and mythical vision.

The only weakness of this reading is that it makes "Coole Park and Ballylee, 1931" into a rather recondite and not very tightly organized poem. Perhaps one can attribute to overgenerosity the somewhat embarrassing comparison between Lady Gregory and Homer, and forget, too, Yeats's pomposity in heralding himself, linked to Lady Gregory as the river links Ballylee to Coole Park, as one of the last representatives of heroic grandeur in a decaying world. Such considerations are, after all, extraneous to the poem—as is the rather trite definition of romanticism as a union between nobility and the true "people." But—always assuming that our proposed reading is the correct one—the economy of the poem is open to criticism on purely formal and intrinsic grounds; a great deal of superfluous detail in the descriptive passages rather seems to blur the movement which they are to convey; the development on the "soul" and the reference to the *Phaedo* may appear like a very elaborate windup to deliver a rather weak pitch; the link between the natural stream and the myth of the swan, though outwardly motivated by real incident, is not organically necessary, nor does it enrich the meaning of the poem as much as could be expected from such a striking and authoritative symbol. One could also quarrel with a discrepancy between tone and statement: this would indeed be a poem of rather grim despair, predicting no less than the end of a civilization with

which Yeats has entirely identified himself. Yet the poem does
not sound desperate, not even elegiac. The river and the swan
do not behave as if they were symbols of destruction, although the text leaves no doubt that they have forever departed from this earth. They could easily have been made into
poignant death symbols and made to utter the "swan-song"
of a vanishing world, but they appear instead as a welcome
relief to the eye among the tragically barren trees of the wood.
On the whole, the poem renders a decidedly heroic ring, which
makes even the final stanza appear altogether plausible. This
supposes an assertive assurance which nothing that is being
said would seem to warrant.

Before thus censoring Yeats, as poet or as courtier, one
should remember that this reading is founded on a literal
interpretation of the opening landscape. We assumed the stream
to be a description of an actual scene in nature; it gains symbolic significance later in the poem by analogy with other
events, but it was a natural fact *prior* to becoming symbolic.
This was certainly also the case for Wordsworth's landscape.
Everything in "Composed by the Side of Grasmere Lake" grows
directly out of the landscape; the sonnet is entirely self-contained, and no need exists to bring other texts, whether by
Wordsworth or someone else, to bear on the interpretation
(unless, of course, one wanted to show that the poem is typical of Wordsworth in general). Nor does the reader have to
possess any special knowledge beyond the most commonplace mythological information. Even this is less essential than
the careful attention which Wordsworth demands for his natural setting. Coming from this kind of romantic nature poetry,
one is inclined to expect a similar primacy of the natural landscape in Yeats.

There can be no doubt, however, that a richer reading of
a poem like "Coole Park and Ballylee, 1931" can only be obtained by giving up the illusion of natural realism. Yeats's
landscapes have a symbolic meaning prior to their natural appearance, and act as predetermined emblems embedded in a
more or less fixed symbolic system which is not derived from

the observation of nature. One therefore has to go outside the poem to find the "key" to such symbols. The point is, of course, still highly controversial in the interpretation of Yeats, and this is certainly not the place to argue it more extensively. I merely want to give some indication of what happens to this poem if one extends the perspective in this manner.

The concluding line of the first stanza "What's water but the generated soul?" marks the sudden intrusion of expository language into pure description. It acts as a signal to the reader that a more elaborate kind of symbol is being used. The theme of "generation" is a very frequent one in Yeats, who likes to treat it in Platonic terms, as a descent of the immortal and divine soul into the finite world of nature and matter. The recurrent emblem for this process is described at length in the early volume of prose essays *Ideas of Good and Evil*—a much richer source of information on Yeats's symbolism, be it said in passing, than the later and much more devious *A Vision*. It derives from Porphyry's esoteric interpretation of the Homeric ode "The Cave of the Nymphs," in which the Cave is said to represent the descent of the soul into matter by means of the act of generation. (Other uses of this myth occur in several of Yeats's major poems, for instance in "Among School Children"—where it is explicitly referred to in a footnote—in "Meditations in Time of Civil War" and so on.) Alerted by line 8, we recognize the description of the river to be a modified and personal version of Porphyry's Cave: the " 'dark' cellar" corresponds to the obscurity of the cavern" (*Ideas of Good and Evil*, p. 119); the underground course of the water corresponds to the actual Cave, bounded by the gates of generation and of death. The successive stages of the river above and below ground mark the different incarnations which according to Yeats's poetic mythology extend the existence of the individual soul over several lives; the subterranean stretches correspond to life on earth, the others presumably to a partly immaterial, purgatorial state. In its final return to the divine principle, the ultimate death of the body, the soul drops into the "hole" of the lake. The "moor-hens on the top" are the divine principle, which Yeats generally associates with birds, while the "otters below" are the animal principle, indicating the composite nature of the generated world. The entire construction is not more or less fantastic than, for instance, Spenser's Garden of Adonis in Book III of *The Faerie Queene* (with which it shares Platonic sources), except for the fact that it is presented as a reality and not as a fiction.

If one grants the identity of the river scene with the Cave of the Nymphs, a new dimension is introduced into the poem. For it marks Yeats's allegiance (whether real or apparent cannot concern us at this point) to a body of doctrine that considers the incarnate state of the soul as a relative degradation, and looks upon death as a return to its divine origin and, consequently, as a positive act. The allusion to the *Phaedo*, one of the main sources of esoteric Neoplatonism, now becomes altogether understandable. In opposition to the generated "water" of stanza 1, the swan "But seems a concentration of the sky"— air being an element closer to the divine than water—joyously "mounting" from the decaying wood of matter toward its true abode. Its purity and its loveliness are due to the desire for the eternal that inhabits the swan's breast, and make it impervious to those who think that divine essence can be found on this natural earth.

After this, the second half of the poem takes on a very different significance. The "great glory" (l. 39) of the historical world created by a successful culture is bound to become an ambiguous compliment, since we now must assume that no earthly achievement, no matter how impressive, can have absolute value. The passing of the Irish gentry, Yeats's most closely personal experience of the mortality of civilizations, becomes a much less momentous and definitive event when any death, whether individual or collective, marks in fact a desirable escape from earthly embroilments. Like all earth-bound civilizations, the Irish aristocracy made the mistake of imagining that its world of marriages, houses, and "generations" was "more dear than life" (l. 34), whereas the only thing dearer than life can be the immortal and immaterial soul, loosened from earthly fetters. Faced with the tragic decay of history, the man of true wisdom can only cry out, as Yeats proclaims in another poem, " 'Let all things pass away' " ("Vacillation"). Here, in a *poème de circonstance*, written in homage to his benefactor and her class, the reservations are of course expressed in a much more oblique and allusive way. They are tacitly implied by the values established in the first three stanzas. Moreover, in a poet who makes deliberate ironic use of the technique of repetition, it is revealing that the two ear-striking words "stick" and "spot," when they appear in reference to Lady Gregory and her kind (ll. 25 and 33), have previously been given derogatory connotations associated with the decaying and misleading world of matter (ll. 10 and 24).

But it is in the last stanza that the esoteric symbolism makes its greatest contribution to an enriched complexity of statement. On a first level, the passage indeed expresses the extravagant compliment of Yeats to his patron and fellow writer, and his apocalyptic pessimism about the decadence of the Western world. Much is added, however, to complicate Yeats's own attitude toward this assertion. Two verbal echoes from the earlier stanzas help to give access to a difficult section. The "last romantics"—and nothing in the syntax indicates that "we," in line 41, necessarily refers to Yeats and Lady Gregory—are said to have chosen ". . . for theme / Traditional sanctity and loveliness." The adjective "lovely" has been prominently used before as an attribute of the liberated soul (l. 21), in opposition to the earthbound, natural beauty of the woods and the waters. Those who glorify the beauty of the soul are called "romantics," and "traditional sanctity" surely indicates the wisdom of the esoteric tradition to which Yeats claims allegiance. The "romantics" are those initiated in that tradition or spontaneously attracted to it, not the "natural" romantics like Wordsworth or Keats. The true "romantics" know "Whatever's written in what poets name / The book of the people . . ." and from Yeats's essays on folklore we know that what he and

other "poets" find there is precisely the esoteric tradition in a
particularly otherworldly form—so otherworldly, in fact, that
it rejects much of Plato himself as too earthbound.

The final line, "Where the swan drifts upon a darkening
flood," echoes the "darkening" of line 4 (". . . darkening
through 'dark' Raftery's 'cellar' drop") and takes us back, closing the cycle, to Homer, whose ode "The Cave of the Nymphs"
actually began the poem in a disguised version. The swan
drifting on a "darkening flood" refers to a soul still impris-
oned in generated matter (water) (unlike the "mounting swan"
in line 14), and Yeats is suggesting that ever since men have
been willing to found their values upon the incarnate world
and to praise the act of generation, Pegasus has been riderless—there has been no truly great poetry. This came about
with Homer, a transitional figure who, in his esoteric aspects
(as in "The Cave of the Nymphs") still belongs to an uncor-
rupted past, but in his exoteric aspects stands at the dawn of
a literature which will get increasingly enmeshed in the ser-
vitudes of original sin. The passage repeats what Yeats had
explicitly been saying about Homer in an early essay, "The
Autumn of the Body" (*Ideas of Good and Evil*, pp. 301ff.); it now
uses symbolic language to mask a direct statement on which
Yeats has not changed his mind over the years. Homer is in
fact the real "last romantic," the last representative of a tradition that nearly died with him, and Yeats pretends to see himself in a somewhat similar situation, as one of the few to have
kept contact with "traditional sanctity." In a sense, the "we"
in "We were the last romantics . . ." refers to Homer and Yeats,
whereas the statement that follows "But all is changed . . ."
(l. 46) points not so much to the present, the 1931 of the poem,
as to the entire time span of Hellenic and Christian civilization. Tragic as it is, the threatening destruction of the West can
be contemplated with the kind of heroic gaiety for which Yeats
is striving—perhaps in vain—in the *Last Poems*. For if ever since
"all is changed" (that is, ever since Homer) the "high horse"
of poetry has been "riderless," a poetic rebirth can only be expected in an altogether new type of civilization. We have moved

a long way beyond Lady Gregory into speculations for which this very practical lady would have had little sympathy but which, for poetic reasons, obsessed Yeats during his entire life.

Two distinct readings thus become apparent. They do not necessarily cancel each other out, but represent very different attitudes toward a common situation. Each of these readings, however, depends on altogether divergent uses of imagery, as epitomized in the role played by the opening landscape; in the first interpretation it acts as a natural analogical image, in the second as an emblematic "key." The descriptive, mimetic use of landscape remains quite similar to Wordsworth's first kind of vision, in which nature is seen as an exterior object. But Yeats's symbolism has nothing in common with Wordsworth's second or symbolic kind of language. The emblematic landscape, in which a familiar river is used to mask an esoteric text, differs entirely from Wordsworth's transcendental vision, as we encountered it in the first poem. Both, it is true, lead from material to spiritual insights, but whereas Wordsworth's imagination remains patterned throughout on the physical process of sight, Yeats's frame of reference, by the very nature of his statement, originates from experiences without earthly equivalence. The texture of his language, in the poetry written after 1900, thus depends on an altogether composite style, held together by almost miraculous skill. On the one hand, the poems seduce by the sensuous "loveliness" of their natural landscapes and images, while gaining their deeper structural unity and most of their intellectual content from nonnatural or even antinatural uses of language. The juxtaposition of two truly incompatible conceptions of style is much more precarious even than Wordsworth's delicate balance between perception and imagination. In Yeats, the imagination in fact scorns the perception, but seems unable to do without it; stripped of its natural attributes the poem would become a lifeless skeleton. The result, in Yeats's masterful hands, can be intensely dramatic, but it could certainly never end, like Wordsworth's sonnet, in a promise of "tranquillity."

8
Image and Emblem
in Yeats

WITH STRIKING critical insight,
Yeats has described his own poetic development by opposing
it to the concept of *Bildung*, as it appears in the German romantic tradition. He knew this tradition only through Goethe,
one of his father's favorite authors, but the reference to *Wilhelm Meister* is singularly apt: "I still think that in a species of
man, wherein I count myself, nothing so much matters as Unity
of Being, but if I seek it as Goethe sought, who was not of that
species, I but combine in myself, and perhaps as it now seems,
looking backward, in others also, incompatibles. Goethe, in
whom objectivity and subjectivity were intermixed . . . could
but seek it as Wilhelm Meister seeks it, intellectually, critically, and through a multitude of deliberately chosen experiences; events and forms of skill gathered as if for a collector's
cabinet; whereas true Unity of Being, where all the nature
murmurs in response if but a single note be touched, is found
emotionally, instinctively, by the rejection of all experience not
of the right quality, and by the limitation of its quantity."[1]

It is well to bear this in mind when trying to impress a
framework of order on Yeats's work. We cannot expect the
gradual development of a Mallarmé, a consciousness which

comes to know itself by observing the reflections of its own experiences, but rather an *a priori* commitment that maintains itself in the face of all attacks and temptations. The movement of *Bildung* is one of repeated defeats, never altogether wasteful because, no matter how tragic the damage to individuals, they result in an enrichment of the spirit. Blind hope rushes into action to meet disaster; Faust embarks forcefully on the impossible, causes ruin and destruction to others and to himself, with no gain but some increased wisdom of his limitations. The impossibility of the quest unveils gradually, and an awareness of the ultimate absurdity of the enterprise appears as the crowning achievement, at the end of the drama. The pattern of Yeats's poetic development, however, is Quixotic rather than Faustian. The irrevocable commitment seems to be made from the start, absurdity and all, and the subsequent test is merely one of loyalty and perseverance.

Such a pattern could be simple enough, much simpler, in fact, than the succession of assertions and denials that characterize a movement of becoming. But in Yeats's case, the original commitment is particularly elusive. There is bound to be a fundamental complication associated with an ideal which is persistently referred to as Unity of Being, but most frequently expressed, as in the above quotation, by such terms as "to reject" or "to limit"—terms that suggest plurality rather than unity. And there may well be true incoherence at the core of a system which, like *A Vision,* claims to be both cyclical, a mere repetition of a movement resulting from tensions between irreconcilable opposites, and dialectical, a progression of antinomies toward their ultimate reconciliation. A "Unity of Being" which has to be understood in opposition to another "Unity of Being" is certainly not of a kind which can easily be defined. Behind the term "Unity of Being" is hidden a long history of conflicts and contradictions; when Yeats uses it to describe his poetry, an interpretation of the entire work is needed to know why he chooses to state it in this manner.

Yeats's actual commitment, which determines the intricate verbal strategy of his poetry, cannot be deduced, as was the case for Mallarmé, from his own explicit statements. Mallarmé's obligation is to the *truth* of his language; therefore, the complication of his intention is always exactly equal to the complication of his statement: this makes him, in spite of so many opinions to the contrary, into the very opposite of an "obscure" poet—although it certainly does not make him into a simple one. Yeats is very articulate about his poetic theories and discourses eloquently and abundantly on the subject, but his statements, whether they appear in the poetry or in his dramatic or critical writing, always have to be considered in the light of an intent that reaches beyond their particular meaning. His language is not the language of truth; it is determined by an intent which uses language and in which language is deeply involved, but which nevertheless finds its ultimate justification in a meta-logical and, at times, anti-logical realm.

In the case of a poet of this type, when no works or passages can be singled out and given true exegetic value, the best way to gain access to their true meaning is often to observe local accidents and anomalies of language by means of which actual intentions or commitments, hidden behind the statement, are revealed. By far the most conspicuous of such accidents are the several stylistic changes and incessant revisions that mark Yeats's career. His avowed opinions and convictions, as well as his public conception of his role as a poet, remain remarkably stable, but his poetry keeps varying in texture and in tone until the very last poems. These changes are not primarily thematic, even though they sometimes seem to be: Yeats's themes are in fact much less varied than his styles, and it is not always possible to establish a correlation between thematic and stylistic shifts. A strong feeling exists among commentators that if it were possible to account for the changes in manner, true insight would be gained in Yeats's fundamental hopes and preoccupations. The stylistic experimentations are prompted by his deepest concern; themes, declarations of purpose, aesthetic or pseudo-philosophical theories are subsidiary to this concern, put to use in its service. The key to a real understanding of Yeats's poetic enterprise, as well as of his place in the tradition of nineteenth-century poetry, is to be found in his stylistic evolution. This is true of all poets, to some extent, but it is true in a special sense for Yeats. In some—and Mallarmé is a case in point—the distinction between theme and style is not apparent, and one is free to move from stylistic to thematic considerations without encountering discontinuities; Yeats, on the other hand, consciously uses and exploits this very distinction for strategic purposes. By ignoring the formal aspects of his language, one allows oneself to be deliberately misled by the author's own devices.

Critics have been well aware of the importance of the stylistic element in Yeats, and most attempts at a general interpretation have actually been interpretations of the stylistic changes. Although no systematic study of the problem is as yet available, the more or less fragmentary and intuitive descriptions of the changes stress similar elements: the contrast between the vocabulary of the early and the later poetry; the passage from a purely lyrical to a more dramatic medium; the difference between the esoteric, hieratic imagery of the early and the much more concrete and natural imagery of the later poetry; the change from repetitive and incantatory rhythms to intricately varied and abrupt metrical patterns; the increased use of irony and ambiguity; the passage from a neoromantic Victorian "poetic" diction to a hardened "modern" form of address often said to be close to actual speech. There is at least some measure of agreement as to the general trend of these changes, although the findings are based, in general, on quick impressions rather than on exhaustive analysis.[2] Stylistic criticism of Yeats would complicate this relatively simple picture a great deal.

Beyond this point, agreement vanishes. When it comes to an interpretation of the changes, opinions vary widely, quantitatively, qualitatively, and historically. Some see a total contrast between the early and the late Yeats,[3] others maintain that it ". . . is a development rather than a conversion, a technical change rather than a substantial one."[4] Some, a majority, see it as a movement toward a more "realistic," socially responsible, publicly committed poetry,[5] while others stress the increased esotericism and hermeticism of the later poetry, less conventionally "literary" and more avowedly occult and initiatory.[6] Some consider Yeats as the culmination and fulfillment of the romantic tradition,[7] others as moving definitely outside of this tradition.[8]

Before any other consideration, it should be pointed out that the change cannot be so easily observed as its obvious existence may lead one to believe. There is not one single change but several, and it is not certain that they tend in the same direction. Neither is it certain that objective characteristics of style (assuming even—which is not the case—that they had been accurately defined and described) can be easily and immediately translated in terms of poetic intent; that the prevalence of a more or less colloquial vocabulary, for instance, necessarily indicates a poetry closer to earth than conventionally "poetic" word choice; or that the frequent presence of natural imagery necessarily implies a concretization of experience; or that a dramatic syntax and structure is necessarily more socially concerned than a lyrical one. All such outward characteristics of style have to be placed within a highly complex network of motives and intentions before their tentative significance can be stated with some chance of accuracy.

For instance, to take a simple and well-studied example, Yeats's style underwent a considerable transformation between 1889, the date when his first volume of verse was published, and 1895, when he revised his early poems for a new edition (*Poems,* London, 1895); the alterations offer excellent material for a study of the development at that point. The conclusions are clear; the changes are attempts to eliminate the remnants of conventional romantic diction: inflected verb forms, partially elided prepositions, inversions, etc.[9] In a way, this makes the language more natural and brings it closer to ordinary speech; words such as "you," "the," "always," "no," "from" are certainly closer to ordinary speech than "ye," "thy," "ever," "nay" "o'er," etc. But it could hardly be argued that this shift from conventionally "poetic" language to normal usage was accompanied by a parallel thematic change from an otherworldly realm back to earth; whatever the difference between the 1889 and the 1901 versions of a poem like "The Indian to His Love,"[10] they hardly make it less ethereal, though they make it a great deal less ridiculous. As for the new poems which Yeats is writing around 1895 and which will be printed in book form in 1899 under the title of *The Wind among the Reeds*, they are certainly not to be called earth-bound or realistic. This change, although it is doubtlessly oriented toward "natural" diction, occurs at a moment when the "substantial" evolution, as revealed by the imagery, moves more and more radically away from nature. We understand, then, that this particular change in diction (not in imagery) between the 1889 edition of *The Wanderings of Oisin and Other Poems* and the 1895 edition of *Poems*, marks a development in technical skill. Yeats has come into contact in London with his English fellow poets[11] and he is "learning his trade" *with* (not *from*) them, following a trend which was generally prevalent among his contemporaries; a similar difference exists between the diction of Swinburne and that of Dowson and Symons (both great admirers of Verlaine) or between that of Tennyson and Lionel Johnson. This is indeed a "technical change rather than a substantial one," but it is complicated by the fact that at the same time a "substantial" development has taken place (between *The Wanderings of Oisin and Other Poems* of 1889 and *The Countess Kathleen and Various Legends and Lyrics* of 1891) that tends in the direction opposite from the evolution in technique.

Later, when the major change occurs which is generally mentioned in speaking of the transition from Yeats's early to his mature period (between *The Shadowy Waters*, 1900, and *In the Seven Woods*, 1903), the hardening of texture, the introduction of contemporary, topical allusions, a new abundance of natural imagery all have prompted the prevalent interpretation of a definitive return to a certain form of realism. The stylistic equivalence of this return is found in a parallel return to a syntax and diction that imitate natural speech. So oversimplified are our notions of style, and so strongly influenced by loose historical categories, that we tend to call "realistic" any diction which is no longer Victorian. One commentator, at least, has been curious enough to take a closer look,[12] and drawn attention to the fact that Yeats's mature diction is anything but mimetic, that it introduces again many of the more "literary" forms of style which the early revisions had been eager to eliminate, especially archaisms and inversions. Of course, they are not the same kind of archaisms or inversions and they fulfill a different expressive function, but their fundamental characteristic remains: they accentuate the distinction between spoken and written language and widen the gap between mimetic and expressive diction.[13] In the middle and the later Yeats, one is very far removed indeed from the Preface to the *Lyrical Ballads*. The vocabulary and syntax of the poetry after 1904 is certainly not sufficient proof that the change ought to be interpreted as a return to reality.

Our point is merely that if the study of stylistic changes is indeed the best way of access to the interpretation of Yeats, it is a key that should be used with great caution and with a steady awareness of the intentional principle that determined stylistic peculiarities. It is this pattern of intentions (which, in Yeats, differs from the thematic structure) which we want to observe. And, as in all romantic poetry, the most revealing stylistic unit will be the image.

Yeats's early poetry is, in his own words, "covered with embroideries," and much of its imagery is purely decorative. It is often similar in texture to this passage from *The Wanderings of Oisin:*

> A citron colour gloomed in her hair,
> But down to her feet white vesture flowed,
> And with the glimmering crimson glowed
> Of many a figured embroidery;
> And it was bound with a pearl-pale shell
> That wavered like the summer streams,
> As her soft bosom rose and fell.
>
> (*Var.*, pp. 3–4)[14]

This is pictorial, Pre-Raphaelite writing, with a picture-book delight in colors that exist merely for the color's sake; citron, white, and crimson, all in the span of three lines. In this context, the "pearl-pale shell" seems hardly more than another picturesque detail—although it could be more than this. Niamh, who is being described, is something of a siren, a water creature who rides the waves, and the decorative shell could point to her elemental nature. Very early in the poem, we are perhaps already dealing with an image which belongs to a much more complicated species; it refers, by means of a traditional pictorial emblem to a complex experience (the sea, and its dark attraction on Oisin); it contains mythological elements (the siren); and it refers to a specific natural element (water). But it appears among so much descriptive detail, devoid of metaphorical or emblematic depth, that it escapes notice in the crowded picture.

A little further along in the poem, the image of the shell reappears, when Niamh and Oisin are about to land on the first of their three islands:

> . . . we rode on,
> Where many a trumpet-twisted shell
> That in immortal silence sleeps
> Dreaming of her own melting hues,
> Her golds, her ambers, and her blues,
> Pierced with soft light the shallowing deeps.
>
> (*Var.*, p. 13)[15]

This image starts from the perception of an actual thing, the eye catching sight of the shells as the water grows shallow. The late version (which dates from a 1933 edition) still strengthens this effect by means of the exact visual detail "trumpet-twisted," but it is clear from the unaltered line, "Pierced with soft light the shallowing deeps," that the encounter with the natural, outward world has always been an essential part of the image. It grows, however, into much more than a descriptive or decorative detail. The transfer of the material attributes of shape and color into consciousness, which makes up the perception, is accompanied by a symmetrical transfer of acts of consciousness into the object: the shell is said to be "dreaming" and the verb "pierced" changes the passive process of being perceived into an act of volition; by then, the shell has both imagination and will, the main faculties of a conscious mind, and it has received them from a mere figure of speech.

This kind of image is very frequent in the early Yeats.[16] It differs from mere personification, which has primarily a descriptive purpose and is based on mimetic devices; to say that the wind howls or that the sun smiles is to say something about the wind and the sun, but to write of shells "dreaming of their own hues" is to say something about the act of dreaming, not to describe the shells. Or rather, it is to say something about the power of symbolic language, which is able to cross the gap between subject and object without apparent effort, and to unite them within the single unit of the natural image. Behind such imagery stands the conception of fundamental unity of mind and matter, expanding from the particular oneness of the single image into universal unity, the *"ténébreuse et profonde unité . . . Ayant l'expansion des choses infinies"* of Baudelaire's famous sonnet "Correspondances."

Baudelaire can be mentioned with relevance at this point, certainly not as a source (for whatever contact Yeats had with French symbolism occurred later and even then Baudelaire was not the major influence), but because the conception of imagery, at the beginning of Yeats's work, places him so clearly within the general European tradition of symbolism. None of Yeats's immediate predecessors or contemporaries in England, even those, like Symons or Dowson, who came into much closer contact with France, is as closely akin to the symbolic language of Baudelaire and his successors. This becomes more apparent still in the lines

> . . . a trumpet-twisted shell . . .
> Dreaming of her own melting hues,
> Her gold, her ambers, and her blues . . .

The verb "dreaming" transfers attributes of consciousness into
the natural object and establishes the unity of a correspondence, but the content of the dream is itself of great importance for the structure of image: the shell is dreaming, not only
of itself, but of its own most striking formal, material features:
the very colors by which it was originally perceived. The
movement of the image, which started in perception, then fused
the perceived object and the perceiving consciousness into one
by means of a verbal transfer, now returns to the original perception, making the object itself into the perceiver. From purely
perceptual, then metaphorical (or symbolic), the image has become one of self-reflection, using the material properties of the
object (the colors) as a means to allow a self-reflective consciousness to originate. In the process, the center of interest,
which first resided in the colors as the qualities by which the
object was perceived, has shifted: the idea of a shell endowed
with the highest form of human consciousness (self-reflection)
is in itself so striking that the colors have lost most of their
prominence; what arrests the mind, no doubt, are no longer
the "melting hues" but the shell dreaming of its own beauty.
The structure of the image has become that of self-reflection.
The poet is no longer contemplating a thing in nature, but the
workings of his own mind; the outside world is used as a pretext and a mirror, and it loses all its substance. Imagery by
"correspondences" ends up in self-reflection, and the dominant mood of Yeats's earliest poetry is one of narcissistic self-
contemplation:

> . . . they are always listening,
> The dewdrops, for the sound of their own dropping.
> ("The Sad Shepherd," *Var.*, p. 68)

> A parrot sways upon a tree,
> Raging at his own image in the enamelled sea.
> ("The Indian to His Love," *Var.*, p. 77)[17]

One could speculate at length how a young poet, living
in the peripheral, eccentric atmosphere of Dublin and the J. E.
Yeats family,[18] came to write as by instinct in a style which

has no immediate antecedent in the English poetry of his day. It was natural enough for Mallarmé to think of himself as one who had to begin where Baudelaire left off,[19] but much more difficult to explain how Yeats found himself unknowingly in the same predicament. His early poetic manner bears the obvious marks of the English romantic and post-romantic tradition, of Tennyson and Swinburne, of the romantic conception of Spenserian sensual imagery as it appears in Keats and in the Pre-Raphaelites, of Shelley's near-emblematic symbolism.[20] None of these influences, however, can account for the combination of imagery founded on correspondences between mind and matter, with conscious self-contemplation, a combination which characterizes French rather than English poetry of the second half of the nineteenth century. Later, Yeats will discover his affinities with the *symbolistes,* but his poetry is never closer to theirs than before 1885, when he had little or no knowledge of their work.

The answer lies for the main part in the universal nature of the poetic consciousness, which is bound to encounter similar problems and to attempt similar stylistic devices, regardless of actual contact or influence. Some very general common sources exist, however, which, if they do not explain the deeper affinity, give it at least some basis in historical fact. The speculations of the Dublin Theosophical Society, even before Yeats's initiation to the *Prophetic Books* of Blake,[21] were his means of access to the Neoplatonic and occult tradition (and, indirectly, to the poetry of the Renaissance), a tradition which had acted deeply on late French romanticism and on symbolism, but found few adepts among the English poets of the same period. The current, it seems, was strong enough to steer Yeats closer to a French movement which he did not know than to the English tradition in which he was raised. Theosophy led to Blake and his Swedenborgian origins, and Yeats's theoretical justifications for his early style sound remarkably like Baudelaire's often quoted statement on Swedenborg:

. . . D'ailleurs Swedenborg, qui possédait une âme bien plus grande (que Fourier), nous avait déjà enseigné que *le ciel est un très grand homme;* que tout, forme, mouvement, nombre, couleur, parfum, dans le *spirituel* comme dans le *naturel,* est significatif, réciproque, converse, *correspondant.* Lavater, limitant au visage de l'homme la démonstration de l'universelle vérité, nous avait traduit le sens spirituel du contour, de la forme, de la dimension. Si nous étendons la démonstration . . . nous arrivons à cette vérité que tout est hiéroglyphique, et nous savons que les symboles ne sont obscurs que d'une manière relative, c'est-à-dire selon la pureté, la bonne volonté ou la clairvoyance native des âmes. Or, qu'est-ce qu'un poète (je prends le mot dans son acception la plus large), si ce n'est un traducteur, un déchiffreur? Chez les excellents poètes, il n'y a pas de métaphore, de comparaison ou d'épithète qui ne soit d'une adaptation mathématiquement exacte dans la circonstance actuelle, parce que ces comparaisons, ces métaphores et ces épithètes sont puisées dans l'inépuisable fonds de l'*universelle analogie,* et qu'elles ne peuvent être puisées ailleurs.

> ("Réflexions sur quelques-uns de mes contemporains:
> Victor Hugo")

Yeats's defense of his style dates from 1900, but it fits his earliest manner, before 1885, better than his writing at the turn of the century:

All sounds, all colours, all forms, either because of their pre-ordained energies or because of long association, evoke indefinable and yet precise emotions, or, as I prefer to think, call down among us certain disembodied powers, whose footsteps over our hearts we call emotions; and when sound, and colour, and form are in a musical relation, a beautiful relation to one another, they become as it were one sound, one colour, one form, and evoke an emotion that is made out of their distinct evocations and yet is one emotion. The same relation exists between all portions of every work of art, whether it be an epic or a song, and the more perfect it is, and the more various and numerous the elements that have flowed into its perfection, the more powerful will be the emotion, the power, the god it calls among us.

(*Ideas of Good and Evil,* "The Symbolism of Poetry," p. 243)

The formal elements mentioned as the starting point of the image appear as the most striking similarity between the two quotations: "All sounds, all colours, all forms" in Yeats, "forme, mouvement, nombre, couleur, parfum" and later "contour, forme, dimension" in Baudelaire. As the image of the shell started with an actual perception of a natural shell

> Not such as are in Newton's metaphor,
> But actual shells of Rosses' level shore

—as Yeats will put it in a much later poem—so the deciphering of the poet starts in his "reading" of *nature* as the direct emanation of the divine, leading, from analogy to analogy, to the revealed unity of the epiphany, "the god it calls among us." Such images are natural images in the sense stated by Hölderlin's line, images which originate "like flowers" originate, as emulators of nature. It remains problematic how analogies between sensual, material elements (as in synaesthesia) can expand to become analogies between the material and the spiritual. Baudelaire speaks of *"traduire le sens spirituel du contour"* and of correspondences *"dans le spirituel comme dans le naturel,"* but he does not mention the much more problematic analogy *"du spirituel au naturel"* which is to make the translation possible. In "Correspondances," for instance, the analogy remains confined between properties of finite matter, "Les parfums, les couleurs et les sons se répondent," until the transition to the spiritual is made by the word *"infini"* in the line, "Ayant l'expansion des choses infinies."

"Infini" is an ambiguous term in this context; it has, of course, strong transcendental connotations but, in the material reality of the poem, it refers to the tenuous, volatile nature of "parfums." One could say that the presence of the divine is discovered by the material imagination meditating on the experience of "parfums." A sensibility which operates in this manner is perfectly consistent as long as it remains pantheistic and admits to the ontological supremacy of the natural object. From the moment, however, that it transfers the power of epiphany into words, into the constitutive rather than the mimetic power of language, it necessarily becomes ambivalent— like the phrase *"choses infinies"* in this poem. The experience, as such, is altogether coherent, but its linguistic equivalence

falls prey to the logical discontinuity that disrupts the natural image.

This discontinuity, often concealed within the image itself, becomes explicit on the thematic level, in the complicated attitude of such poets toward nature. One does not have to go beyond the first two of Yeats's collected poems to observe this discrepancy in "The Song of the Happy Shepherd" and its counterpiece "The Sad Shepherd."[22] The first poem is a complex juxtaposition of themes, but in terms of material imagery it has a very clear programmatic purpose: it states the superiority of the self-reflective, "symbolist" image over its romantic forerunner. The latter is Arcadian, pastoral, a song "of old earth's dreamy youth,"[23] the expression of a nostalgic pantheism in a mimetic image of earth, flowers, and woods. Yeats opposed the image of the "shell" to the pastoral symbols of wood and earth; the superiority of the shell resides in its echo-harboring structure; it is no longer sheer nature, impressing itself upon a passively receptive, awe-inspired consciousness, but the nature-as-mirror which appears in the formerly quoted passage from *Oisin*. Echo suggests Narcissus and "The Song of the Happy Shepherd" can serve as a poetically successful statement of Yeats's earliest, narcissistic conception of the image. The shell is only a mirror for a dream which is no longer that of nature, but the subjective dream of a human imagination; consequently the interest has shifted from the shell to the human words spoken to the shell by the shepherd-poet. Nevertheless, in spite of the apparent replacement of the object by its reflection, the image remains altogether conditioned by the existence of this object and the poem has to be presented as a natural scene:

> Go gather by the humming sea
> Some twisted, echo-harbouring shell,
> And to its lips thy story tell . . .
>
> (*Var.*, p. 66)

We are *told* about the miracle of reflection, but what we *see* is a scene by the seashore. To the extent that the shell is a thing in nature, the image remains in essence natural, although it is mediated by reflection and thus at least once removed from nature. "The Song of the Happy Shepherd" still remains a pastoral poem in praise of nature.

It is also an ironic poem, since shells are not likely to re-word "in melodious guile" stories told to their lips. The juxtaposition of a natural setting with a supernatural event (the shell's replying) is self-defeating and the poem reveals the inner absurdity of the natural image in its unwarranted assertion

> Go gather by the humming sea
> Some twisted, echo-harbouring shell,
> And to its lips thy story tell,
> And they thy comforters will be,
> Rewording in melodious guile
> Thy fretful words a little while . . .

The failure is made explicit in "The Sad Shepherd" where the same shell behaves as a natural shell would behave, and shatters the "song" of consciousness into confusion:

> Then he sang softly nigh the pearly rim;
> But the sad dweller by the sea-ways lone
> Changed all he sang to inarticulate moan . . .
>
> (*Var.*, p. 69)

Taken together, the two songs constitute an exact retelling of the Narcissus myth: the reflection can be left to exist as a mere phantom of the self without substantial existence, but when reached for as if it were a material thing it dissolves into chaos:

> Mais ne vous flattez pas de le changer d'empire.
> Ce cristal est son vrai séjour;
> Les efforts mêmes de l'amour!
> Ne le sauraient de l'onde extraire qu'il n'expire . . .
>
> (Paul Valéry, "Fragment du Narcisse")

The treatment of nature remains contradictory: as the necessary starting point of the image, "la première en date, la nature . . ." (Mallarmé, "Bucolique,"), it is indispensable, but as the entity which, by its mere presence, voids the poet's hope to find permanence in words, it is his worst enemy. It throws him back upon himself, in sterile self-contemplation, "Raging at his own image in the enamelled sea."

The same paradoxical combination occurs in Baudelaire: a unity founded on a problematic analogy between matter and spirit: praise of the artifice and of reflected *forms* in a language whose poetic tenor is conditioned by material and tactile sensations. The resulting equilibrium is a paralysis rather than a resolution, as if the author of "Correspondances" were bound to become, by the same token, also the author of "L'Irrémédiable":

> Un navire pris dans le pôle,
> Comme en un piège de cristal,
> Cherchant par quel détroit fatal
> Il est tombé dans cette geôle;
>
> . . .
>
> Tête-à-tête sombre et limpide
> Qu'un coeur devenu son miroir!
> Puits de Vérité, clair et noir,
> Où tremble une étoile livide, . . .

The contradiction is spelled out as a conscious theme in a famous Baudelaire poem much admired by Valéry, "L'Homme et la Mer":

> Homme libre, toujours tu chériras la mer!
> La mer est ton miroir; tu contemples ton âme
> Dans le déroulement infini de sa lame,
> Et ton esprit n'est pas un gouffre moins amer.
>
> Tu te plais à plonger au sein de ton image;
> Tu l'embrasses des yeux et des bras, et ton coeur
> Se distrait quelquefois de ta propre rumeur
> Au bruit de cette plainte indomptable et sauvage.
>
> Vous êtes tous les deux ténébreux et discrets:
> Homme, nul n'a sondé le fond de tes abîmes;
> Ô mer, nul ne connaît tes richesses intimes,
> Tant vous êtes jaloux de garder vos secrets!

Et cependant voilà des siècles innombrables
Que vous vous combattez sans pitié ni remord,
Tellement vous aimez le carnage et la mort,
Ô lutteurs éternels, ô frères implacables!

Yeats stresses the struggle with nature rather than the brotherhood, the "lutteurs éternels" rather than the "frères implacables." One does not expect pantheistic bliss from a poet who deliberately made his collected poems start with two lines that are like the epitaph of romantic pastoralism:

The woods of Arcady are dead,
And over is their antique joy . . .[24]

(*Var.*, p. 64)

Allusions to natural harmony occur only in the youthful correspondence: as early as 1888, Yeats already looks back nostalgically toward the time when he was writing *The Island of Statues:* "I was then living a quite harmonious poetic life. Never thinking out of my depth. Always harmonious, narrow, calm. Taking small interest in people but most ardently moved by the more minute kinds of natural beauty . . . The 'Island' was the last. Since I have left the 'Island,' I have been going about on shoreless seas . . ."[25] The predominant mood of the early poems is a combination of an unwanted tranquillity, very different from the peaceful, simple harmony with nature alluded to in this letter, and the restlessness that forces all Yeats's early heroes out on aimless wanderings, "made / To wander by their melancholy minds" (*Var.*, p. 72) in order to escape, no doubt, from their narcissistic predicament. The first five lines of "The Indian to His Love" summarizes this mood:

The island dreams under the dawn
And great boughs drop tranquillity;
The peahens dance on a smooth lawn,
A parrot sways upon a tree,
Raging at his own image in the enamelled sea.[26]

To set out on a poetic career with a style that is so hyperconscious, so obviously "late" or even decadent, might well have led to total paralysis, to the conviction that little was left to discover although the existing predicament was well-nigh intolerable. Whether inherited by way of his followers, by direct contact with the work, or intuitively rediscovered, Baudelaire's situation is a difficult legacy to bear. Mallarmé's "solution," regardless of whether it can be called successful, allows for no imitation. The works of most modern poets—Valéry, Claudel, Rilke, George, Hofmannsthal—are instances of the struggle to escape from the narcissistic imagery ingrained in symbolism, and the difficulty of their poetry reflects, often enough, the failure of their attempt. Yeats's second and third volumes of poetry, *The Countess Kathleen and Various Legends and Lyrics* (1892) and *The Wind among the Reeds* (1899), represent *his* attempt to overcome the contradiction inherent in the natural image, a contradiction of which symbolist imagery is well aware but which it cannot resolve.

So little change in general theme, tone, and rhythm separates Yeats's first from his second volume of poetry that both are often linked together, with *The Wind among the Reeds,* under the general heading of his "early manner," in contrast to the poems written after 1900. However, the change in image structure that occurs at this point is perhaps more important than any other stylistic change in Yeats's development. Some of the most important characteristics of the entire work are determined by the transformation that takes place at this time; it is the first clear appearance of a problem which will never be overcome.

At first sight, it might seem as if many of the images from the first volume are simply carried over to the second. Two poems like "Ephemera" (from the 1889 volume) and "The White Birds" (from the 1892 volume) are not only strikingly similar in theme—earthly love first destroyed by time, then transcended by a promise of eternal love in some other, supernatural realm—but they have some of the main images in common. Stars and meteors appear in both:

How far away the stars seem, and how far
Is our first kiss . . .

(*Var.*, p. 80, "Ephemera," ll. 8–9)

The woods were round them, and the yellow leaves
Fell like faint meteors in the gloom, and once
A rabbit old and lame limped down the path . . .

(*Ibid.*, ll. 13–15)

As in the other instances from the earliest poetry, the images of stars and meteors appear here, among several other natural things (leaves, rabbits, woods, etc.), as details in a landscape. The meteor is used as the second term of a simile to make a certain detail more vivid, more picturesque, and the entire poem is set up as a visible scene, organized in terms of the graphic reality of a picture.

Consider now the following passage from "The White Birds":

I would that we were, my beloved, white birds on
the foam of the sea!
We tire of the flame of the meteor, before it can fade
and flee;
And the flame of the blue star of twilight, hung low
on the rim of the sky,
Has awaked in our hearts, my beloved, a sadness that
may not die.

A weariness comes from those dreamers, dew-
dabbled, the lily and rose;
Ah, dream not of them, my beloved, the flame of the
meteor that goes,
Or the flame of the blue star that lingers hung low
in the fall of the dew:
For I would we were changed to white birds on the
wandering foam; I and you!

(*Var.*, p. 121–22)

The poem is inspired by a remark made by Maud Gonne at a specific time and place,[27] but nothing of the concrete circumstance remains. "Meteor," "star," "lily," "rose," "white birds," etc. are still names of objects in nature, but no suggestion is made that the poet or his beloved are actually seeing any of them. The original perception of the object is entirely lacking. Nor is the poem organized in terms of a concrete and natural arrangement of things, as is the case for the landscape of "Ephemera"; instead, the structure is determined by a pattern of relationships between the key images themselves. The meteor and the blue star are associated as both partaking of the elemental nature of fire; they seem to correspond to the rose and the lily respectively, and are transcended by the white birds, whose elemental nature is that of water as opposed to fire:

> Soon far from the rose and the lily and fret of the
>   flames would we be,
> Were we only white birds, my beloved, buoyed out
>   on the foam of the sea!
>
> *(Var.,* p. 122)

Subtler shades are conveyed by the properties of the images; the nature of the distinction between the realm of the meteor and that of the star is never stated, but one is led to believe that the second is closer to the final reconciliation than the first. The star "lingers . . . in the fall of the dew," and is thus clearly of a less fiery nature than the meteor; it also corresponds to the lily, which is white like the birds, and thus in all respects closer to the ultimate fulfillment. The autobiographical pretext for the poem bears this out; the plea for the rejection of passionate and sensual love in favor of platonic contemplation is a continuing obsession in Yeats's relationship with Maud Gonne.

A remarkable new element appears here; a functional and structural difference distinguishes words like "star" and "meteor" as they appear in "Ephemera" from those same words in "The White Birds." In "Ephemera," they are mimetic nouns referring to natural objects which the poet claims to present to us as perceived by him. In "The White Birds," the same nouns have no mimetic referent whatever; in no way can it be said that the poem is "about" actual stars or actual meteors; the images have given up all pretense at being natural objects and have become something else. They are taken from the literary tradition and receive their meaning from traditional or personal, but not from natural associations—in the same way that the colors of a national banner are determined, not by analogy with nature, but by the decree of an independent will. Since this distinction is of crucial importance in an interpretation of Yeats, we need a word to discriminate the natural image from the kind of image that appears in "The White Birds." Yeats himself, groping for a term, sometimes uses "symbols" or "profound symbols" or "images that are living souls" before settling, quite consistently, for "emblems." In Yeats's vocabulary—and we do not have to inquire here as to whether this usage is in conformity with the history of the word—an emblem is defined as "having its meaning by a traditional and not by a natural right"[28]—to which must be added that, in this context, "traditional" is synonymous with "divine." I will henceforth use the term "emblem" in this particular sense, which is Yeats's own.

Literary associations are obvious in the case of the lily and the rose, hackneyed emblems that abound in the Pre-Raphaelites.[29] But the meteor comes from Shelley, who uses it not as an emblem, but as a natural image often associated with the sun:

> The sanguine Sunrise, with his meteor eyes,
>   And his burning plumes outspread,
> Leaps on the back of my sailing rack,
>   When the morning star shines dead;
>
> ("The Cloud")

Association of the meteor with the sun implies association of the blue star with the moon; such emblematic patterns receive added meaning from related passages in Yeats's early prose: "In ancient times, it seems to me that Blake, who for all his protest was glad to be alive, and ever spoke of his gladness,

would have worshipped in some chapel of the Sun, and that
Keats, who accepted life gladly though with 'a delicious dili-
gent indolence,' would have worshipped in some chapel of the
Moon, but that Shelley, who hated life because he sought 'more
in life than any understood,' would have wandered, lost in a
ceaseless reverie, in some chapel of the Star of infinite desire"
(*IoGE*, "The Philosophy of Shelley's Poetry," p. 137). The same
thematic and emblematic pattern that is in "The White Birds"
is repeated and one becomes aware that such a conventional
appearing poem is linked to an intricate cluster of emblems:
fire and water, lily and rose, meteor and star transcended by
the white birds, sun and moon transcended by the "star of infinite desire," red and blue by white, Blake and Keats by Shelley, etc. Those associations remain far from constant, but they
always remain in existence, even when they change or diver-
sify their meaning. The sun-moon opposition undergoes baf-
fling, but highly revealing, variations; Keats appears in *A Vision* associated, as he would be here, with beautiful women;
and the birds, an early appearance of a central emblem, recur
in an infinite variety of forms until the very last poems. One
is tempted to organize and interpret Yeats's poetry in terms of
his manipulation of emblems.

In so doing, however, one would not reach the central intent out of which this poetry originates. Yeats's work, seen in
its entirety, is not a closed system of emblems that gain in
meaning and depth as he meditates on their mythological or
religious universality. He often claims this to be the case, and
in *The Wind among the Reeds* as well as in essays written around
the same time and gathered in *Ideas of Good and Evil*, he comes
very close to practicing what he advocates. A certain image born
as by chance out of a natural perception, or a literary reminiscence, or an arbitrary act of the imagination becomes meaningful when its universality is revealed, either because it recurs, like a Jungian archetype, in a variety of separate traditions,
or because its association with a certain experience is sanctioned by a supernatural vision; in both cases, the "meaning"
of the emblem is determined by a divine decision and it ap-

pears as the means of access to an understanding of the will of God. The natural images of the earliest volume are transformed into emblems which claim to be the divine *logos*. The natural image is in fact an emblem which the poet has not yet deciphered and identified as such. Shelley, for instance, was writing in terms of emblems without being altogether aware of it, still half deluded in his belief that his divinely inspired, *recurrent* symbols were natural images:

> One finds in his [Shelley's] poetry, besides innumerable images that have not the definiteness of symbols, many images that are certainly symbols, and as the years went by he began to use these with a more and more deliberately symbolic purpose. I imagine that, when he wrote his earlier poems, he allowed the subconscious life to lay its hands so firmly upon the rudder of his imagination, that he was little conscious of the abstract meaning of the images that rose in what seemed the idleness of his mind. Any one who has any experience of any mystical state of the soul knows how there float up in the mind profound symbols, whose meaning, if indeed they do not delude one into the dream that they are meaningless, one does not perhaps understand for years. Nor I think has any one, who has known that experience with any constancy, failed to find some day in some old book or on some old monument, a strange or intricate image, that had floated up before him, and grown perhaps dizzy with the sudden conviction that our little memories are but a part of some great memory that renews the world and men's thoughts age after age . . . Shelley understood this . . . but whether he understood that the great memory is also a dwelling-house of symbols, of images that are living souls, I cannot tell.
>
> (*IoGE*, "The Philosophy of Shelley's Poetry," pp. 112–14)

Yeats sees himself, at that time,[30] as a more conscious Shelley who would be well aware that his spontaneous images are signals that reach him from a divine realm, and that the task of his poetry consists in recording those signals and using them as the key to decipher the ordered system of which they are the visible part. In 1908, he describes the genesis of *The Wind among the Reeds* in the same manner: "When I wrote these poems I had so meditated over the images that came to me in writing 'Ballads and Lyrics,' 'The Rose,' and 'The Wanderings of Oisin,' and other images from Irish folk-lore, that they had become true symbols. I had sometimes when awake, but more often in sleep, moments of vision, a state very unlike dreaming, when these images took upon themselves what seemed an independent life and became part of a mystic language, which seemed always as if it would bring me some strange revelation" (from a note in vol. 1 of the Stratford edition, p. 227, also in *Var.*, p. 800).

Images of this kind differ radically from the Baudelairian symbol. The use of emblems is alien to French symbolism; Baudelaire is persistently obsessed with the texture of matter and of sensation; as for Mallarmé's highly intellectualized images, they are still founded on the ontological priority of natural things, and his conception of the work as a historical reality is aimed primarily toward the future, with no consideration of the tradition except as a record of failures. He represents even such an obviously emblematic object as a tombstone as if it were a natural thing: "Calme bloc ici-bas chu d'un désastre obscur . . ." ("Le Tombeau d'Edgar Poe,"). With the exception of Gérard de Nerval, who is an isolated and very special case,[31] the symbolists use emblems only as ornament and decoration, while their original inventions always stem from the domain of the image.

It may seem a minor matter when Yeats calls natural images nothing but disguised, not yet understood emblems, but it represents a radical departure from one of the main tenets of the Western poetic tradition. This tradition conceives of the *logos* as incarnate and locates divine essence in the object, not in the unmediated *word* of God. Romanticism and symbolism, with their avowed or occult pantheistic overtones and nostalgias, belong in that tradition. But when nature itself is considered a mere sign, or a mouthpiece without actual substance, then one has left the mainstream of the tradition and embarked "on strange seas of thought." We can understand and share in Hölderlin's nostalgia for a time when words will originate like flowers; but it is much more difficult to understand a conception of the emblem which reverses the process and wants flowers to originate as if they were words. *"Aussi peut-être un jour,"* writes Balzac in *Louis Lambert,* *"le sens inverse de l'Et verbum caro factum est sera-t-il le résumé d'un nouvel évangile qui dira: Et la chair se fera le Verbe, elle deviendra la Parole de Dieu."* This would indeed require a "nouvel évangile" and it would lead to a very different poetry from the one we know at present. It is not surprising that Yeats has to go far afield and make ample use of his imagination in order to find examples and antecedents for this kind of imagery. When Western art made extensive use of emblems, during the Middle Ages, it was to illustrate a dogma which states the withdrawal of the divine from anything but matter; afterward, poets could only celebrate the divine in natural images of earth and light. The Renaissance poets of the sixteenth century try in vain to keep their emblems from turning into pantheistic, Hellenic images—a predominant tension from Spenser to Milton, from Ronsard to Racine—and romanticism, experiencing divine absence in the form of an alienation from nature, makes the natural image into its foremost stylistic device. Yeats's return to the emblem would seem to represent a very radical reaction.

He had, of course, the very recent example of the Pre-Raphaelites behind him, who had been writing emblematic poetry of a kind. But, as one would expect from a group so closely related to the plastic arts, their neo-medieval emblems are predominantly decorative and inspired by a concern for graphic values. It is one of the ironies of Yeats's situation that when, in *The Wind among the Reeds* and in the poetic drama *The Shadowy Waters,* he is experimenting with a very different and new kind of poetry, he appears more derivative, more conventionally Pre-Raphaelite than before. His claims for the emblem, however, go far beyond anything dreamed of by his predecessors; he intends to write divine voices into existence and to rediscover the long-lost unity between man and the gods, of which traces have been preserved in the literary tradition: "If I watch a rushy pool in the moonlight, my emotion at its beauty is mixed with memories of the man that I have seen ploughing by its margin, or the lovers I saw there a night ago; but if I look at the moon herself *and remember any of her ancient names and meanings,*[32] I move among divine people, and things that have shaken off our mortality . . ." (*IoGE,* "The Symbolism of Poetry," p. 251). This is no longer an epiphany, for it substitutes "names and meanings" for the thing itself and, in gnostic fashion, searches for Being not in the divinely created thing, but in language as the vessel of divine intellect. Because he is aware of the ontological assumptions that stand behind emblematic imagery, Yeats reaches out far beyond his Pre-Raphaelite forerunners.

It is important to remember that Yeats's emblematic style was preceded, in his development, by a kind of imagery more in keeping with the romantic and symbolist tradition. This casts a different light on the reasons that may have prompted the change; instead of being the result of an irresistible command similar to a divine annunciation or, at the very least, a spiritual exercise leading up to such an annunciation, the evolution from image to emblem might well be Yeats's strategic attempt to disentangle himself from the predicament reflected in his earliest style. Hence the effort, in the later work, to bridge or, rather, to conceal the gap that separates the emblem from the natural image. Apparently, Yeats's "conversion" to an emblematic conception of language is never complete. In the last analysis, he remains loyal to natural things and to the poetic tradition of which he is the heir, although he fully realizes that it can only lead him to a narcissistic paralysis. The resulting conflict determines the subsequent development of his poetry.

Evidence of this conflict appears already during the period of *The Wind among the Reeds* in certain hesitations and dissatisfactions expressed in the critical essays. The articles from *Ideas of Good and Evil* do not openly make the distinction between the two kinds of imagery; the previous quotation from "The Symbolism of Poetry," for instance, contains a claim of unity rooted in the experience of matter, but the essay as a whole states the superiority of emblems over images, without apparent awareness of the contradiction between the two attitudes. A revealing passage from "Symbolism in Painting" however, shows that Yeats is aware of the problem: ". . . the other day, . . . I sat for my portrait to a German Symbolist in Paris, whose talk was all for his love for Symbolism and his hatred for Allegory . . . The only symbols he cared for were the shapes and motions of the body; ears hidden by the hair, to make one think of a mind busy with inner voices; and a head so bent that back and neck made the one curve, as in Blake's 'Vision of Bloodthirstiness,' to call up an emotion of bodily strength; and he would not even put a lily, or a rose, or a poppy into a picture to express purity, or love, or sleep, because he thought such emblems were allegorical, and had their meaning by a traditional and not by a natural right" (*IoGE,* pp. 227ff.). This puts the case of image versus emblem very clearly, and indicates some impatience on Yeats's behalf with what is still, in 1898, his dominant manner. He goes on to offer an equally revealing defense of the emblem: "I said that the rose, and the lily, and the poppy were so married, by their colour and their odour, and their use, to love and purity and sleep, or to other symbols of love and purity and sleep, and had been so long part of the imagination of the world, that a symbolist might use them to help out his meaning without becoming an allegorist. . . ."

A very characteristic shift occurs in this argument: if the image of the lily suggests purity because of its whiteness, then the imagination will create the metaphor by meditating on the particular texture of whiteness proper to the lily, and expand this material perception until it becomes linked with a certain experience of consciousness, such as purity. What matters is the connection between whiteness and purity and, to be successful, the metaphor has to discover the link anew, make it originate at this moment, purity originating "as flowers originate." The distortion in Yeats's argument is introduced by putting the "use" of the symbol lily on the same plane with its odor and color, when both belong to altogether different realms. The permanence of the odor and the color resides in the thing itself, while that of the use resides in the will of man, or of a god acting through man. The former leads to a (problematic) vision of unity that transcends the opposition between object and subject, while the latter finds unity preserved in language as the carrier of a divine, and therefore permanently repeated, pattern of experience; it postulates as an act of faith that the divine is immediately and audibly present to human consciousness in the very entity—language—that is the distinctive attribute of this consciousness.

A poetics based on this faith will, like most medieval art, be allegorical without being in the least apologetic about it: the meaning of the emblem is revealed by a key and this key is given *a priori,* as the divine order itself. It may be realistic, as much allegorical art is realistic, not because it desires to equal nature by imitation, but in order to make certain that the emblems will be easily recognized and read, like a clear handwriting; medieval realism is a form of calligraphy. But it will not be metaphorical like Hölderlin's "words," or Baudelaire's "parfums" or Yeats's "shells." Therefore, Yeats soon wearies of a purely emblematic style, dismisses it as allegory or more "embroideries" and returns, after 1900, to what seems to be a more natural kind of image. This would suffice to indicate that, although he is conscious of the redeeming power that the emblem might possess for him, it cannot satisfy him; his real torment remains that of the romantic alienation from matter. *The Wind among the Reeds* failed to bring to its author the exhilaration of self-renewal: the style is not really new because the underlying problem has not changed and because the emblems are in reality pseudo-emblems, dead allegories that cover up the defeat of the natural image.

The conflict between image and emblem leads to the development of a thematic pattern which comes into full view around this time. From *The Countess Kathleen and Various Legends and Lyrics* on, there prevails an almost obsessive recurrence of the theme of apocalyptic death as the climactic dénouement of almost all poems. This thematic development reflects what is in reality a stylistic tension—keeping in mind that style, as well and often more candidly than theme, is shaped by intent.

In the earliest work, the theme of death appeared in close association with that of stillness and repose. "The Island of Statues" has to do with death as the price one has to pay to move from a natural, Arcadian world into another realm, very dimly and vaguely characterized in some of the most promising bad verse since Keats's early "I stood tip-toe . . ." or "Sleep and Poetry."[33] Among the rewards of the supernatural world, the most specific is a form of eternal peace:

> hast thou never heard
> Mid bubbling leaves a wandering song-rapt bird
> Going the forest through, with flutings weak;
> Or hast thou never seen, with visage meek,
> A hoary hunter leaning on his bow,
> To watch thee pass? Yet deeper than men know
> These are at peace.
>
> (*Var.*, p. 672, ll. 153ff.)[34]

This quiet is a counterpart for the restlessness which makes Yeats's early heroes embark on impossible quests, passively lured away, as by a supernatural temptation, from their own selves or their own countries, longing for what they never really had to leave, though refusing to accept as their own what is immediately accessible. They are voluntary exiles, whose eagerness to leave is only surpassed by their desire to return, and who remain condemned to aimless "wanderings." Their restlessness is accompanied, naturally enough, by a simultaneous longing for the exact opposite: total quiet and repose. The theme of quiet is abundantly present in Yeats's earliest poetry, both explicitly designating the ideal mood to which he aspires, and implicitly, in the repetitive, lilting rhythms and sound of several—though by no means all—among his early poems.[35] Answering a friend who had asked for an explanation of one of the poems in this vein, Yeats writes: "You ask me what is the meaning of 'She who dwelt among the Sycamores.' She is the spirit of quiet. The poem means that those who in youth and childhood wander alone in woods and in wild places, ever after carry in their hearts a secret well of quietness and that they always long for rest and to get away from

the noise and rumour of the world."[36] The pursuit of quiet or
its corollary, the disturbance of quiet by the intrusion of the
world, is an ever-recurring theme throughout the early poems.
"The Wanderings of Oisin" itself is an outstanding example.
As Russell K. Alspach has shown,[37] the main source for this
poem, Michael Comyn's *The Lay of Oisin*, has a closely similar
plot; however, though mention is made of a Land of Victories
next to the traditional Land of the Young, there is no trace of
what becomes with Yeats the third and final realm visited by
Niamh and Oisin, the land of repose and forgetfulness. This
is his own invention. Moreover, from a letter to Katherine
Tynan (after September 6, 1888),[38] we know that the third part
gave him by far the greatest satisfaction; for the second edition in 1895 (the first is from 1889), he rewrote and improved
the two first parts extensively; but, except for minor changes,
the third remained as it was. Clearly, the theme closest to him
had "got itself expressed" much better than the others. The
quietest mood has an almost irresistible tendency to push itself into the foreground, and it is closely associated with the
theme of death.

There is nothing new or unusual about this association of
themes, or about the ambiguity which makes quiet appear as
both desirable and dangerous: this is a dominant pattern in
romantic poetry. One thinks of Keats's "cold pastoral":

> Thou still unravish'd bride of quietness,
> Thou foster-child of silence and slow time

where the eternity of the work of art implies a funeral urn and
a sacrifice; or of the symbol of the nightingale, the "immortal"
bird whose song is the desire for death; or perhaps most of all
of the Cave of Quietude in *Endymion:*

> But few have ever felt how calm and well
> Sleep may be had in that deep den of all.
> There anguish does not sting; nor pleasure pall:
> Woe-hurricanes beat ever at the gate,
> Yet all is still within and desolate.
> Beset with plainful gusts, within ye hear

> No sound so loud as when on curtain'd bier
> The death-watch tick is stifled . . .
>
> (*Endymion* IV.524ff.)

Or one thinks of Wordsworth, whose states of suspended, fragile immobility and silence have a strangely superhuman quality as if they, too, could only occur on the far side of death. Still, in *Igitur*, the same association is present when the "death" of truth is described as "un calme narcotique de *moi* pur longtemps rêvé" (I.3).

The allusion to Mallarmé helps us to understand how the association between quietness and death, so frequently found in romanticism, must be distinguished from the same association in Yeats, when natural images begin to give way to emblems. Death in *Igitur* is the sacrifice of the natural part of man to the truth of conscious poetic language. With less emphasis on truth and consciousness but no essential difference, this is also what death means for Keats: the necessary sacrifice of the gods of nature to the gods of art, of Saturn to Apollo. Keats chose the myth of the battle of the Titans as the subject for his projected romantic epic, and this myth contains the archetype of the romantic experience, with all its tragic and elegiac connotations. The all-pervading stillness in the opening lines of *Hyperion*

> Deep in the shady sadness of a vale
> Far sunken from the healthy breath of morn,
> Far from the fiery noon, and eve's one star,
> Sat gray-hair'd Saturn, quiet as a stone,
> Still as the silence round about his lair; . . .

is indeed the stillness of Yeats's dead woods of Arcady. But Apollo's song is the reward for this sacrifice: it narrates this death in the language which survives after the sacrifice has been accomplished. Saturn's death marks the end of all hope that a natural image could contain natural objects as presences, i.e., without mediation, but it creates the possibility of another kind of mediable poetic language. Wordsworth, too, with his unshakable faith in the mimetic power of natural speech, postpones the restoration of innocence till the passage of a cosmic cataclysm has cleansed the world as it now exists.[39] In all those cases, language remains as the lone survivor after the tragic death of the gods that inhabit natural substances, and it becomes the sole carrier of time. It contains the potential future of a new beginning, the next gyre in Mallarmé's spiral. *"Tout existe,"* said Mallarmé, *"pour aboutir à un Livre"* and this *"tout,"* as Mallarmé's work and the entire romantic tradition testifies, emphatically includes death, our death to the extent that we partake in the existence of natural things.

But the death that appears in Yeats's *The Wind among the Reeds* is different. It is not the *cost* one has to pay for a possible fulfillment, as was still the case in "The Island of Statues"; it is in itself that fulfillment. *"Tout existe,"* Yeats could have said in paraphrase of Mallarmé, *"pour aboutir à la mort."* Whether death be dreaded in terror or fervently prayed for, it always appears as an absolute annihilation beyond which nothing earthly can survive. Practically all the poems in the book gravitate around the single theme, "the battle between the manifest world and the ancestral darkness at the end of all things" in which "darkness . . . will at last destroy the gods and the world."[40] This "end of all things" is represented by a variety of emblems drawn from several traditions: the cry of the curlow, the death-pale deer, the galloping horses, the boar without bristles, etc. The title of the volume itself, which originally appears in connection with the idea of eternity,[41] more and more acquires an apocalyptic significance: "God will accomplish his last judgment, first in one man's mind and then in another. He is always planning last judgments. And yet it takes a long time and that is why he laments in the wind and in the reeds and in the cries of the curlews."[42] The last judgment means cosmic annihilation—"God burning Nature with a kiss"—*as well as* the end of language, man "struck dumb in the simplicity of fire," his tongue become a stone.[43] In its most extreme form, as in Mallarmé's *Coup de Dés*, the language of the image also has a destructive power on a cosmic scale, but there always remains the tenuous counterweight of the Work, the "constellation," as a possible survival. The nihilism of *The*

Wind among the Reeds is more absolute, without any positive counterpart, although it does not stem from a *fin-de-siècle* decadence, or a weariness of the creative faculties. No such concerns torment Yeats, a young and successful poet in search of a new style at a moment when self-renewal is particularly difficult. What looks like romantic agony is primarily the symptom of a stylistic problem common to all post-romantic poetry. In Yeats's case, the nihilism is a consequence of the unresolved conflict between image and emblem.

Theoretically, the emblem should convey a message of hope and joy, the "good tidings" that the voice of God has again been heard, rediscovered in a tradition that was only dimly aware of its eschatological power. Even if the poet feels only on the brink of this discovery, he should speak with the expectation and the fervor that sometimes appear, though rarely without reservations, when Yeats, in his essays, speaks of the great memory as the storehouse of emblems in which divine presence has been preserved. Why is it then that the poetry of *The Wind among the Reeds* is a poetry of terror and annihilation, apocalyptic rather than eschatological? It can only be because Yeats still experiences the Annunciation as an intolerable destruction of nature. The advent of the emblem marks the end of the ontological supremacy of natural substances as repositories of the divine, but this should be a matter of indifference to the poet who no longer expects a revelation to come from the world of nature. "Words alone are certain good . . ." provided they be divinely inspired, and it will be of little moment if the "vegetable glass" of nature will disappear into nothing if touched by their fire, for all reality resides in the flaming word of God. The poet who has really overcome his nostalgia for natural things will be able, as Yeats says of Blake,[44] to face the Last Judgment without any terror. But Yeats has not freed himself from the latent pantheism which is so deeply rooted in the tradition of the West, and for him the "flaming word" of God is still, throughout his poetry, nothing more than the fear of death. The paralysis of death is apparent in the stilted stiffness of his allegorical language. Yeats rebelled, to some

extent, against the style of *The Wind among the Reeds;* the publication of a collection of poems by young Irish poets, edited
by George Russell and entitled *New Songs,* confirmed him in
his decision, by showing how his own manner would be corrupted by clumsy imitators. He was so sensitive on this point
because it brings into the open what he had in fact been doing
himself; instead of recording "some strange revelation," he had
merely ransacked the tradition and his own early work for images which he could only passively imitate.

The advent of the emblem can still only be celebrated in
what fundamentally remains a natural imagery: as long as we
see nature being burned up, we cannot feel the "kiss of God."
This leads to curious contradictions. A poem like "The Man
who Dreamed of Faeryland" (*Var.,* p. 126) is quite unambiguous in its explicit statement: the necessity for complete renunciation of all worldly pleasures and aspirations, love, wealth,
fame, and the peace of death, all of them far surpassed by corresponding supernatural experiences. This message is conveyed by creatures—fish in stanza 1, a lug-worm in 2, a knot-
grass in 3, worms in 4—that one must assume to be purely
emblematic, pertaining to the realm of "sweet, everlasting
voices" where no matter exists. Instead, they possess a vivid
reality, strengthened by the precise and specific place-names
which suggest that they stem from actual observation; there is
a fish market, indeed, at Dromahair and there are plenty of
lugworms on the sands of Lissadell; as for the "worms that
spired about his bones," they are almost naturalistically plausible. Still, it is those very substantial, real things which are
made to announce the utter vanity of anything natural. What
makes the poem expressively as well as logically odd is that it
derives its undeniable effectiveness precisely from the reality
of the images; certainly, one remembers the "little silver heads"
of the fishes, the "lug-worm with its grey and muddy mouth,"
"the sands of Lissadell" where "his mind ran all on money
cares and fears," the crowd in Dromahair where "his heart hung
all upon a silken dress," much better than the vague people

of Faeryland—and that is the very opposite of what the poem sets out to convey.

Yeats will learn to make use of such contradictions later, and play skillfully on the ambiguous status of an imagery which seduces the reader as a natural image while trying to convince him as an emblem—but at this point, several of the best poems from "The Rose" have an attractive but involuntary aura of absurdity about them. In *The Wind among the Reeds* such mixed imagery is no longer tolerated, and all becomes emblem. Still, even here, the emblems have an irresistible tendency to acquire a life of their own, not as the archetypal experiences which they are supposed to reveal, but as slightly ludicrous, plastically picturesque objects—as when, in an altogether otherworldly poem, a deer with no horns becomes, by metamorphosis, a hound with specifically *one* red ear, while a fierce mythological boar without bristles is last seen very realistically, and understandably, exhausted and grunting, after having rooted sun, moon, and stars out of the sky. In later poems, such absurdities will become controlled ironies, but at this time they illustrate the failure of a style which Yeats is soon to abandon, at least in appearance.

When Yeats's next volume of poetry appears in 1903,[45] it contained the first awkward version of a play that introduces a different character: Cuchulain, the man who has ". . . the touch of something hard, repellent yet alluring, self-assertive yet self-immolating."[46] Cuchulain replaces the passive and yielding Oisin as the main hero, and remains so, by and large, till the end. Introducing his new play, Yeats writes: "The first shape of it came to me in a dream, but it changed much in the making, foreshadowing, it may be, a change that may bring a less dream-burdened will into my verses."[47] The accompanying lyrical poems, as well as the play itself, indicate that the change has already taken place: some of the lyrics differ considerably from *The Wind among the Reeds* in texture, with biting, topical allusions and at times an abrupt diction that treats language

cavalierly with nothing of the elaborate decorum of the previous, hieratic manner:

> new commonness
> Upon the throne and crying about the streets
> And hanging its paper flowers from post to post, . . .
>
> ("In the Seven Woods," *Var.*, p. 198)

> I thought of your beauty, and this arrow,
> Made out of a wild thought, is in my marrow.
>
> ("The Arrow," *Var.*, p. 199)

While he remained silent about the crucial change that took
place between his two preceding books, we now have Yeats's
own announcement that a new style is being created. The difference, indeed, is made as conspicuous as possible. Such an
attitude should inspire caution before accepting an interpretation which Yeats himself seems almost overeager to suggest.

This interpretation is obvious enough. It appears as if Yeats
wanted to free himself from the morbid, decadent obsessions
of the early poetry by assuming at last his share of worldly
responsibilities (*Responsibilities* being indeed the title of one of
his next volumes). In this he seems to be following in the footsteps of such other repentant decadents as, to borrow an enumeration from Praz, Swinburne, Barrès, and d'Annunzio.[48] In
terms of imagery, the conversion is reflected in a return to the
use of natural imagery, a return which can undoubtedly be
observed from this volume on. But such tidy and simple
schemes have little chance to apply to a poet of genuine complexity; neither was Yeats the man to abandon the transcendental hopes that inspired his early poetry for a mere compromise with reality, on reality's own terms. Even the biographical
facts contradict such a notion.[49] One cannot enlist Yeats's work
or life in the cause of an attack on aestheticism in the name of
social or existential commitments, however noble and desirable they may be. It could be questioned, of course, if the motives that inspire the early work enter under the category of
aestheticism. If by aestheticism one means Oscar Wilde, d'Annunzio, or des Esseintes, the practice of a fastidious poetic

discipline as a means of emancipation from moral restrictions, then the answer is negative. But if by aestheticism is meant the use of poetic language as a means to overcome the kind of alienation characteristic of romanticism, then Yeats remains a representative of what could be called, if the term had not been corrupted, the "aestheticism" of all romantic and post-romantic poetry. At any rate, the interpretation of the change in manner that took place around 1900 is best understood in terms of the different kind of imagery that precedes it. The change is decisive in the sense that it leads, after a long period of gestation, to the masterly poetry written after 1916.[50]

It is very revealing that this change, far from being an exhilarating experience, is felt by Yeats himself as a sacrifice and a loss, the loss of what he most wanted to possess. Yeats's own versions of his transformation, in his later autobiographical writings, are ambiguous to the point of incoherence, and complicated by the use of a cryptic emblematic language, very difficult to decipher.[51] But in *On Baile's Strand* itself, we are offered a hardly veiled statement of his true feelings at that time; indeed, most of the poems from *In the Seven Woods* deal with the tragedy of having had to abandon the emblematic style of *The Wind among the Reeds*.

On Baile's Strand, like many of the plays, contains an intimate confession, expressed by means of a rather transparent and somewhat mechanical pattern of symbols and emblems.[52] It is a dramatization of Yeats's inner conflict at that time, having to do, in part, with personal matters: his relationship to Maud Gonne and, no doubt, Lady Gregory's well-meaning attempts to make his life more stable and orderly. Much more prominently, however, it deals with problems of poetic style, for the events in Yeats's life tend to become very quickly inseparable from his literary concerns.[53] On one level of meaning, the characters in the play correspond to the different types of style with which Yeats has been experimenting, and the action—Cuchulain unwittingly slaying his son at the instigation of Conchubar—reflects Yeats's despair at having to abandon the purely emblematic style of *The Wind among the Reeds*. The new poetry will be successful, as Conchubar and his comic equivalence, the blind man, are successful in securing their position as unchallenged rulers. But the true tradition has only contempt for this kind of success, the stability of ordered government and domestic happiness, of natural order and natural imagery. It can only be satisfied by supernatural revelation, direct unity with the Sun to whose realm Cuchulain belongs, in opposition to the lunar, reflected light of Conchubar's rationality.[54] The transmission of the true esoteric tradition is represented in Cuchulain's wish to pass on to his son and heir the "coat" which Yeats will later identify, derisively but explicitly, as representing his early emblematic style ("I made my song a coat / Covered with embroideries / Out of old mythologies / From heel to throat"—*Var.*, p. 320). Cuchulain himself has received it from his solar father, as emblems are inherited from the gods by ways of the literary tradition:

> (Spreading out cloak)
> Nine queens out of the Country-under-Wave
> Have woven it with the fleeces of the sea
> And they were long embroidering at it . . .
>
> (*Plays*, p. 270)

> My father gave me this.
> He came to try me, rising up at dawn
> Out of the cold dark of the rich sea.
> He challenged me to battle, but before
> My sword had touched his sword, told me his name,
> Gave me this cloak, and vanished. It was woven
> By women of the Country-under-Wave
> Out of the fleeces of the sea.
>
> (*Plays*, p. 268)

Cuchulain killing his son corresponds to Yeats's turning away from his true heritage, at the instigation of his older, wiser self that knows of the dangers to which his allegiance to the emblem may lead. But this defensive victory of the natural image turns out to be a tragedy: Cuchulain, by his own hand, destroys the tradition of which he was the recipient and, fooled by a false loyalty to the natural order of things, he fails to see his own strength. The final image of his hopeless fight against the waves can be interpreted in various ways but it is not, at any rate, a symbol of appeased reconciliation. As in "The White Birds" the ultimate destiny is death in the infinity of the sea, but instead of the passive, contented quietism of the early poem, death is now a bitter, absurd, heroic act. And, also as in the early poems, two roads lead to this fulfillment: the solar route of the emblem and the lunar route which is closer to the order of nature. In this particular text, the natural image appears as the unmitigated villain, and all Yeats's sympathies go to the emblem, the loser in the play as well as in the poetry. This stands in contradiction, of course, to the nostalgic longing for natural imagery when, as in *The Wind among the Reeds*, Yeats adopts the solar road of the emblem. Such contradictions are to be expected from a poet who, in his own words, "vacillates" between two extremes that permit of no synthesis or dialectical mediation. At a moment when his work seems to come back to a more concrete kind of poetry, the nostalgia for the supernatural is at its strongest.

Even statements that seem to herald the new manner with unreserved conviction and enthusiasm are still loaded with the particular sophistry which allows Yeats to say two contradictory things at the same time. As stated before, the open, public polemic against the early manner was instigated in part by Yeats's impatience with the anthology of *New Songs*, edited by George Russell; on that occasion, he wrote AE a letter which sounds like a powerful manifesto against his early manner (although the target of his attack is the mawkish *Land of Heart's Desire*, not *The Wind among the Reeds* or *The Shadowy Waters*): "I have been fighting the prevailing decadence for years, and have just got it under foot in my own heart—it is sentiment and sentimental sadness, a womanish introspection . . . Let us have no emotions, however abstract, in which there is not an athletic joy."[55] But this very Nietzschean outcry carefully avoids including the real substance of the early work in the condemnation; Yeats insists that "my own early subjectiveness rises at rare moments[56] . . . . above sentiment to a union with a pure energy of the spirit," and makes a revealing distinction between the spirit, which inspires his early poetry and leads to ecstasy, and the will, which inspires epic and dramatic poetry and leads to joy; the gradation from joy to ecstasy suggests a hierarchy in which the emblematic poetry ranks the highest.[57] The "athletic joy" may at times come close to the ecstasy of divine revelation, but it can be no substitute for it.

Perhaps Yeats's own reservations about his new manner should not be pressed too far; they could be a passing nostalgia, a tolerant fondness of the older for the younger poet. They are a part, however, of a much larger bundle of evidence: not only in his statements *about* the change, but in actual practice, Yeats never really abandoned the emblematic style of *The Wind among the Reeds*. Learning from the failure of this book, he now becomes much more cautious, strategically avoids some of the stylistic pitfalls and masks his real predicament behind a screen of ambiguities which has succeeded in convincing a majority of readers that he is a much more assertive and self-confident, though a much less considerable poet than he really is.

In "Adam's Curse," a poem from *In the Seven Woods* which sounds unlike anything in *The Wind among the Reeds*,[58] appears the following passage:

> We sat grown quiet at the name of love;
> We saw the last embers of daylight die,
> And in the trembling blue-green of the sky
> A moon, worn as if it had been a shell
> Washed by time's waters as they rose and fell
> About the stars and broke in days and years.
>
> (*Var.*, pp. 205–6)

If this image of the moon is compared with earlier examples of Yeats's imagery—the shell from *Oisin*, the meteor from "The White Birds"—it may seem closer to the earlier of the two. This moon is like the shell in that it does not point to ". . . any of [the moon's] ancient names and meanings" and does not refer us to a myth preserved in the literary tradition. Like the descriptive "trumpet-twisted" that gave the shell visual presence and reality, the "trembling blue-green of the sky" coupled with the indefinite and very un-allegorical article "*a* moon," makes this into a very specific object, perceived at one particular time by Yeats and his friends, in a real, concrete setting. Unlike the meteor, the moon is a natural presence, and the passage seems to start out from the perception of this presence. In this respect, it is indeed very similar to the natural imagery of *Oisin* and very different from the allegorical emblems of *The Wind among the Reeds*.

Natural presences like the moon from "Adam's Curse" will henceforth appear very frequently. The poems are often given a natural setting and start with the description of a natural scene or a situation of unmistakable reality. Examples abound; "The Wild Swans at Coole" can be taken as typical:

> The trees are in their autumn beauty,
> The woodland paths are dry,
> Under the October twilight the water
> Mirrors a still sky;
> Upon the brimming water among the stones
> Are nine-and-fifty swans.
>
> (*Var.*, p. 322)[59]

and "Among School Children" is a clear case of a poem starting not with a natural setting, but with a concrete situation:

> I walk through the long schoolroom questioning;
> A kind old nun in a white hood replies; . . .
>
> (*Var.*, p. 443)[60]

Even when an altogether supernatural realm is being evoked, it is often done in a matter-of-fact, circumstantial manner, as if it were a perception in ordinary time and space—as in "Byzantium"

> The Emperor's drunken soldiery are abed;
> Night resonance recedes, night-walkers' song
> After great cathedral gong; . . .
>
> (*Var.*, p. 497)

or in "News for the Delphic Oracle"

> There all the golden codgers lay,
> There the silver dew, . . .
> Plotinus came and looked about,
> The salt-flakes on his breast, . . .
>
> *(Var.,* pp. 611–12)

From those few examples, taken among many others, it seems indeed as if Yeats solved the dilemma of his *fin-de-siècle* manner by reintroducing the natural imagery to which the later poems owe, in part, their superiority over the earlier ones. Instead of inheriting emblems from the literary and esoteric tradition, the mature poetry goes back to the particular perception in the poet's own experience from which the metaphor originates, "as flowers originate." This original experience may grow into an altogether supernatural vision, but the very fact that, within the span of a single poem, the two can exist side by side without destroying the coherence of the whole, establishes the possibility of unity between them: "Natural and supernatural with the self-same ring are wed" ("Supernatural Songs," *Var.,* p. 556). The return to natural images coincides, moreover, with several explicit statements pleading for the necessity to root the image in the concrete substance, the "body" of this world. One does not have to look for examples in the less accessible prose or in the plays, for they appear conspicuously in the most famous poems:

> Labour is blossoming or dancing where
> The body is not bruised to pleasure soul . . .
>
> ("Among School Children," *Var.,* p. 445)

> Paul Veronese
> And all his sacred company
> Imagined bodies all their days
> By the lagoon you love so much,
> For proud, soft, ceremonious proof
> That all must come to sight and touch; . . .
>
> ("Michael Robartes and the Dancer," *Var.,* p. 386)

Often at evening when a boy
Would I carry to a friend—
Hoping more substantial joy
Did an older mind commend—
Not such as are in Newton's metaphor,
But actual shells of Rosses' level shore.
("At Algeciras—A Meditation upon Death," *Var.*, p. 494)

What if I bade you leave
The cavern of the mind?[61]
There's better exercise
In the sunlight and wind.
("Those Images," *Var.*, p. 600)

For what but eye and ear silence the mind
With the minute particulars of mankind?
("The Double Vision of Michael Robartes," *Var.*, p. 384)

God guard me from those thoughts men think
In the mind alone;
He that sings a lasting song
Thinks in a marrow-bone;
("A Prayer for Old Age," *Var.*, p. 553)

To such statements must be added an obvious thematic development: as the imagery becomes more and more concrete and as Yeats grows in years as well as in mastery, the theme of love does not only become much more important, but it becomes much more frankly sexual. This is so evident that it requires no illustration. Love is certainly present as a theme in *Oisin* and in *The Wind among the Reeds*, but, whatever interpretation one chooses to give it, those works are certainly far from being ribald, while one can easily think of the later poems as an exaltation of the body, be it as a way of access to the divine. The gradual sexualization of the poetry, which reaches its extreme point in *Last Poems*, would seem to be one more confirmation of a definitive return to the world of natural images.

Backed by this impressive amount of evidence, it is

tempting to see Yeats as the poet who went further than any in overcoming the separation between mind and matter, the "dissociation of sensibility" that characterizes the romantic heritage. This has been the prevalent opinion among his closest interpreters. It is in this sense, presumably, that Richard Ellmann refers to Yeats as a great "realist"[62] and emphasizes his "affirmative capability,"[63] or that Graham Hough speaks of Yeats as "in love with experience, with the world as it has been"[64] and compares him with Blake, whose salvation "is so deeply attached to the phenomenal world that it cannot bear to think of it except as eternally recurrent"—in opposition to the Buddhist salvation which escapes from the cycle of material reality. The thesis is most consistently argued in Frank Kermode's *Romantic Image* where Yeats is presented as the successful seeker for "the reconciling image." The image of the dancer is said to be the supreme instance of the reconciliation (a reconciliation which presupposes, of course, an initial severance) because it contains the ideal attributes of both body and imagination. The author willingly concedes that the reconciliation is not painless, and that it has to happen at some expense to the natural world; hence the morbidity, the death-in-life aspect of the resulting symbol.[65] But the world of reality is never really annihilated, partly because—always according to Mr. Kermode's very convincing argument—the tension between body and imagination becomes itself the subject matter of the poem; life, body, and matter thus enter the work as a necessary part and, although they may at times be under attack or in jeopardy, they can never altogether cease to exist: they are forces in a dialectic able to meet their antithesis on equal terms. Yeats is praised for having begun "Among School Children" with the concrete situation of the first stanza; the passage is necessary because "the Image belongs to life in so far as the artist suffers for it."[66]

Some extrinsic facts prevent unqualified acceptance of this opinion. The first fact, nowise decisive by itself, is Yeats's own description of the new style as a capitulation—but this could be relegated to the "cost" side of the balance sheet and dismissed as temporary discouragement, overcome in the obvious gusto of the later work. More disturbing, however, is the predominant tone of the late poetry. Mr. Kermode's main text, understandably enough, is "Among School Children," with its seductively dazzling imagery of unity. But even this poem acquires very different overtones when read within a somewhat larger context. One may well dislike the violence, the invective, and the fundamental strangeness of so many poems, especially (but not only) among the latest ones; one can gloss over the obsessive image, in the last plays, of the poet being murderously cut into pieces by queens and beggarmen, calling this a literary memory of romantic decadence, a late version of Wilde's *Salomé* or Mallarmé's "Hérodiade." The fact remains that one enters here into a world of cold terror and strident dissonance, far removed from the essentially attractive and reassuring image of the "great-rooted blossomer" and the "body swayed to music." No interpretation will do Yeats justice that fails to account for the controlled violence of the late work.

The main discrepancy in the interpretation of Yeats was again clearly demonstrated on the occasion of a recent book, F. A. C. Wilson's *W. B. Yeats and the Tradition*. Because Mr. Wilson has a strong philosophical interest in Yeats's Neoplatonic sources, he is keenly aware of the use of traditional emblems stemming from that tradition. Consequently, when he comes to the refrain from Part VI of "Meditations in Time of Civil War"

> O honey-bees
> Come build in the empty house of the stare
>
> (*Var.*, p. 425)

he naturally refers to the well-known passage in "Among School Children"

> What youthful mother, a shape upon her lap
> Honey of generation had betrayed, . . .
>
> (*Var.*, p. 444)

where Yeats himself supplies a note mentioning Porphyry's commentary on the Homeric ode "The Cave of the Nymphs." On the assumption that Yeats uses recurrent emblems, Mr. Wilson concludes that "we are justified in interpreting 'The Stare's Nest by my Window' from the same source."[67] A reviewer took issue with this and protested that all the beauty of the image is lost if one does not see it as a lyrical development founded on an actual perception,[68] and indeed, a note by Yeats mentions a real starling which, at that time, built his nest by his bedroom window. Yeats's notes cannot even be trusted to be necessarily unreliable,[69] but regardless of the authenticity of the starling or the bees, their relevance to this particular poem depends to a large extent on an emblematic reading derived from Porphyry. In the context of Section VI, the bees are treated in antithesis to the violence and destructiveness of the war; read as natural images, they appear as symbols of peace and abundance:

> . . .
> We are closed in, and the key is turned
> On our uncertainty; somewhere
> A man is killed, or a house burned,
> Yet no clear fact to be discerned:
> Come build in the empty house of the stare.
>
> A barricade of stone or of wood;
> Some fourteen days of civil war;
> Last night they trundled down the road
> That dead young soldier in his blood:
> Come build in the empty house of the stare.
>
> (*Var.*, p. 425)

A reading that extends the context to include the entire poem will recall the "ancestral houses" in the first part ("some marvellous empty sea-shell . . .") emptied and burned by war and internal decay, and notice the analogy with the "empty house" of the starling. In addition to being a symbol of peace, the bees become a symbol for the possible rebirth that may occur after the forces of destruction have taken their toll. This is how far the natural image will take us, and it is quite a way toward an understanding of this poem. If, however, we wish to relate the passage to the theme that gives a deeper unity to "Meditations in Time of Civil War" as a whole, an emblematic reading becomes necessary. Bees, in Yeats's reading of Porphyry, signify "pleasure arising from generation"[70] and generation is the descent out of the realm of the divine, which is eternal and continuous, into the fallen realm of matter and nature, which is subject to discontinuity and decay. The various birds that appear throughout the work are among Yeats's prevailing emblems of the soul's longing for the divine, and the eternal manifestation of the divine will in this world is often represented by the infallible knowledge with which birds build their nests.[71] This emblem appears in "Meditations . . .", first in Part IV, in connection with birds (owls) that build their nests in the cracked masonry of the house

> The Primum Mobile that fashioned us
> Has made the very owls in circles move; . . .
> (*Var.*, p. 423, ll. 17–18)

and it is taken up again later, with the starling's nest in the refrain of Part VI. The prayer, then, for bees to take over after the birds have left, becomes a prayer that the natural order of man, kept alive by the pleasure of procreation, may achieve the same kind of continuity that existed in a divine order with which we have lost contact. This fits in with Yeats's hopes at that time as the "founder" of an estate and a family (Parts II and IV, respectively "My House" and "My Descendants"), but from a bitter passage in Part IV we know this hope to be a vain illusion:

> And what if my descendants lose the flower
> Through natural declension of the soul,
> Through too much business with the passing hour,
> Through too much play, or marriage with a fool?
> May this laborious stair and this stark tower
> Become a roofless ruin that the owl
> May build in the cracked masonry and cry
> Her desolation to the desolate sky.
> (*Var.*, p. 423, ll. 9ff.)

A further enrichment of meaning is brought in by another emblematic association. Bees are related, through Porphyry, to
Homer who, for Yeats, is the poet of "pleasure arising from
generation"—"What theme had Homer but original sin?"—and
thus the poet of the incarnate, Western, Hellenic world of
"bodies" and natural images. This cluster of emblems provides the link with the Christian emblem of "the lion and the
honeycomb" in "Vacillation"

> Homer is my example and his unchristened heart.
> The lion and the honeycomb, what has Scripture
>   said? . . .
>
> (*Var.*, p. 503)

and suggests the kind of Jungian unity of emblematic arche-
types in which Yeats finds the main confirmation of his be-
liefs. Homer is mentioned in "Meditations . . ." in Part I, expressing the conviction that life can be sufficient to itself, that
"profane perfection of mankind" is not in need of divine assistance or intervention:

> Mere dreams, mere dreams! Yet Homer had not sung
> Had he not found it certain beyond dreams
> That out of life's own self-delight had sprung
> The abounding glittering jet; . . .
>
> (*Var.*, p. 417)

The Western conception of art and poetry is founded on this
belief; in emblematic terms, it is the belief that the bees will
be able to "build" as if they were divine like the birds, that the
natural image may accomplish what only the emblem can
achieve. What this belief leads to is revealed in Part I, where
the gradual decline of Western art, a decline that began with
Homer,[72] is represented in terms of the decline of the Irish
gentry, ending up, with perfect emblematic consistency, with
the "sea-shells" of Yeats's earliest poetry, the emblem for the
narcissistic, decadent natural image:

> . . . though now it seems
> As if some marvellous empty sea-shell flung
> Out of the obscure dark of the rich streams,

> And not a fountain, were the symbol which
> Shadows the inherited glory of the rich.
>
> (Var., pp. 417–18)

The ephemeral instability of Western art is contrasted, in Part III, with the permanence of an art that never gives in to the "pleasure of generation" and remains purely emblematic, like the art of the East that produced Sato's sword. By comparison, the Western art of Homer seems to be on the verge of collapse, about to disappear in the apocalyptic destruction heralded by the cry of Juno's peacock, "the last surrender, the irrational cry, revelation . . ." (*Vision*, p. 268): "it seemed / Juno's peacock screamed."

The refrain "O honey-bees, / Come build in the empty house of the stare . . ." acquires a very different function in this wider context. It stands in a deliberate and ironic contrast to the concluding section, which has its own innumerable complications but has to do, at any rate, with "the half-read wisdom of daemonic images" (i.e. emblems) and stands under the sign of the East, of a moon "that seems unchangeable, / A glittering sword out of the east . . ." The refrain expresses the vain and desperate hope of Western, romantic poetry, that divine presence will return in nature, a hope from which Yeats, too, can not disentangle himself, although he knows of the existence of another road. Hence the pathos of the section, which typifies the pathos of all Yeats's mature work.

A poem like "Meditations in Time of Civil War" is built on an intricate network of emblems: our quick analysis of one single line suffices to reveal some of them. No reader can perceive the larger unity of the work, carried by the natural suggestiveness of the imagery alone: real birds and bees cannot take one to Homer or to the *Primum Mobile*, and without this link the poem would only consist of parts haphazardly assembled under a common title, contrary to all we know about Yeats's method of poetic composition. This does not prevent the reviewer who censored Mr. F. A. C. Wilson from being altogether right on the naive plane of immediate appreciation; we all prefer the perception of things to the manipulation of emblems, and we receive much more pleasure from authentic, live bees at Thoor Ballylee than from Porphyry's bookish images—just as we obtain much more satisfaction from reading the poem, with all its personal overtones and memories and its dramatic setting so masterfully conveyed, as if it were a casual diary rather than as a kind of puzzle of esoteric emblems. Yeats's entire effect is calculated to seduce the reader by the apparent realism of his narration. But since it is much easier to construct a seemingly real setting around a system of emblems than to discover a coherent set of emblems in a real situation, one may well conjecture that the reality here is artifice, while the emblematic network is the real starting-point. A definite stylistic pattern thus begins to appear; the poem uses natural imagery and gains its immediate appeal and effectiveness from this imagery; the true meaning, however, is only revealed if the images are read as emblems, and one is lead to believe that it consists of emblems masquerading as images rather than the opposite.

The dual role of the emblem image does not appear in the form of a discontinuity in texture; the two versions dovetail perfectly with each other and with the larger context of the poem. They fit neatly within the picture of the concrete scene, as well as in the network of emblems. Various techniques achieve this unity of texture, while preserving the duality of function. The technique is at times quite explicit and mechanical, as when Yeats uses the artificial device of a footnote to tell us that the starling is a "real" bird, or when he openly tells us that a natural object in a landscape is *also* to be read emblematically:

> An acre of stony ground,
> Where the *symbolic* rose can break in flower, . . .
>   ("Meditations . . . ," *Var.*, p. 419, emphasis added)

or

> At sudden thunder of the mounting swan
> I turned about and looked where branches break
> The glittering reaches of the flooded lake.

> Another *emblem* there! . . .
> ("Coole Park and Ballylee, 1931," *Var.*, p. 490, ll. 14 ff., emphasis
> added)

or a slightly more complicated example:

> Under my window-ledge the waters race,
> Otters below and moor-hens on the top,
> Run for a mile undimmed in Heaven's face
> Then darkening through 'dark' Raftery's 'cellar' drop,
> Run underground, rise in a rocky place
> In Coole demesne, and there to finish up
> Spread to a lake and drop into a hole.
> What's water but the generated soul?
> (*Ibid.*, ll. 1 ff.)

The last line makes it clear that every detail in what sounded exactly like a realistic description is chosen for its place in an emblematic picture, transposed into reality. And this emblem, as the word "generated" suggests, is Porphyry's cave in another version: the "dark" "cellar" corresponds to the "obscurity of the cavern" (*IoGE*, p. 119), the underground stream to the two gates, that of generation and that of death, where the body "drop[s] into a hole"; the otters are the animal principle "below" and the moor-hens the divine principle "on the top," etc.[73] The very discomfort one experiences in thus destroying a wonderful picture is an essential part of Yeats's statement.

Moreover, when the ambiguity between image and emblem occurs, as in the above passage on the honey-bees, Yeats, who by then has sufficient mastery to write just as "beautifully" as he wishes, charges his language with a maximum of natural seduction. The emblematic reading, however, leads to a statement that proclaims the irrevocable inferiority and defeat of the natural image; in the case of "Meditations . . ." it does so by undermining all hope in the continuity of an art founded on "life" or on the body. The passage states the destruction of the stylistic device by means of which it functions and exists. This is a recurrent strategy in Yeats's mature work, his particular way of coping with the dilemma of the natural image. Two more examples will indicate the recurrence of the pattern.

In the earlier "Adam's Curse," the charm of the poem is also conveyed by the natural setting: the casual scene, the tone of civilized conversation with touches of urbane wit, the two handsome women, the evening light in an atmosphere of refined emotions and courtly love. The title remains something of an enigma: why such a ponderous reference for such a personal poem? And the unity of the poem, too, is by no means obvious: it develops as a somewhat rambling conversation, moving from the hardships of the misunderstood poet to considerations on feminine beauty, to end up with a statement of renunciation that may seem ill-prepared by what comes before. Remembering, however, that the poem appears in *In the Seven Woods* and that most poems of that period deal, like *On Baile's Strand*, with the change of style, a possible reading emerges. One of the two women, Maud Gonne, has always been associated with renunciation of this world, renunciation of the "pleasure of generation"; her literary archetype is Sarah in Villiers de l'Isle-Adam's *Axël*, in whose destiny Yeats found the equivalence of their own relationship. Her beauty is of divine origin and stands above worldly decay and weariness; in terms of style, she corresponds to the emblem which stems, as she does, from "precedents out of beautiful old books" ("Adam's Curse," *Var.*, p. 205, l. 26). She belongs to the realm of revealed divine presence that precedes all labor; the labor of generation and childbirth, the labor to keep the decaying body beautiful as well as that of the poet condemned to write in natural images,[74] all of which began when Adam discovered the "pleasure of generation." The other woman in the poem (identified by Hone as being Maud's sister),[75] who has gently and mildly resigned herself to being a natural body, corresponds to the natural image.[76] The poet, too, has resigned himself, though bitterly, to write in the labored language of images instead of in the inspired language of revelation, but there is no doubt as to what beauty he rates highest:

> I had a thought for no one's but your ears:
> That you were beautiful, and that I strove
> To love you in the old high way of love; . . .
>
> (*Var.*, p. 206)

The lines which we singled out earlier as typifying the return to natural imagery ("And in the trembling blue-green of
the sky / A moon, worn as if it had been a shell . . .") now
also appear as the emblematic analogy for the fall from a divine into a natural state. The moon being hollowed out by the
waters of the sky as if it were eroded by time constitutes a
perfectly consistent image of a natural process, but in Yeats's
emblematic language, the shell is a recurrent emblem for the
failing natural image. In contrast, the moon represents at least
a possible way of access to the divine, with qualifications that
need not be stressed at this point. The metamorphosis of the
moon into a shell marks a regression back to the unsolvable
problems of the period when *Oisin* was being written, the period before the "solution" of the emblem; the same regression
is experienced in falling from ecstasy to labor, from Maud
Gonne to a "beautiful mild woman" who "must labour to be
beautiful." The pattern is the same as in "Meditations in Time
of Civil War": a striking natural image, "A moon . . . , in the
trembling blue-green of the sky" functions also as an emblem
that states the inadequacy and the downfall of precisely that
type of natural image.

A final example comes from "Among School Children,"
the poem singled out by Kermode as heralding the triumph of
the reconciliatory image:

> O chestnut-tree, great-rooted blossomer,
> Are you the leaf, the blossom or the bole?
> O body swayed to music, O brightening glance,
> How can we know the dancer from the dance?
>
> (*Var.*, p. 446)

It might seem far-fetched or even perverse to find here anything but a splendid statement glorifying organic, natural form,
its sensuous experience and fundamental unity. Tracing back

the images of the dancer and the tree in romantic and symbolist poetry, Mr. Kermode adds the testimony of history[77] to
the instinctive delight with which one welcomes a climax for
which everything in the poem, the imagery as well as the
drama, seems to be a perfect preparation. Yeats calls these images "presences"

> O Presences
> That passion, piety or affection knows,
> And that all heavenly glory symbolise- . . .

and, in the three beginning stanzas, the poem describes how
such an image originates through an act of memory, by thinking of a past experience:

> And thinking of that fit of grief or rage
> I look upon one child or t'other there
> And wonder if she stood so at that age—
> . . . .
> And thereupon my heart is driven wild:
> She stands before me as a living child.
>
> (*Var.*, pp. 443–44)

Memory starts in a concrete perception, the spectacle of the
children in the schoolroom; hence the necessity for the first,
descriptive stanza and the importance of the "real" setting.
Many poems about memory, in the romantic tradition, start
like this, from a physical perception that widens into the infinite expansion of accumulated memories:

> Andromaque, je pense à vous! Ce petit fleuve,
> Pauvre et triste miroir où jadis resplendit
> L'immense majesté de vos douleurs de veuve,
> Ce Simoïs menteur qui par vos pleurs grandit,
>
> A fécondé soudain ma mémoire fertile,
> Comme je traversais le nouveau Carrousel.
>
> (Baudelaire, "Le Cygne")

or Hölderlin's poem "Andenken" (An-denken like Yeats's
"*thinking of* that fit . . ." or Baudelaire's "Je *pense à* vous . . ."),
which starts out with a sense perception in the present:

Der Nordost wehet,
Der liebste unter den Winden
Mir, weil er feurigen Geist
Und gute Fahrt verheisset den Schiffern.
Geh aber nun und grüsse
Die schöne Garonne,
Und die Gärten von Bourdeaux . . .

The deepening of a perception through memory offers a perfect analogy with the structure and intent of the natural image: memory is engendered as an act of consciousness freed from the restrictions of time and space, but entirely contained in the original, material perception. Memories originate out of perception "as flowers originate"; the perception is, as it were, the epiphany of the accumulated memories that give it meaning.[78] Hence that memory is a favorite theme in symbolist writing. It acts as a reconciling agent by providing the link with a natural identity from which the poet is alienated: the exile remembers his homeland as possessing the physical, natural well-being which he has lost. It stands in contrast to his present state as winter contrasts with summer, aridity with abundance, consciousness with matter:

Un cygne qui s'était évadé de sa cage,
Et, de ses pieds palmés frottant le pavé sec,
Sur le sol raboteux traînait son blanc plumage.
Près d'un ruisseau sans eau la bête ouvrant le bec

Baignait nerveusement ses ailes dans la poudre,
Et disait, le coeur plein de son beau lac natal:
"Eau, quand donc pleuvras-tu? quand tonneras-tu,
    foudre?"

("Le Cygne")

and the same swan, in Mallarmé

Un cygne d'autrefois se souvient que c'est lui
Magnifique mais qui sans espoir se délivre
Pour n'avoir pas chanté la région où vivre
Quand du stérile hiver a resplendi l'ennui.[79]

("Le vierge, le vivace et le bel aujourd'hui")

The intent of memory, like that of the natural image, is always directed toward matter, toward the need to "communicate substantially with what is substantial in things."[80] With its "substantial" images of the chestnut tree, the dancer's "body swayed to music" and the poet's memory of his beloved in her youth, "Among School Children" seems to fit perfectly in the general pattern of romantic poems on memory. It seems even more affirmative, though with no easy concessions, than Baudelaire and less exclusively mental than Mallarmé.

If read as emblems, however, the final lines acquire very different connotations. One naturally assumes that the questions "Are you the leaf, the blossom or the bole?" and "How can we know the dancer from the dance?" are to be read as rhetorical questions that express unity and state the impossibility of distinguishing the part from the whole, the action from the actor, or the form from its creator. Assuming however that a difference exists between what is represented by the dancer and what is represented by the dance, by the leaf, and by the blossom, the question could just as well express the bewilderment of someone who, faced with two different possibilities, does not know what choice to make. In that case, the questions would not be rhetorical at all, but urgently addressed to the "presences" in the hope of receiving an answer.

The emblems of the "tree," the "dancer," and the "dance" are not too difficult to identify. Emblematic trees abound in Yeats's poetry, but the most explicit is doubtlessly the reference to the tree from *The Mabinogion;* it is mentioned in an essay from 1897, "The Celtic Element in Literature" (*IoGE,* p. 275) and it returns in a poem written not long after "Among School Children":

> A tree there is that from its topmost bough
> Is half all glittering flame and half all green
> Abounding foliage moistened with the dew;
> And half is half and yet is all the scene;
> And half and half consume what they renew,
> And he that Attis' image hangs between

That staring fury and the blind lush leaf
May know not what he knows, but knows not grief.
("Vacillation," *Var.*, p. 500)

The Tree of Life is divided in two parts, one part being the green way of nature and the incarnated world, the other that of divine fire, unmediated by material things. The leafy part corresponds to the nature image, the fiery part to the emblem. Neither of them is practicable by itself, each leading to its own kind of failure, but a synthesis is suggested by Attis' image or, more precisely, by the poetic act of hanging Attis' image between the two halves. Attis is a highly ambiguous reference that weighs the balance heavily in favor of the emblem; not only is he a sun god, and thus definitely on the side of fire, but his myth, as Yeats knew it, is precisely that of the renunciation of matter in order to achieve unity with the divine: Attis is castrated before he can return to Cybele, the mother of the gods.[81] What appears as a synthesis is thus only one more veiled statement of the absolute superiority of the emblem over the image. The same tree appears in the "chestnut tree" of "Among School Children," in which the leaf corresponds to the green foliage, the blossom to the fire, and the bole to Attis' image. No hierarchy or preference is expressed in this case, but the question is asked whether the presence celebrated in the poem is to be reached and held by natural or by supernatural—and also anti-natural—ways; in stylistic terms again, whether it is to be an image or an emblem.

The same question is asked in the final line: "How can we know the dancer from the dance?" The dance is a recurrent emblem for contact with the divine; the following early quotation describes it well: "Men who lived in a world where anything might flow and change . . .[82] had always, as it seems, for a supreme ritual that tumultuous dance among the hills or in the depths of the woods, where unearthly ecstasy fell upon the dancers, until they seemed the gods or the godlike beasts, and felt their souls overtopping the moon; and, as some think, imagined for the first time in the world the blessed country of the gods and of the happy dead."[83] The state of the dance can only be evoked in the divinely sanctioned language of the emblem. The "dancer" on the other hand, in this poem at least, is associated with the symbol of the "body" and appears as a real woman in the generated world of matter, capable of giving the "pleasure of generation." More equivocal in other poems, the "dancer" of "Among School Children" is doubtlessly oriented toward the seduction of physical beauty; she appeals by means of a "body swayed to music," a "brightening glance," a "Ledaean body." All the temptation in the poem emanates from nature and suggests sensuous pleasure. But this might well be the serpent's trick all over again, and by giving in to this temptation, one may trade eternity for a world of decay and weariness. It would make a big difference, in that case, how one chose; to choose the dancer means to fall into the transient world of matter for the sake of a few moments of illusive pleasure; to choose the dance means to renounce all natural joys for the sake of divine revelation. The ways of the image and of the emblem are distinct and opposed; the final line is not a rhetorical statement of reconciliation but an anguished question; it is our perilous fate not to know if the glimpses of unity which we perceive at times can be made more permanent by natural ways or by the ascesis of renunciation, by images or by emblem.

Under the guise of preparing a reconciliation, the foregoing stanzas lead up to this unsolvable predicament. Structurally and stylistically, they seem to emphasize the natural power of memory, of bodies and of physical things, but they state in fact the opposite throughout. When memory is named, in what seems like a casual aside,

> What youthful mother, a shape upon her lap
> Honey of generation had betrayed,
> And that must sleep, shriek, struggle to escape
> As recollection or the drug decide, . . .

> (*Var.*, p. 444)

it is not the Arcadian memory of romanticism but prenatal Platonic recollection, stemming from a stage of being that precedes all descent into matter. This same recollection is present as an ironic contrast in the opening stanza: in the *Meno* (81 b to 86 c) as well as in the *Phaedo* (72 e to 73 b), the doctrine of recollection is associated with a system of education that proceeds by divine revelation, the very opposite of the children's plodding labor in "the best modern way," under the guidance of servants of a religion founded on incarnation. When the sexual act, to which so much in the poem invites, is mentioned, it is as an aberration into which the soul is tricked by the fallacious "drug" of sexual pleasure. There is much emphasis throughout on the extreme stages of human life, childhood and old age, when the soul is closest to its divine origin and least disturbed by erotic temptations. The soul is pleased by the body's bruises (a line which, on one level, refers to the asceticism of the nuns, but much more significantly to the liberation of the soul once it ascends out of this world)[84] because it knows that it is drawing near to its real abode. The actual reminiscence of Maud Gonne mentions a Ledaean body and alludes to the Eros of the *Symposium*, but it occurs over a "sinking fire," by means of a tale that reminds one of the escapism of "The White Birds." In fact, it is not a real memory at all but a Platonic recollection, not of Maud Gonne as Yeats knew her but of her in the shape of a child, and it is all too easily superseded by the real memory of her present appearance.[85] The predominant theme of the poem becomes the cancellation of divine messages by the destructive power of nature, as it appears in the absurd hope for a "happy" generation, in the naive faith of a religion founded on an epiphany, or even in the work of art itself.[86] We are very far removed from a reconciliation between image and reality.

Yeats's mature style is founded on a curiously complex duality of substance and function. He often treats the dance as if it were the dancer, that is, he presents emblems disguised as natural images. On the other hand, when the poems

are more openly emblematic in imagery, this is often counter-
balanced by a thematic insistence on the value of incarnated
beauty. The result is a tenuous equilibrium, in itself an ex-
traordinary feat of style and rhetoric, but no reconciliation, not
even a dialectic. The reader vacillates between two extremes,
reflected in the two main trends that dominate in Yeats's
interpretation: the tendency to give in to the natural seduction
of the images, to read the poems without afterthought and to
protest against any intrusion of "systems" or pedantic erudition; or, on the other hand, the tendency to read them as if
they were esoteric puzzles accessible only to the initiates as a
reward for an act of faith. The two approaches are hard to reconcile. The resulting image is never truly natural, as Baudelaire's or Keats's images are natural; they remain oddly void
of substance and texture. They have about them something
transparent and discarnate, reminiscent, in their extreme styl-
ization and the precision with which they focus upon a few
outstanding details to evoke an entire landscape or mood, of
Chinese scroll-painting. The imagery is overwhelmingly visual, with hardly a suggestion of the warmer, tactile sensations that pertain to the realm of pure matter. The vision is
not one that tries, like Baudelaire's or Rilke's, to mold the form
in its spatial dimensions, to make it stand out as a sculptural
unit. A passage like the following, very close to being pure
landscape

> The trees are in their autumn beauty,
> The woodland paths are dry,
> Under the October twilight the water
> Mirrors a still sky;
> Upon the brimming water among the stones
> Are nine-and-fifty swans . . .
>   ("The Wild Swans at Coole," *Var.*, p. 322)

appears strictly as a two-dimensional picture, with a strong
emphasis on linear contour (one is reminded of Yeats's admiration for Blake's sense of contour), but none at all on texture.
Unlike the impressionists, whose light almost possesses vol-

ume, Yeats's light is pure transparency, the fitting lack of texture for the *sign* which is there to reveal, not itself, but what stands behind it. It would be impossible to apply to Yeats the categories of the material imagination suggested by Gaston Bachelard that fit Baudelaire so well.[87] The very carefully gauged brittleness of the image is necessary, lest the natural attraction would grow so powerful that the opposite, emblematic reading would be overcome.

If this rhetoric is able to deceive the reader, it can never deceive the author, whose fundamental bewilderment is bound to emerge sooner or later. It does emerge in the late poetry, not so much in the structure of the imagery, which undergoes no other important transformations, but in the form of a thematic crisis, closely related to the problems of the image, and which gives to the late work its strident tone.

From the failure of *The Wind among the Reeds,* Yeats learned not only that a purely emblematic style was impracticable as long as his own commitments remained divided, but also that the thematic pattern resulting from this conflict could not be stated too openly. Significantly, after his poetry had been almost exclusively centered on the apocalyptic vision of annihilation, the first poem in the new manner, the introduction to *The Shadowy Waters,* turns away to silence when it reaches the point where previous poems would have taken up this very theme:

> And more I may not write of, for they that cleave
> The waters of sleep can make a chattering tongue
> Heavy like stone, their wisdom being half silence.[88]

The same poem puts in the form of a question what in the preceding volume would have been unreservedly answered in the affirmative: "Is Eden out of time and out of space?" (*Var.,* p. 218, l. 36).

This change in attitude toward one of the major themes does not take place because Yeats has given up the convictions so openly and candidly stated in the essays from *Ideas of Good and Evil.* The rhetorical strategy, as our examples showed, remains organized around emblematic patterns. They are, however, no longer immediately apparent, but are enveloped in a pseudo-hermetic and esoteric language, less forbidding and inaccessible than it may at first appear (since it suffices, in general, to know Yeats's work to obtain a key), but nevertheless somewhat hidden below the surface. Other statements, definitely oriented in the opposite direction, appear in full evidence, such as to receive the full attention and solicit the assent of even a casual reader. Among those statements, the theme of erotic love is probably the most prominent.

The reconciling symbol of the "body," the loosely Platonic notion that the divine is manifest in the incarnated world as Eros, has a long and tortuous history in Yeats's work. It can be traced back to his early heroines' wavering between a divine and a natural status, a familiar romantic theme much in evidence, for instance, in Keats's *Endymion*. Similar hesitations befall several of Yeats's heroines: Naschina in *The Island of Statues*, Niamh in *The Wanderings of Oisin*,[89] the Countess Kathleen, Dectora in *The Shadowy Waters*, the heroine of the Hanrahan stories, etc. Sometimes, the heroine is divided within herself, sometimes she becomes two opposed symbolic characters (as in the novel *John Sherman*), or she appears as committed to one side (Niamh to the supernatural, the Countess to the real world), but then the conflict is transferred to the tragic decision of the lover who has to renounce her. In the romantic tradition, the theme appears predominantly as the sacrificial death of the beloved, a death which becomes a necessary tragedy in the initiation of the hero: one thinks of Goethe's Gretchen, of Hölderlin's Diotima in *Hyperion*, of Keats's Indian Maiden in *Endymion*, and also of Julie's death in *La Nouvelle Héloïse* with its innumerable offspring of romantic love-deaths. The death often marks the hero's transcendence of the world of personal experience and his entrance upon the larger stage of a creative life on a metapersonal level; more deeply, the sacrifice symbolizes the cost, the tragedy of all becoming, which proceeds by the negation of what it overcomes. In its most spiritualized form, the dead heroine becomes the subject of a romantic elegy, the equivalence of an Arcadian symbol recaptured in a natural image that originates out of memory. She is the lost experience of natural unity and the romantic love-death at its most extreme, as in Novalis' *Hymnen an die Nacht* or Wagner's *Tristan und Isolde*, is a half-morbid version of the pantheism which receives unadulterated expression in Wordsworth's Lucy Gray sonnets; the theme has its Satanic counterpart in Poe, in Sade, and in certain aspects of Baudelaire. Later, in the more language-obsessed world of symbolism and aestheticism, the Eros becomes the linguistic symbol itself and the relationship between the poet and his own language gains erotic overtones. Mallarmé remains committed to this conception: the poem originates in a manner analogous to sexual generation ("Telle que vers quelque fenêtre / Selon nul ventre que le sien, / Filial on aurait pu naître." "Autres Poëmes et Sonnets," III) and its failure is called impotence or sterility.

Yeats's treatment of the same theme grows into a curious conglomeration of personal and traditional elements, biographical self-justification and symbols drawn from various sources. It often sounds like orthodox Platonism, an impression which is reinforced by the frequent use of emblems stemming from the Platonic and Neoplatonic tradition.[90] At other times, however, it resembles Wagner or Villiers de l'Isle-Adam's love-death and, frequently enough, it seems to be a mere restatement of Pater's conception of art for art's sake. It is not easy to disentangle a cluster of themes that seem to derive from a variety of not altogether compatible sources, all the more so since Yeats's thematic strategy is not unlike his ambivalent use of imagery: he uses the language of Neoplatonism, romanticism, and aestheticism in order to undermine a belief which these traditions have in common: the belief in the Eros as a reconciliatory force.

Because of the attractive richness of his profane values, it requires some argument to show that Yeats's approach to the Eros is, on the whole, negative—as negative, for instance, as in Balzac's *Louis Lambert* or in Gérard de Nerval's *Aurélia*, where

sexual consummation is an obstacle to divine insight. Granted
the obvious fact that his poetry is never voluptuous in the
manner associated with Baudelaire, or even sensuous like
Keats's, it certainly remains open to question whether it can
be called anti-erotic. When, in *The Wind among the Reeds*, one
comes upon passages like the following:

> And when you sigh from kiss to kiss
> I hear white Beauty sighing, too,
> For hours when all must fade like dew,
> But flame on flame, and deep on deep,
>   ("He remembers Forgotten Beauty," *Var.*, p. 156)

or

> . . . *O women, bid the young men*
>   *lay*
> *Their heads on your knees, and drown their eyes with your*
>   *hair,*
> *Or remembering hers they will find no other face fair*
> *Till all the valleys of the world have been withered away* . . .
>   ("He tells of a Valley full of Lovers," *Var.*, p. 163)

or

> *Until the axle break*
> *That keeps the stars in their round,*
> *And hands hurl in the deep*
> *The banners of East and West,*
> *And the girdle of light is unbound,*
> *Your breast will not lie by the breast*
> *Of your beloved in sleep* . . .
>   ("He hears the Cry of the Sedge," *Var.*, p. 165)

or when he entitles a poem "He wishes his Beloved Were Dead"
or, in *The Shadowy Waters* makes his heroine leave a world of
riches and glory to follow a poet on a quest for death—in all
those cases, the theme seems to be that of love as the only
human experience extreme enough to equal or to overcome
death. And when, in the later work, one comes upon the numerous statements that hold up the "body" as the supreme
value

All dreams of the soul
End in a beautiful man's or woman's body . . .
("The Phases of the Moon," *Var.*, p. 374)

this seems very close to the humanistic Neoplatonism of the Renaissance, as it explicitly appears in "Michael Robartes and the Dancer":

Paul Veronese
And all his sacred company
Imagined bodies all their days
By the lagoon you love so much,
For proud, soft, ceremonious proof
That all must come to sight and touch;
While Michael Angelo's Sistine roof,
His 'Morning' and his 'Night' disclose
How sinew that has been pulled tight,
Or it may be loosened in repose,
Can rule by supernatural right
Yet be but sinew.

(*Var.*, p. 386)

Finally, when in the Crazy Jane poems from "Words for Music Perhaps," a harlot reproves a pompous bishop, or when, in the *Last Poems*, we are offered a ribald story about an enterprising chambermaid ("The Three Bushes"), it may seem difficult to conceive of Yeats as a poet who speaks evil of erotic love. Some examples, taken from different periods, will show that this is nevertheless the case.[91]

Most of the early works, up to *The Shadowy Waters*, place considerable emphasis on the theme of love. *The Wanderings of Oisin*, for instance, has all the aspects of a story of erotic wish-fulfillment, even without the authority of Yeats's late poem for confirmation

But what cared I that set him on to ride,
I, starved for the bosom of his faery bride?
("The Circus Animals' Desertion," *Var.*, p. 629)

Certain symbolic passages in the poem still strengthen this impression: when Niamh and Oisin ride away, they see a vi-

sion of a deer chased by a white dog with one red ear (*Var.,*
pp. 11–12, ll. 139ff.) and of a lady with a golden apple followed by a young man; the emblem, as we know from Yeats's
notes to *The Wind among the Reeds,* represents "the desire of
the man, and . . . the desire of the woman 'which is for the desire of the man,' and . . . all desires that are as these." (*Var.,* p.
153). The interpretation can only be that Oisin's quest, which
moves from a worldly, natural realm to supernatural experiences, is prompted by desire. The Eros awakens a longing for
the divine and kindles dissatisfaction with the world as it is;
but it is by no means certain that it is to be the guide in man's
upward striving, nor is it altogether certain that "desire" refers to the natural need for sexual pleasure. Even in this early
poem, doubt is clearly in evidence. When Oisin notices the lady
and young man following each other in pursuit, he asks Niamh:

> "Were these two born in the Danaan land
> Or have they breathed the mortal air?"
>
> (*Var.,* p. 12, ll. 146–47)

The question is of crucial importance, foreshadowing the later
question of "Among School Children": "How can we tell the
dancer from the dance?" If these symbols of desire are a transcendental form of a natural experience, if, in other words, these
two *have* breathed mortal air, then the progression toward the
divine, as Diotima teaches in the *Symposium,* can start in the
pleasure of the body and move upward in continuous progression from man to god. If however the kind of longing by
which Oisin is driven belongs exclusively to the godlike inhabitants of supernatural realms, then the earthly counterpart
is deceptive and, by giving in to it, one would be betraying
the call of the gods. In that case, true desire is not for the body
and sexual pleasure could never be a foreboding of divine bliss.
Niamh does not answer Oisin's question directly

> "Vex them no longer," Niamh said,
> And sighing bowed her gentle head,
> And sighing laid the pearly tip
> Of one long finger on my lip.
>
> (*Ibid.,* ll. 148ff.)

but in the opening scene of Book II, when the same vision reappears, her answer is more openly negative and suggests that Oisin should turn away from all intercourse with his own human kind:

> And now fled by, mist-covered, without sound,
> The youth and lady and the deer and hound;
> "Gaze no more on the phantoms," Niamh said,
> And kissed my eyes, and, swaying her bright head
> And her bright body, sang of faery and man
> Before God was or my old line began; . . .
>
> (*Var.*, p. 29)

However, when it comes to expressing the contact between man and the gods, the imagery is still overwhelmingly erotic:

> Wars shadowy, vast, exultant; faeries of old
> Who wedded men with rings of Druid gold;
> And how those lovers never turn their eyes
> Upon the life that fades and flickers and dies,
> Yet love and kiss on dim shores far away
> Rolled round with music of the sighing spray: . . .
>
> (*Var.*, pp. 29–30)

The "dim shores far away" are all that nature is not, and none of the pleasures experienced there should bear any resemblance to the joys of this world; the erotic imagery seems to be a weakness of the language, unable to reach beyond the limits of nature in its attempt to express what is supernatural. Later poems, such as "Byzantium," attempt to evoke the union with the gods in an imagery that is no longer sexual, but in *Oisin*, the all-pervading erotic symbolism blurs the actual statement.[92] This statement is quite unambiguous: "Gaze no more on the phantoms" can only mean that Oisin's quest implies the renunciation of sexual desire; the union between man and woman is futile and, in a sense, evil. Oisin is one of the Yeatsian heroes who reject the possibility of a union with the gods and prefers to return to earth, partly because the traditional story demands it, partly out of patriotic loyalty; most of his other heroes accept the renunciation as their only possible destiny.[93] But many begin by sharing in the fallacious conception of this union as a mere extension of an earthly experience.

Similar thematic hesitations appear in all of Yeats's early treatment of the love theme. Niamh is the daughter of Aengus, the god of love, and Edain (*Var.*, p. 5, ll. 46ff.) and thus the offspring of an adulterous relationship (Edain is the wife of Midhir). Yeats refers to this myth in an introductory poem to *The Shadowy Waters* (*Var.*, p. 219), which originally was a part of the first version of the play (*Var.*, p. 762), and also, indirectly, in the narrative poem "Baile and Aillinn." He ignores the adulterous element in the myth and centers instead his attention on the emblematic details of the "tower of glass" where Aengus took Edain and the *"boughs where apples made / Of opal and ruby and pale chrysolite / Awake unsleeping fires; . . ."* (p. 219) under which they lay. The emblem of the apple is particularly revealing because it is linked, by contrast, with the apple of Genesis. Eve's apple suggests the profane pleasure of original sin and "honey of generation,"[94] but Aengus's jeweled fruit has very different connotations. It may remind one of Parnassian and Baudelairian artifice, of *Émaux et Camées*, Mallarmé's *Hérodiade* and the lines from Baudelaire's "Rêve parisien":

> J'avais banni de ces spectacles
> Le végétal irrégulier, . . .

Remembering, however, that the enumeration of precious stones ("Of opal and ruby and pale chrysolite . . .") stems from a biblical passage describing the New Jerusalem (Revelation 21.19–20) and that Baudelaire himself possibly inherited it from there by way of Swedenborg,[95] it becomes apparent that Aengus's apples are not merely a negation of nature, but apocalyptic emblems which take us beyond any natural being whatsoever. This is even more clearly apparent when they reappear in "Baile and Aillinn":

> They know undying things, for they
> Wander where earth withers away,
> Though nothing troubles the great streams

> But light from the pale stars, and gleams
> From the holy orchards, where there is none
> But fruit that is of precious stone,
> Or apples of the sun and moon.
>
> (*Var.*, p. 196)[96]

"Sun" and "moon" are among the cornerstones of Yeats's emblematic system, and their fruit is bound to have nothing in common with nature. To love under these "apples," as do Aengus and Edain, is to experience the very oblivion of earthly love. Aengus is said to be watching ". . . over none / But faithful lovers" (*Var.*, p. 763), but "faithful" has the same meaning here as in the poem "The Grey Rock" when Yeats says of himself

> *I have kept my faith, though faith was tried,*
> *To that rock-born, rock-wandering foot, . . .*

or the goddess, Aoife, by man "betrayed"[97] moans

> "Why are they faithless when their might
> Is from the holy shades that rove
> The grey rock and the windy light? . . ."
>
> (*Var.*, pp. 276 and 275, ll. 124–25 and 109–11)

A "faithful" lover is one who rejects the temptation of erotic love and pursues fearlessly his quest for the divine. Like Forgael in *The Shadowy Waters*, he stands under Aengus' guidance and, as a poet, plays Aengus' harp—that is, writes entirely unnatural, nonerotic, emblematic poetry. Baile and Aillinn are "faithful" lovers, helped in this by Aengus who uses every trick to prevent an earthly consummation of their love:

> *Their love was never drowned in care*
> *Of this or that thing, nor grew cold*
> *Because their bodies had grown old.*
> *Being forbid to marry on earth,*
> *They blossomed to immortal mirth.*
>
> (*Var.*, p. 189)

Mongan, one of the mythical speakers in the original version of *The Wind among the Reeds*, is an example of a lover who was not "faithful."[98] Though initiated into divine wisdom, he chose to become ". . . a man, a hater of the wind" (i.e. afraid of the mystical 'death in God') and to remain entangled in erotic desire:

> I was looking another way;
> And now my calling is but the calling of a hound;
> And Time and Birth and Change are hurrying by.
> ("He [originally Mongan] mourns for the Change
> that has come . . . ,"
> *Var.*, p. 153)

The hound, as a note specifies, is the hound from *Oisin*, an emblem of sexual desire. As punishment for his betrayal

> his head
> May not lie on the breast nor his lips on the hair
> Of the woman that he loves, until he dies.
> (*Var.*, p. 177)

What appears as a Wagnerian Tristan theme turns out to be something entirely different: instead of the Eros finding complete fulfillment in death, it is Eros being surmounted by means of death. The punishment befalls Mongan because he has given in to desire: the "woman that he loves" is a supernatural being, and she can only be recaptured when he will be restored to his previous condition of greatness, by means of total renunciation. Another persona in the same volume, Aedh, is said to be purged of all worldly involvement, pure "fire burning by itself" like the "flames begotten of flame" in "Byzantium." In his case, the situation between sexes is reversed: it is his task to purify the woman, instead of having to concern himself, like Mongan, with his own salvation. He is made to wish for the death of his beloved, so that she may join him in a realm where no sexual desire exists. One misreads a poem like "He wishes his Beloved were dead" (*Var.*, p. 175), which pleads for an entirely spiritual unity far beyond the world of the body, in looking for necrophilic elements: there is nothing here of Poe or Baudelaire.

None of these poems seem to be aware that they describe

an ideal in the very language of the experience least compatible with that ideal. A rather complicated passage in the first version of *The Shadowy Waters*, a work more than any other concerned with the love relationship between man and woman, indicates that this problem is growing more and more pressing, and marks the beginning of a transition to a more complex conception of the erotic in the later poetry. The passage describes the various stages that lead to the full initiation of the woman into the mysteries of divine love. The situation is analogous to Aedh's rather than to Mongan's: Forgael, the hero of the play, has no hesitation about his supernatural calling, but his companion, Dectora, is not freed from worldly ties. Forgael uses his poetry as a means to win her for his cause, and begins by taking her back in memory to the day she first discovered the emotion of love in herself:

> She has begun forgetting. When she wakes,
> The years that have gone over her from the hour
> When she dreamt first of love, shall flicker out
> And that dream only shine before her feet.
>
> (*Var.*, pp. 760–61)

Like Milton's Eve, the revelation of love came to her when she discovered the beauty of her own image mirrored in a natural stream:

> Look on this body and this heavy hair;
> A stream has told me they are beautiful.
>
> (*Var.*, p. 767)[99]

The desire that this vision awakes in her, however, is not the longing for the self as nature, not even in its extreme, narcissistic form. Desire is demonic and opposed to nature; it destroys at once the moment of natural revelation:

> I will drink out of the stream. The stream is gone:
> Before I dropped asleep, a kingfisher
> Shook the pale apple-blossom over it;
> And now the waves are crying in my ears,
> And a cold wind is blowing in my hair.
>
> (*Var.*, p. 761)

The familiar emblem of the red-eared hound appears as a destructive, antinatural force:

> A hound that had lain in the red rushes
> Breathed out a druid vapour, and crumbled away
> The grass and the blue shadow on the stream
> And the pale blossom; . . .

This is the second stage in Dectora's growth, during which she is following the red hound as her guide, sexual love trying to be sufficient to itself.[100] It is the specific function of the poet (Forgael's song), to take her beyond this stage and to "overturn" the demon-hound, sublimating, like Aedh, what there still remains of earthly attachments in her:

> . . . but I woke instead
> The winds and waters to be your home for ever;
> And overturned the demon with a sound
> I had woven of the sleep that is in pools
> Among great trees, and in the wings of owls,
> And under lovers' eyelids.
>
> (*Var.*, pp. 761–62)

The "winds" and "waters" among which this song transports her are not the natural stream and sky where her desire first awakened, but supernatural emblems: the "wind" among the reeds that heralds annihilation and the "waters" on which one embarks for another world. This world will contain the peace that is lacking here; therefore, the song will be made of substances associated with rest and sleep, including the lover's sleep, when full sexual consummation has killed all desire in him. This theme to which Yeats often returns in the last poems[101] is taken up again and developed a little later in the same scene:

> Even that sleep
> That comes with love, comes murmuring of an hour
> When earth and heaven have been folded up;
> And languors that awake in mingling hands

> And mingling hair fall from the fiery boughs,
> To lead us to the streams where the world ends.
>
> (*Var.*, p. 765)

Desire (which, it must be stressed, is itself already opposed to nature and to the body as part of nature) longs for the sexual act, not for the pleasure that it gives, but as the best means to kill desire itself. This most negative conception of the pleasures of sex remains constant throughout the entire work.

The "progression" from nature to the divine, by ways of the destruction of natural and erotic love, expresses Yeats's conviction at the height of his "emblematic" period. Some of the doubts that will lead to the partial abandonment of this attitude are already evident in the same scene from *The Shadowy Waters*. After Dectora has awakened from her dream and Forgael has interpreted it for her, they experience a kind of relapse into their mortal condition; even if they now both have a clear vision of their supernatural destiny, they are still creatures of flesh and blood, and Dectora, especially, is not fully detached from the world. The dramatic interest of the play resides in her final conversion to Forgael's quest, a climax which is not handled very convincingly in either version. But the movement is interesting from a thematic point of view, illustrating Yeats's hesitations about the Eros theme: somewhat later in the scene, Forgael takes Dectora in his arms, and this gesture, which one may assume to be instigated by her, reawakens desire and brings back the hound that Forgael's song had removed. It is, says Forgael, as if the gods had suddenly decided to love as mortals and thus reawakened the temptation:

> F.   Aengus has seen
> His well-beloved through a mortal's eyes;
> And she, no longer blown among the winds,
> Is laughing through a mortal's eyes.
>
> D. (*Peering out over the waters*) O look!
> A red-eared hound follows a hornless deer.
>
> (*Var.*, pp. 763–64)

In the ambiguous state of desire, which is half out of nature but still tied to it, a strong temptation exists to return to the easy joys of the natural world. Dectora succumbs to it:

> The gods weave nets, and take us in their nets,
> And none knows wherefore; but the heart's desire
> Is this poor body that reddens and grows pale.
>
> (*Var.*, p. 764)

but Forgael knows this to be a deceptive trick the gods play on men, like the "cup of oblivion" which causes us to forget prenatal memory and leads to the "betrayal" of generation. He wins out, although it is not too clear why Dectora, who has been eloquently extolling the dangers of divine love and praising the limited blessings of its human counterpart, changes her mind at the last minute.[102] To judge by its thematic content, it is not altogether clear either that Forgael has won out in Yeats's work during the twenty years that follow *The Shadowy Waters*. For this is the period, marked by continuous labor on *The Player Queen* and culminating in *The Wild Swans at Coole* (1917) and *Michael Robartes and the Dancer* (1921), during which many statements seem to give substance to the current image of Yeats as a highly sophisticated but genuine poet of the reconciliatory power of the Eros and the body.

It is difficult to imagine Forgael speaking to Dectora as Yeats wrote to Florence Farr in 1906: ". . . I once cared only for images about whose necks I could cast various 'chains of office' as it were. They were so many aldermen of the ideal, whom I wished to master the city of the soul. Now I do not want images at all, or chains of office, being content with the unruly soul . . . I have myself by the by begun eastern meditations—of your sort, but with the object of trying to lay hands upon some dynamic and substantialising force as distinguished from the eastern quiescent and supersensualizing state of the soul—a movement downwards upon life, not upwards out of life" (*Letters*, p. 469). One is inclined to take this for Yeats's final pronouncement, forgetting all too easily that such statements occur during periods when his inventive powers are at a low ebb. As far as the poetic style is concerned, this return "downwards upon life" results in the devious manner in which natural images reappear in the work; as far as the theme of love is concerned, it results in an apparent descent from the otherworldliness and renunciation of *The Wind among the Reeds* to the concrete and sensuous realm of the "body."

The texts in which the symbol of the body receives the most emphasis are generally associated with the persona of Michael Robartes: "The Double Vision of Michael Robartes," "Michael Robartes and the Dancer," "The Phases of the Moon," etc. This is no doubt deliberate. In the enigmatic notes to *The Wind among the Reeds,* Michael Robartes is described as "fire reflected in water" or "the pride of the imagination brooding upon the greatness of its possessions or the adoration of the Magi." The Magi are those who offer worldly riches and power to the divinity; opposed to the other mythical figures from *The Wind among the Reeds,* Aedh and Hanrahan, Robartes is the one who proudly wishes to "possess" images:

> When my arms wrap you round I press
> My heart upon the loveliness
> That has long faded from the world; . . .
> ("He remembers Forgotten Beauty," *Var.,* p. 155)

In the prose story *Rosa Alchemica* he appears again as the leader of a secret order that searches for God alchemically, by trying to change the common metal of matter into gold; initiation in the order involves a dance with the goddess Eros. Are we to conclude that he considers man and nature as the direct reflection of God (as he is the *reflection* of the divine fire in the "water" of generation) and thus advocates a search for divine knowledge, not in the ascetic disciplines of the mind, but in the sensuous experiences of the body? He is steadily opposed to the monkish Owen Aherne who is "stout and sedentary-looking, bearded and dull of eye" (a striking resemblance of George Russell), while Robartes, not altogether unlike Yeats, is "lank, brown, muscular, clean-shaven, with an alert, ironical eye." [103] This opposition between two personalities, the one active, questioning, and energetic, the other dreamy, passive, and introverted, is at the basis of the polarity on which *A Vision* is founded, the contrast between what Yeats calls antithetical and primary men, or civilizations. Throughout *A Vision*, he manipulates his tone and his symbols in such a way as to make it appear as if he favored the antithetical, which is—at least at the present moment in history—secular and "natural," over the primary, which is religious and "emblematic"; he thus makes his book into an oblique and immensely involved plea in favor of the later poet over the earlier. Since, however, the mechanics of the symbolism are set up as a closed system, in which any value affirmation is immediately canceled out by a symmetrically opposed countervalue, the entire statement is self-destructive; there is, in fact, no value judgment at all. One gains the strong impression, for instance, that the book is an attack on the asceticism and the indiscriminate universality of Christian love, to which it opposes a religious revelation that would have all the characteristics which we associate with the profane. It is the familiar conflict between *Eros* and *Agape:* to the "primary" civilization of Christianity will succeed an "antithetical" civilization which, being favorably inclined toward the body, will be conducive to the kind of artistic creation that Christian morality prevents; Yeats appears then as the prophet of the new, "aesthetic" dispensation. But this is not how the logic of *A Vision* works. If such were indeed Yeats's unqualified conviction, Western art would have to be celebrated by the achievements that come closest to this ideal, namely the profane art of Greece and of the Italian Renaissance. Those two periods are indeed considered to be high points, but the originality of Yeats's panorama of the arts consists in the introduction of another, counterbalancing climax, not, as one might expect, medieval art (which is said to tend toward the profane!), but the art of Byzantium, described as purely emblematic and dependent, for its existence, on the "primary" Christ. "The painter, the mosaic worker, the worker in gold and silver, the illuminator of sacred books, were almost impersonal, almost perhaps without the consciousness of individual design, absorbed in their subject-matter and that the vision of a whole people. They could copy out of old Gospel books those pictures that seemed as sacred as the text, and yet weave all into a vast design, the work of many that seemed the work of one, that made building, picture, pattern, metal-work of rail and lamp, seem but a single image; and this vision, this proclamation of their invisible master, had the Greek nobility, Satan always the still half-divine Serpent, never the horned scarecrow of the didactic Middle Ages."[104] No more exalted praise of the emblem can be found in Yeats, including the claim that this art can outdo the Greeks at their own game and defeat the enemy, the serpent of natural temptation, without having to degrade it. "To me it seems that He, who among the first Christian communities was little but a ghostly exorcist, had in His assent to a full Divinity made possible this sinking-in upon a supernatural splendour, these walls with their little glimmering cubes of blue and green and gold." The greatness of this art stems from its total inhumanity: Christ is exalted as the One who dared to give himself entirely to the divine, and the Divine Principle is so little associated with nature that it can be said, at this point, that there was no incarnation at all, no human body of Christ: ". . . wherever Christ is represented by a bare Cross and all the rest is bird and beast and tree, we may discover an Asiatic art dear to those who thought Christ contained nothing human." At such moments, the passivity of the total "assent to a full Divinity" appears as a high virtue, because it is clear that the Divinity has nothing in common with natural or human norms. A book that contains such passages can not possibly be a plea for incarnated beauty. More than anything else, it is this very Yeatsian mixture: a pseudo-theory of reality which is to exorcize reality. It shows reality to be an absurd realm, where all determinations or values are pseudo-truths canceled out by their opposites; only direct interventions of the divine have the power to shape and determine the content of things and events, and of these we have no knowledge, for they escape the causal network of the system altogether. Reality is ours, body and mind, but precisely insofar as it is accessible to us, it is nothing. The pseudo-exploration and pseudo-ordering that takes place in *A Vision*, the theories of personality, of history, and even of the afterlife (which is made part of reality as soon as it is said to be known) have considerable exegetic value for the poems (like all Yeats's prose texts), but they do not reveal a true commitment. The fundamental intent can only be derived from the poems themselves, considered in their entirety.

The "body," which, according to Michael Robartes, can bring perfection, outdance thought, prove that all must come to sight and touch and even be the Eucharist, would have all the attributes of the Eros if it were also a real, actual substance. It is, however, only an apparition in a dream or, more often still, in a mirror. As such, it is reminiscent of the Narcissus myth in Yeats's earliest poetry, and one remembers that Dectora's initiation also started in self-contemplation. But an important difference separates the narcissistic predicament of Yeats's earliest poetry from the "discipline of the looking glass" which Michael Robartes recommends to beautiful women who ". . . may / Live in uncomposite blessedness, / And lead us to the like—. . ." ("Michael Robartes and the Dancer," *Var.*, p. 387). Narcissus discovers his own presence and reality as a consciousness (reflection) of himself, revealed by a perception; the perception is possible because he is also a natural object. As a natural object, he awakens desire for self-knowledge, and the failure of his attempt at self-possession (the dispersion of the reflection in the water when he tries to seize it or, in Yeats, the echoing shell shattering the "song" of consciousness into chaos)[105] corresponds to the impossibility for consciousness to become its own object and leave the natural status of the self undisturbed. Narcissus is the myth of the dialectic between object and consciousness, and the myth necessarily implies that the reflection be perceived as being that of a thing in nature. Yeats's mirror, however, in "Michael Robartes and the Dancer," reflects the element in the woman that is not her natural self, but that is supernatural—not her material, incarnate being but whatever, as a direct emanation of the divine, remains "out of nature." The "body" is precisely what is not embodied or, to put it less paradoxically, the mirrored body itself has become pure emblem. All that binds the woman to earth, her cares, affections, and especially her "opinions"[106]—one remembers the catastrophical opinions of the Countess Kathleen and of Maud Gonne—are eliminated from the mirrored form, and this includes whatever is material in the body. Only her contour, her form emptied of all substance, remains and it is as such, as pure form, that she appears to the light of perception. We "perceive" the divine in the pure transparency of a form which, being a mere shadow in a mirror, has no material reality whatsoever. In the same manner, an emblem appears to the eye or to the ear as a pure sign, without having to become matter. The mirror asserts the priority of the shadow over the object, because the shadow, not the object, is the product of divine fire and light.[107] To the real woman, trapped in her own opinions and desires, the mirrored image is the most alien of visions, as remote as the sight of a strange god:

> I rage at my own image in the glass
> That's so unlike myself that when you praise it
> It is as though you praised another, or even
> Mocked me with praise of my mere opposite; . . .
> ("The Hero, the Girl, and the Fool," *Var.*, pp. 447–48)

The echo from the early poem, the parrot "raging at his own image in the enamelled sea," isolates and contrasts two symmetrically balanced predicaments: that of the narcissistic poet of the image, who fails to unite with the body as a natural object, and that of the poet of the emblem, who fails to unite with the body as a supernatural form of the divine.

Being mere shadow and entirely out of nature, the image of the dancer is also out of reach of erotic desire. It represents a highly refined kind of beauty, revealed to the inner eye of vision, but that does not appeal to the senses and does not invite possession. It is Athena rather than Venus, Shelley's intellectual beauty rather than Keats's "sensation." Like the be-

loved which Aedh wishes to lead beyond life, the dancer has
". . . danced her life away, / For now being dead it seemed /
That she of dancing dreamed" ("The Double Vision of Michael Robartes," *Var.*, p. 383). In "Michael Robartes and the
Dancer," which is an urbane and personal love poem,[108] aside
from being written partly, as Yeats puts it, "for exposition"
(*Var.*, p. 821), Robartes himself has not altogether escaped from
desire, hence his insistence on sight and *touch* instead of eye
and ear, hence also his references to the later painters of the
Renaissance, Veronese and Michelangelo, whose work is capable of arousing sexual desire. The dancer herself is closer to
Quattrocento, to Botticelli ("we had not desired to touch the
forms of Botticelli or even Da Vinci"—*A Vision*, p. 293), who,
as Yeats insists, was a purely emblematic painter. An orthodox disciple of Pater and Pre-Raphaelite taste, Yeats dates the
beginning of decadence from Michelangelo; from his time on
"all is changed, and where the Mother of God sat enthroned,
now that the Soul's unity has been found and lost, Nature seats
herself, and the painter can paint only what he desires in the
flesh . . ." (*A Vision*, pp. 293–94). Supernatural beauty can be
revealed through the Eros only if the lover, unlike Robartes or
Michelangelo, can refine his desire out of existence. If Narcissus had seen God where he saw only nature, he would never
have broken the mirror. In spite of the reversal in language,
the statement remains very close to that of *The Shadowy Waters:*
the way of the Eros and of nature appears as a preparatory
stage on one of the roads toward greater perfection, a dangerous stage, because it is particularly easy, at this point, to take
the dancer for the dance and to fall back into the condition of
matter out of which one is trying to rise. Similarly, the natural
images that have been introduced in the poetry can take the
reader some way toward their understanding, but if he confines himself to them, he will be led astray. It is the task of
poetic language to transform mere desire into authentic vision.

Many of the passages on bodily perfection, in *A Vision* and
in the poems from the middle period, seem to resemble the

reconciling ideal of symbolism and aestheticism: language acting as a mediator between mind and matter because it partakes of both. Frequent references to the Renaissance remind one of Pater (Yeats started out his late *Oxford Book of English Modern Verse* with Pater's description of the Mona Lisa), and the same is true of sentences that appear in the description of Unity of Being (at phase 15): "Thought has been pursued, not as a means but as an end—the poem, the painting, the reverie has been sufficient of itself"; or "The being has selected, moulded and remoulded, narrowed its circle of living, been more and more the artist, grown more and more 'distinguished' in all preference" (*A Vision*, pp. 135–36). But whereas for Pater, as for Baudelaire and still, negatively, for Mallarmé, the "body" of language is derived from the sensation of natural things, the "body" of Yeats's *logos* is celestial; in the condition which he considers ideal, "love knows nothing of desire" (*A Vision*, p. 136). The poets of the romantic and symbolist tradition are all poets of desire, whose dream is not the suppression, but the eternal fulfillment and renewal of desire after a seemingly endless period of starvation; they rejoice in things that originate "as flowers originate," green foliage after the desert. Yeats remains among them only in his failure, although his frustration stems not so much from the excessive barrenness of his wasteland as from the fact that it never grew barren enough to be left without regret. His ideal is no longer that of aestheticism, but it does not suffice to change the ideal in order to escape from the predicament.

Whether one should call it Platonic (or Neoplatonic) will depend on the kind of Platonism one chooses to take as a norm. Yeats certainly shared with this intellectual tradition—with which he was well acquainted[109]—the elements that stress the supernatural aspects of the soul and the spiritual character of the divine, and he often uses Platonic or related myths and emblems in preference to their Christian equivalences. But if one considers as essential to Platonism the notion of a continuous universe in which all individual entities are emanations of the same divine spirit and thus, to some degree, analogous to that spirit, then Yeats is not a Platonist. His ambiguous treatment of the Eros and the conception of physical and divine love as mutually exclusive are not Platonic; for all his sexual bravado, Yeats has a very protestant and un-Greek sense of the degradation of matter and of the body—as his ferocious treatment of old age, for instance, testifies. And it would be exceedingly difficult to make a statement like the following, which expresses a very genuine conviction, fall within the boundaries of Platonism: "Life is no series of emanations from divine reason such as the Cabalists imagine, but an irrational bitterness, no orderly descent from level to level, no waterfall but a whirlpool, a gyre."[110]

Coming upon such "Platonic" lines as these: "Natural and supernatural with the self-same ring are wed" or "For things below are copies, the great Smaragdine Tablet said" ("Supernatural Songs," *Var.*, p. 556), their aphoristic quality makes them stand out in memory, and one tends to think of them as Yeats's own credo. In the context of the poem from which they are taken, far from representing the author's belief, they represent a rejected heresy. "Supernatural Songs," Yeats's most far-reaching attempt at a personal theology, are said to be spoken by the hermit Ribh, who, as a later suppressed note tells us, speaks for the element in Christianity that came to the foreground in Byzantium and denied all notion of Christ as an incarnated being: "one could be a devout communicant and accept all the counsels before the Great Schism that separated Western from Eastern Christianity in the ninth century . . . For the moment I associated early Christian Ireland with India; Shri Purohit Swami, protected during his pilgrimage to a remote Himalyan shrine by a strange great dog that disappeared when danger was past, might have been that blessed Cellach who sang upon his deathbed of bird and beast;[111] . . . Saint Patrick must have found in Ireland, for he was not its first missionary, men whose Christianity had come from Egypt, and retained characteristics of those older faiths that have become so important to our invention . . ." (*Var.*, p. 837). Ribh is one of those "Asiatic" Christians and his denunciation of

Patrick, in which the alleged quotation from the Hermes Trismegistus appears,[112] is founded on his denial of any analogy between the realm of man and the realm of God. His attack is aimed at the doctrine that conceives of earthly and natural things as reflections of a divine order (a doctrine Yeats equates with the Platonic and the Western Christian tradition); in such a universe, God can be known by analogy with natural processes. The human Eros, for instance, can be extended to become the pure Idea of divine unity and permanence:

> Man, woman, child (a daughter or a son),
> That's how all natural or supernatural stories run.
>
> Natural and supernatural with the self-same ring are
> wed.
> As man, as beast, as an ephemeral fly begets,
> Godhead begets Godhead, . . .
> ("Supernatural Songs" II, "Ribh Denounces Patrick,"
> *Var.*, p. 556)

The orthodox Saint Patrick has derived his conception of the Christian incarnation and of the Trinity from this doctrine; without any ambiguity, Ribh condemns it as "An abstract Greek absurdity" which has "crazed the man." He opposes to it the entirely masculine Trinity, God begetting himself on his own self and bearing his own son, the self-begotten generation of the divine, which knows nothing of sex, birth, or death, and is bound to remain entirely incomprehensible to the human mind. The divine, which Yeats calls, by antiphrase, "reality" ("Ravening, raging, and uprooting that he may come / Into the desolation of reality"—*Var.*, p. 563) is a realm in which there is neither generation nor becoming:

> Things out of perfection sail,
> And all their swelling canvas wear,
> Nor shall the self-begotten fail
> Though fantastic men suppose
> Building-yard and stormy shore,
> Winding-sheet and swaddling-clothes.
> ("Words for Music Perhaps," xxiv, *Var.*, p. 530)

Beginnings and endings, births and deaths, are so many human illusions; men can sometimes find salvation out of their world of aberrations, but their attempt to understand God by analogy with their own experience is absurd; a true theology contains nothing of history, sex, or bodily death.

Being self-begotten, the Trinity is in fact a Unity. The Godhead can not be said to "augment (its) kind," for it is always identical with the totality of its own omnipresent self, not, as in nature, a chain or collection of individuals in a species that perpetuates by generation. Humans are multiple, not One, and therefore never complete as long as they remain in nature; our multiplicity is apparent from the fact that we beget on an "other" sex: it takes two of us to create a third who, in his turn (being "a daughter or a son"), will keep on copying copies. Like all extreme experiences, sexual joy contains some foreboding of divine reality, but those glimpses of light are irrevocably dispelled by the impurity of the generated world, represented in this poem by the traditional serpent from Genesis: [113]

> When the conflagration of their passion sinks,
>   damped by the body or the mind,
> That juggling nature mounts, her coil in their
>   embraces twined.
> The mirror-scalèd serpent is multiplicity, . . .
>
> (*Var.*, p. 556)

Michael Robartes' mirror, which was to filter the divine gold from the common matter of nature, is transformed by human love in the mere "copy" of reproduction: "Mirror on mirror mirrored is all the show" (*"The Statues," Var.*, p. 610). The evil power of nature is strong enough to overcome man's aspiration toward the divine; the incarnated body as well as the mind drag him down into generation: divine passion *sinks* as the serpent of nature *mounts*. The "supernatural" songs, which presumably were to praise a God that stands above and beyond nature, end up by being songs of hatred directed against the evil but victorious power of nature.

In the sequence entitled "A Woman Young and Old" appears the poem that fully reveals the failure of the emblem. Yeats's awareness of his defeat might well come as a surprise. The survey of the most earthbound of his themes reveals no wavering in his commitment to a belief that could find poetic expression only in terms of emblems, never of natural images. Yeats's Eros, if it can still be called by that name, is aimed against the body, the senses, and the mind, and it demands that the quest for the divine begin with the denial of whatever natural attributes man may possess—or, to speak in terms of intellectual traditions, that it begin outside of the Christian, Platonist, and humanist tradition. If we can nevertheless speak of a failure of the emblem, it is not by implying that Yeats changed his mind; he did not discover that other endeavors, be it human love, or the pursuits of the intellect, or the actions of history, could serve him better. Instead, he failed to overcome the inimical power of nature itself. After having been treated as an ambiguous poetic device, destined to give texture and appeal to emblems and themes not really strong enough to dispense with its assistance, nature returns in the later poetry in a very different form. No longer does it function as the self-reflecting, narcissistic mirror of the early poetry, but it acts as the brutal strength of matter, a bestial violence which can only find expression in images of blood and torment.

"Her Vision in the Wood," the poem which, perhaps more than any other, contains the essence of the late Yeats, is, in a very literal sense, a poem about "bodies from a picture or a coin" contrasted with actual bodies of men and women. Whereas "Among School Children" ended with a question, "How can we tell the dancer from the dance?," this poem tells what happens beyond the unanswered question, when the dancer is taken for the dance, the body treated as if it were an emblem. Yeats's poetry presents emblems in the guise of natural images; his theory of divine love is stated in terms of a bodily Eros—in the same manner, the man and the woman in "Her Vision in the Wood" have loved each other, not for

themselves, but in a search for archetypal experiences that belong to the gods. From the Michael Robartes poems and, well
before, from *The Shadowy Waters* and *The Wind among the Reeds*,
we know this deliberate confusion to be generally willed by
man, against the resistance of the more human desires of
woman:

> Say on and say
> That only God has loved us for ourselves,
> But what care I that long for a man's love?
> ("The Hero, the Girl, and the Fool," *Var.*, p. 448)

In "A Woman Young and Old," Yeats goes further and describes the solitude of a love in which both partners, the woman
as well as the man, are using each other as a means to escape
from the endless turmoil of physical time and matter. Unlike
the recalcitrant girl from "Michael Robartes and the Dancer,"
the woman in this sequence of poems—presumably Every-
Woman—is quite willing to submit to "the discipline of the
looking-glass," willing to attract a man by what she knows to
be supernatural in herself, though knowing that it is precisely
this unhuman, superhuman element in her that the man pursues:

> If I make the lashes dark
> And the eyes more bright
> And the lips more scarlet,
> Or ask if all be right
> From mirror after mirror,
> No vanity's displayed:
> I'm looking for the face I had
> Before the world was made.
> ("A Woman Young and Old," *Var.*, pp. 531–32)

In his early description of the hound emblem from *Oisin*, Yeats
had already spoken of "the desire of the woman 'which is for
the desire of the man,' " but this sentence takes on a very different meaning when one realizes that man's desire is not for
sexual satisfaction, but for the end of all natural passion in the
stillness that follows his lovemaking, when

> God's love has hidden him
> Out of all harm,
> Pleasure has made him
> Weak as a worm.
>
> ("The Chambermaid's First Song," *Var.*, p. 574)

Vicariously, the woman can achieve the same escape out of time, whenever she admits that her desire is not for the satisfaction of a natural craving, but for the destruction of man's desire:

> If questioned on
> My utmost pleasure with a man
> By some new-married bride, I take
> That stillness for a theme
> Where his heart my heart did seem
> And both adrift on the miraculous stream
> Where—wrote a learned astrologer—
> The Zodiac is changed into a sphere.
>
> ("A Woman Young and Old," *Var.*, p. 535)[114]

One begins to understand, perhaps all too well (though one should beware not to confuse ontology and psychoanalysis), Yeats's interest in the castration myth of Attis. The rejection of all feminine and maternal elements of sex,[115] brings to mind Mallarmé's *Hérodiade*, a resemblance confirmed by the frequent references to the decapitation of Saint John in late plays closely related to this theme. Yeats's Queen and woman, however, are more extreme symbols than Hérodiade: Mallarmé's heroine refuses Venus for the sake of self-contemplative self-knowledge; she overcomes the pantheistic temptation of a fusion with nature and resigns herself instead to the mediated knowledge of her own consciousness as she beholds it acting upon natural substances. Later, in the fully developed version of the drama in which Saint John was to appear, and of which only a few fragments remain, Hérodiade would have accomplished her action as a sacrifice of the female and natural principle to the male and intellectual principle. The decapitation freed John from the weight of the body (a tragic act

which involves the Mallarméan form of death), but only Hérodiade can be said to be actually "killed" by this act; John survives as pure spirit, pure "head";

> Et ma tête surgie
> Solitaire vigie
> Dans les vols triomphaux
> De cette faux

and he can praise Hérodiade as the one who made the radical
separation between mind and body *(rupture franche)* possible:

> Comme rupture franche
> Plutôt refoule ou tranche
> Les anciens désaccords
> Avec le corps

(where *"tranche,"* aside from the literal meaning *"couper,"* also
has the figurative meaning of solving an intellectual problem,
as in *"trancher [résoudre] la question").* Mallarmé's gods still reside in nature and his mythology remains fundamentally
pantheistic, a cult of the physical sun as pure intellect (Saint
John is equated with the sun)—but Yeats's gods are the fierce
destroyers of anything natural or human-bred. The entire concept, essential to Mallarmé, of abstract, intellectual self-knowledge is altogether alien to Yeats, and when his woman ban-
ishes all sexual and natural inclinations from her body, she is
not running away from Venus but engaged in a quest to become Venus, the archetype of her species, instead of a transient, incarnated emanation of this divine principle. "Her Vision in the Wood," with its transparent allusions to the Venus
and Adonis myth, describes what happens when a man and a
woman refuse the call of nature and follow instead that of the
gods.

The unity of imagery in "Her Vision in the Wood" is accomplished by the successive metamorphoses of blood into
wine, "wine" being the emblem of the natural substance
"blood" or, in other words, human blood being wine to the
gods.[116] The action of the poem takes place "in the sacred
wood" which, from Yeats's version of *Oedipus at Colonus,* is

known to be the abode of the Athenian gods and, more specifically, of the Furies and of Dionysos[117]—and it takes place at "wine-dark midnight," another link with Dionysos,[118] as well as an indication that the mortal woman is in a state of vision and able to perceive the supernatural.[119] The connection of "wine" with the divine is established at the very start of the poem ("wine-dark midnight in the sacred wood") and its equation with blood (the extension of the Christ in a Holy Blood symbol to the pagan world) occurs in the Bacchante-like self-immolation of the woman:

> Imagining that I could
> A greater with a lesser pang assuage
> Or but to find if withered vein ran blood,
> I tore my body that its wine might cover
> Whatever could recall the lip of lover.
>
> (*Var.*, p. 537)

Blood is transformed into wine in the offering of her life to the wine god, the violent but voluntary death by means of which, in the reversed movement of Dionysos' own descent into matter, she achieves unity of being with the gods. A similarly irrational and ecstatic surrender, this time acted out by men, is mentioned in *A Vision:* "One knows not into how great extravagance Asia, accustomed to abase itself, may have carried what soon sent Greeks and Romans to stand naked in a Mithraic pit, moving their bodies as under a shower-bath that those bodies might receive the blood of the bull even to the last drop" (*A Vision*, p. 272).[120] Her death is the passion for prenatal light as opposed to *Hysterica Passio*, the passion for the natural womb of nature:

> I—love's skein upon the ground,
> My body in the tomb—
> Shall leap into the light lost
> In my mother's womb.
>
> ("Crazy Jane and Jack the Journeyman," *Var.*, p. 511)

On the other hand, the self-sacrifice to the gods also represents the decay of feminine beauty, the proof that the attempt to escape from the world of time has failed. In the realm of nature, old age only involves a decline, the return of clay to clay, and Wordsworth's elegiac consolation can be effective:

> No motion has she now, no force;
> She neither hears nor sees;
> Rolled round in earth's diurnal course,
> With rocks, and stones, and trees.

But in Yeats's discontinuous universe, where nature and the gods are engaged in a merciless battle, the decline of a woman's beauty becomes the ultimate tragedy, the defeat of the divine at the hand of nature:

> To dream of women whose beauty was folded in
> dismay,
> Even in an old story, is a burden not to be
> borne.
>
> ("Under the Moon," *Var.*, p. 210)

The wine of the "wine-dark midnight" and of the divine libation turns back into the dark blood of old age and withered veins, and the sacrifice—which already was a "lesser pang" compared to the full abandon of a virgin's love—appears as the absurd gesture of an old woman who wants to make certain that she is still alive:

> Or but to find if withered vein ran blood,
> I tore my body . . .

In the visionary stage that follows her death, she "dreams back," in accordance with Yeats's theory of the afterlife, and relives the experience of her youthful love and crime. "Dark changed to red," and the black blood of old age recovers the glow it had when she was "A Woman Homer sung"[121] and would have been "fit spoil for a centaur / Drunk with the unmixed wine" (*Var.*, p. 355). The poem becomes emblematic, with references to Renaissance painting indicating that we are watching "bodies from a picture or a coin" during the narration of the experience of love as it affects man:

And after that I held my fingers up,
Stared at the wine-dark nail, or dark that ran
Down every withered finger from the top;
But the dark changed to red, and torches shone,
And deafening music shook the leaves; a troop
Shouldered a litter with a wounded man,
Or smote upon the string and to the sound
Sang of the beast that gave the fatal wound.

All stately women moving to a song
With loosened hair or foreheads grief-distraught,
It seemed a Quattrocento painter's throng,
A thoughtless image of Mantegna's thought—
Why should they think that are for ever young?
Till suddenly in grief's contagion caught,
I stared upon his blood-bedabbled breast
And sang my malediction with the rest.

That thing all blood and mire, that beast-torn wreck,
Half turned and fixed a glazing eye on mine,
And, though love's bitter-sweet had all come back,
Those bodies from a picture or a coin
Nor saw my body fall nor heard it shriek,
Nor knew, drunken with singing as with wine,
That they had brought no fabulous symbol there
But my heart's victim and its torturer.

(*Var.*, p. 537)

Like the woman, the man has used love as a means to reach the gods, and his divine possession, the equivalence of her self-immolation, is treated by reference to the Adonis myth: Adonis slain by a boar, "the beast that gave the fatal wound." The notes to *The Wind among the Reeds* make explicit the association between the boar that killed Adonis (and also Attis), and the "boar without bristles" or the "black pig," emblems that appear frequently in the early volume, representing the destruction of all natural things at the end of time.[122] What was treated before 1900 as a cosmic annihilation now confines the same destructive power to the individual destiny of every man. As a lover, he chose the divine element in the woman—the beauty of her mirrored form—in order to escape from the wheel of time; in that sense it can be said that he is indeed her "victim," for her body (as Michael Robartes understands the word) represents, as it were, and acts for the god who destroys him. Allusions to Mantegna (whom Yeats classifies with Botticelli and da Vinci at phase fifteen, not with the later Michel angelo) as well as the development on the word "thoughtless" ("A thoughtless image of Mantegna's thought— / Why should they think that are for ever young?") make the link with "Michael Robartes and the Dancer": one remembers Robartes' reference to Renaissance painting and his advice to the girl to "banish every thought" (*Var.*, p. 387, l. 48). To the onlooking woman, the "stately women" appear as so many reflections of her own youthful body when, like the dancer, she had eliminated all thought of worldly involvement and become purely the "body" that lured her lover to his sacrificial death. This extends and clarifies the emblem of the dancer who becomes associated, by the setting in the "sacred wood" of Athens, with the Furies. The etymology of the Eumenides' name connects them also with the "Good People" of Faery,[123] the demonic shape-changers of the Sidhe who "empty [our] heart of its mortal dream" (*Var.*, p. 140). The supernatural figures, dancing in lamentation around Adonis' body, are the completed emblem, constant and identical in the Christian,[124] Greek, and Irish tradition, of the eternal feminine as the destroyer of natural man.

Within the strict orthodoxy of the emblem, the poem should have ended in the apotheosis of this pageant: the woman, having shed her mortal body, becomes a demonic icon, while the man, soon to be purged from "the fury and the mire of human veins" ("Byzantium," *Var.*, p. 497), turns into a "fabulous symbol," far out of reach of bodily pain or human grief. Poems heralding the triumph of the emblem, such as "Byzantium," or "Colonus' Praise," or "All Souls' Night" end in that way. Instead, "Her Vision in the Wood" forcefully returns to the world of blood and mire. "Wine" is mentioned once more near the end, now associated with the half-divine mourners whose "bodies" are sharply contrasted with the human body of the woman:

> Those bodies from a picture or a coin
> Nor saw my body fall nor heard it shriek,
> Nor knew, drunken with singing as with wine,
> That they . . .

They are still close enough to their human origin to lament Adonis' death, but their lament is already far removed from the event, far enough to become the ecstatic grief of "song" compared to the "shriek" of the real woman. We can think of this "song" as the poetry which Yeats would have wanted to write. Instead, we hear only the shriek of the lovers as they discover with horror what the gods have done to them. The turning point that marks the dramatic climax of the poem reintroduces the natural substance of "blood":

> That thing all blood and mire, that beast-torn wreck,
> Half turned and fixed a glazing eye on mine, . . .

and marks a decisive shift from the realm of the emblem back to that of the natural image. That this shift remains possible and becomes necessary indicates the defeat and the fallacy of the entire wisdom derived from the emblem. For if it is true that, for the creatures in the poem and, consequently, for the poet and his readers as well, the man has remained a physical, natural body and not grown into a supernatural emblem

> That they had brought no fabulous symbol there
> But my heart's victim and its torturer

then the entire ritual of love, together with the poetical and stylistic strategy that prompted this ritual, is shown to be an infinitely dangerous deceit. Where we had been promised the eternal peace and ecstasy of divine presence, only the image of a beast-torn wreck remains. The poem records the irrevocable condemnation of Yeats's entire enterprise but offers no alternative.

With this shift of theme, all that is left for the poetry to do is to "shriek" in utter derision. In *The King of the Great Clock Tower*, after the same story is told, this time by means of the myth of Salomé and John the Baptist instead of that of Venus and Adonis, Yeats gives the last word to a sardonic, nihilistic emblem of nature (the *"wicked, crooked hawthorn tree"*) that rebukes and dashes the hopes of a *"travelling-man,"* who contains elements from all Yeats's favorite heroes including his most triumphant self (*Plays*, pp. 640–41). In *The Herne's Egg*, after narrating again, by means of another set of emblems, the same myth of divine possession, Yeats ends his play in utter mockery ("All that trouble and nothing to show for it . . ."—*Plays*, p. 678).

Nowhere is the derision more apparent than in the last of the poems directly concerned with the problem of imagery, "The Circus Animals' Desertion" (*Var.*, pp. 629–30). One has to remember what hopes Yeats had invested in his emblems to measure the bitterness with which he refers to them as

> A mound of refuse or the sweepings of a street,
> Old kettles, old bottles, and a broken can,
> Old iron, old bones, old rags, that raving slut
> Who keeps the till.

They represent not only the sardonic counterpart of his most venerated "holy things" but also, quite literally, the utterly worthless content of reality. The failure of the emblem amounts to total nihilism. Yeats has burned his bridges, and there is no return out of his exploded paradise of emblems back to a wasted earth. Those who look to Yeats for reassurance from the anxieties of our own post-romantic predicament, or for relief from the paralysis of nihilism, will not find it in his conception of the emblem. He cautions instead against the danger of unwarranted hopeful solutions, and thus accomplishes all that the highest forms of language can for the moment accomplish.

9
Anthropomorphism and Trope in the Lyric

THE GESTURE that links epistemology with rhetoric in general, and not only with the mimetic tropes of representation, recurs in many philosophical and poetic texts of the nineteenth century, from Keats's "Beauty is truth, truth beauty" to Nietzsche's perhaps better known than understood definition of truth as tropological displacement: "Was ist also Wahrheit? Ein bewegliches Heer von Metaphern, Metonymien, Anthropomorphismen . . ."[1] Even when thus translated before it has been allowed to run one third of its course, Nietzsche's sentence considerably complicates the assimilation of truth to trope that it proclaims. Later in the essay, the homology between concept and figure as symmetrical structures and aberrant repressions of differences is dramatized in the specular destinies of the artist and the scientist-philosopher. Like the Third Critique, this late Kantian text demonstrates, albeit in the mode of parody, the continuity of aesthetic with rational judgment that is the main tenet and the major crux of all critical philosophies and "Romantic" literatures. The considerable difference in tone between Nietzsche and Kant cannot conceal the congruity of the two projects, their common stake in the recovery of controlled discourse on the far side of even the sharpest denials of intuitive sense-certainties. What interests us primarily in the poetic and philosophical versions of this transaction, in this give-and-take between reason and imagination, is not, at this point, the critical schemes that deny certainty considered in themselves, but their disruption by patterns that cannot be reassimilated to these schemes, but that are nevertheless, if not produced, then at least brought into focus by the distortions the disruption inflicts upon them.

Thus, in the Nietzsche sentence, the recovery of knowledge by ways of its devalorization in the deviance of the tropes is challenged, even at this moment of triumph for a critical reason which dares to ask and to reply to the question: what is truth? First of all, the listing of particular tropes is odd, all the more so since it is technically more precise than is often the case in such arguments: only under the pen of a classical philologist such as Nietzsche is one likely to find combined, in 1872, what Gérard Genette has since wittily referred to as the two "chiens de faience" of contemporary rhetoric—metaphor and metonymy. But the third term in the enumeration, anthropomorphism, is no longer a philological and neutral term, neither does it complement the two former ones: anthropomorphisms can contain a metaphorical as well as a metonymic moment—as in an Ovidian metamorphosis in which one can start out from the contiguity of the flower's name to that of the mythological figure in the story, or from the resemblance between a natural scene and a state of soul.

The term "anthropomorphism" therefore adds little to the two previous ones in the enumeration, nor does it constitute a synthesis between them, since neither metaphor nor metonymy have to be necessarily anthropomorphic. Perhaps Nietzsche, in the Voltairean conte philosophique *On Truth and Lie* is just being casual in his terminology—but then, opportunities to encounter technical tropological terms are so sparse in literary and philosophical writings that one can be excused for making the most of it when they occur. The definition of truth as a collection ("army" being, aside from other connotations, at any rate a collective term) of tropes is a purely structural definition, devoid of any normative emphasis; it implies that truth is relational, that it is an articulation of a subject (for example "truth") and a predicate (for example "an army of tropes") allowing for an answer to a definitional question (such as "what is truth?") that is not purely tautological. At this point, to say that truth is a trope is to say that truth is the possibility of stating a proposition; to say that truth is a collection of varied tropes is to say that it is the possibility of stating several propositions about a single subject, of relating several predicates to a subject according to principles of articulation that are not necessarily identical: truth is the possibility of definition by means of infinitely varied sets of propositions. This assertion is purely descriptive of an unchallenged grammatical possibility and, as such, it has no critical thrust, nor does it claim to have one: there is nothing inherently disruptive in the assertion that truth is a trope.

But "anthropomorphism" is not just a trope but an identification on the level of substance. It takes one entity for another and thus implies the constitution of specific entities prior to their confusion, the *taking* of something for something else that can then be assumed to be *given*. Anthropomorphism freezes the infinite chain of tropological transformations and propositions into one single assertion or essence which, as such, excludes all others. It is no longer a proposition but a proper name, as when the metamorphosis in Ovid's stories culminates and halts in the singleness of a proper name, Narcissus or Daphne or whatever. Far from being the same, tropes such as metaphor (or metonymy) and anthropomorphisms are mutually exclusive. The apparent enumeration is in fact a foreclosure which acquires, by the same token, considerable critical power.

Truth is now defined by two incompatible assertions: either truth is a set of propositions or truth is a proper name. Yet, on the other hand, it is clear that the tendency to move from

tropes to systems of interpretations such as anthropomorphisms is built into the very notion of trope. One reads Nietzsche's
sentence without any sense of disruption, for although a trope
is in no way the same as an anthropomorphism, it is nevertheless the case that an anthropomorphism is structured like a
trope: it is easy enough to cross the barrier that leads from trope
to name but impossible, once this barrier has been crossed, to
return from it to the starting-point in "truth." Truth is a trope;
a trope generates a norm or value; this value (or ideology) is
no longer true. It is true that tropes are the producers of ideologies that are no longer true.

Hence the "army" metaphor. Truth, says Nietzsche, is a
mobile *army* of tropes. Mobility is coextensive with any trope,
but the connotations introduced by "army" are not so obvious, for to say that truth is an army (of tropes) is again to
say something odd and possibly misleading. It can certainly
not imply, in *On Truth and Lie* that truth is a kind of com-
mander who enlists tropes in the battle against error. No such
dichotomy exists in any critical philosophy, let alone
Nietzsche's, in which truth is always at the very least dialectical, the negative knowledge of error. Whatever truth may be
fighting, it is not error but stupidity, the belief that one is right
when one is in fact in the wrong. To assert, as we just did,
that the assimilation of truth to tropes is not a disruption of
epistemology, is not to assert that tropes are therefore true or
on the side, so to speak, of truth. Tropes are neither true nor
false and are both at once. To call them an army is however
to imply that their effect and their effectiveness is not a matter
of judgment but of power. What characterizes a good army,
as distinct for instance from a good cause, is that its success has
little to do with immanent justice and a great deal with the
proper economic use of its power. One willingly admits that
truth has power, including the power to occur, but to say that
its power is like that of an army and to say this within the definitional context of the question: what is therefore truth? is truly
disruptive. It not only asserts that truth (which was already
complicated by having to be a proposition as well as a proper

name) is also power, but a power that exists independently of epistemological determinations, although these determinations are far from being nonexistent: calling truth an army *of tropes* reaffirms its epistemological *as well as* its strategic power. How the two modes of power could exist side by side certainly baffles the mind, if not the grammar of Nietzsche's tale. The sentence that asserts the complicity of epistemology and rhetoric, of truth and trope, also turns this alliance into a battle made all the more dubious by the fact that the adversaries may not even have the opportunity ever to encounter each other. Less schematically compressed, more elaborated and dramatized instances of similar disjunctions can be found in the texts of lyrical poets, such as, for example, Baudelaire.

The canonical and programmatic sonnet "Correspondances"[2] contains not a single sentence that is not simply declarative. Not a single negation, interrogation, or exclamation, not a single verb that is not in the present indicative, nothing but straightforward affirmation: "la Nature *est* un temple . . . Il *est* des parfums frais comme des chairs d'enfants." The least assertive word in the text is the innocuous "parfois" in line 2, hardly a dramatic temporal break. Nor is there (a rare case in *Les Fleurs du mal*) any pronominal agitation: no *je-tu* apostrophes or dialogues, only the most objective descriptions of third persons. The only personal pronoun to appear is the impersonal "il" of "il est (des parfums) . . ."

The choice of "Correspondances" to explicate the quandaries of language as truth, as name, and as power may therefore appear paradoxical and forced. The ironies and the narrative frame of *On Truth and Lie* make it difficult to take the apparent good cheer of its tone at face value, but the serenity of "Correspondances" reaches deep enough to eliminate any disturbance of the syntactical surface. This serenity is prevalent enough to make even the question superfluous. Nietzsche still has to dramatize the summation of his story in an eye-catching paragraph that begins with the question of questions: Was ist also Wahrheit? But Baudelaire's text is all assurance and all answer. One has to make an effort to perceive the opening line as an answer to an implicit question, "La Nature est un temple . . ." as the answer to "Qu'est-ce que la nature?" The title is not "La Nature," which would signal a need for definition; in "Correspondances," among many other connotations, one hears "response," the dialogical exchange that takes place in mutual proximity to a shared entity called nature. The *response* to the sonnet, among its numerous readers and commentators, has been equally responsive. Like the oracle of Delphi, it has been made to answer a considerable number and variety of questions put to it by various readers. Some of these questions are urgent (such as: how can one be innocent and corrupt at the same time?), some more casually historical (such as: when can modern French lyric poetry, from Baudelaire to surrealism and beyond, be said to begin?). In all cases, the poem has never failed to answer to the satisfaction of its questioner.

The serenity of the diction celebrates the powers of tropes or "symboles" that can reduce any conceivable difference to a set of polarities and combine them in an endless play of substitution and amalgamation, extending from the level of signification to that of the signifier. Here, as in Nietzsche's text, the telos of the substitutions is the unified system "esprit/sens" (l. 14), the seamless articulation, by ways of language, of sensory and aesthetic experience with the intellectual assurance of affirmation. Both echo each other in the controlled compression of a brief and highly formalized sonnet which can combine the enigmatic depth of doctrine—sending commentators astray in search of esoteric authority—with the utmost banality of a phrase such as "verts comme les prairies."

On the thematic level, the success of the project can be measured by the unquestioned acceptance of a paradox such as "Vaste comme la nuit et comme la clarté," in which a conjunctive *et* can dare to substitute for what should be the *ou* of an either/or structure. For the vastness of the night is one of confusion in which distinctions disappear, Hegel's night in which $A = A$ because no such thing as A can be discerned, and in which infinity is homogeneity. Whereas the vastness of light is like the capacity of the mind to make endless analytical distinctions, or the power of calculus to integrate by ways of infinitesimal differentiation. The juxtaposition of these incompatible meanings is condensed in the semantic ambiguity of "se confondent," which can designate the bad infinity of confusion as well as the fusion of opposites into synthetic judgments. That "echoes," which are originally the disjunction of a single sensory unit or word by the alien obstacle of a reflection, themselves re-fuse into a single sound ("Comme de longs échos qui de loin se confondent") again acts out the dialectic of identity and difference, of sensory diffuseness and intellectual precision.

The process is self-consciously verbal or mediated by language, as is clear from the couple "se confondent / se répondent," which dramatizes events of discourse and in which, as was already pointed out, "se répondent" should be read as "se correspondent" rather than as a pattern of question and answer. As in "confuses paroles" and "symboles" in the opening lines, the stress on language as the stage of disjunction is unmistakable. Language can be the chain of metaphors in a synethesia, as well as the oxymoronic polysemy of a single word, such as "se confondent" (or "transports" in l. 14) or even, on the level of the signifier, the play of the syllable or the letter. For the title, "Correspondances," is like the anagrammatic condensation of the text's entire program: "corps" and "esprit" brought together and harmonized by the *ance* of assonance that pervades the concluding tercets: from *ayant, ambre, chantent* to *expansion, sens, transport,* finally redoubled and re-echoed in *enc-ens/sens.*

The assertion, or representation, of verbality in "se répondent" (or in "Laissent parfois sortir de confuses *paroles*") also coincides, as in Nietzsche's text, with the passage from tropes—here the substitution of one sense experience by another—to anthropomorphisms. Or so, at least, it seems to a perhaps overhasty reading that would at once oppose "na-

ture" to "homme" as in a polarity of art ("temple") and nature, and endow natural forests and trees with eyes ("regards") and voices. The tradition of interpretation for this poem,
which stresses the importance of Chateaubriand and of Gérard de Nerval as sources, almost unanimously moves in that
direction.

The opening lines allow but certainly do not impose such
a reading. "La Nature est un temple" is enigmatic enough to
constitute the burden of any attempt at understanding and
cannot simply be reduced to a pattern of binary substitution,
but what follows is hardly less obscure. "Vivants piliers," as
we first meet it, certainly suggests the erect shape of human
bodies naturally enough endowed with speech, a scene from
the paintings of Paul Delvaux rather than from the poems of
Victor Hugo. "L'homme," in line 3, then becomes a simple
apposition to "vivants piliers." The notion of nature as a wood
and, consequently, of "piliers" as anthropomorphic columns
and trees, is suggested only by "des *forêts* de symboles" in
which, especially in combination with "symboles," a natural
and descriptive reading of "forêt" is by no means compelling.
Nor is nature, in Baudelaire, necessarily a sylvan world. We
cannot be certain whether we have ever left the world of humans and whether it is therefore relevant or necessary to speak
of anthropomorphism at all in order to account for the figuration of the text. "Des forêts," a plural of what is already, in
the singular, a collective plural (forêt) can be read as equivalent to "une foule de symboles," a figure of amplification that
designates a large number, the crowd of humanity in which it
is well known that Baudelaire took a constant poetic, rather
than humanitarian, interest.

Perhaps we are not in the country at all but have never
left the city, the "rue assourdissante" of the poem entitled "À
une passante," for example. "Symboles" in "des forêts de
symboles" could then designate the verbal, the rhetorical dimension within which we constantly dwell and which we
therefore meet as passively as we meet the glance of the other
in the street. That the possibility of this reading seems far-

fetched and, in my experience, never fails to elicit resistance, or that the forest/temple cliché should have forced itself so emphatically upon the attention of the commentators is one of the cruxes of "Correspondances."

It has been enough of a crux for Baudelaire himself to have generated at least one other text, the poem "Obsession," to which we will have to turn later. For the possibility of anthropomorphic (mis)reading is part of the text and part of what is at stake in it. Anthropomorphism seems to be the illusionary resuscitation of the natural breath of language, frozen into stone by the semantic power of the trope. It is a figural affirmation that claims to overcome the deadly negative power invested in the figure. In Baudelaire's, as in Nietzsche's text, the icon of this central trope is that of the architectural construct, temple, beehive, or columbarium.

This verbal building, which has to celebrate at the same time funeral and rebirth, is built by the infinite multiplication of numbers raising each other to ever higher arithmetic power. The property which privileges "parfums" as the sensory analogon for the joint powers of mind and body (ll. 9–14) is its ability to grow from the infinitely small to endless expansion, "ce grain d'encens qui remplit une église"—a quotation from *Les Fleurs du mal* that made it into Littré. The religious connotation of "temple" and "encens" suggests, as in the immediately anterior poem in the volume, "Elévation," a transcendental circulation, as ascent or descent, between the spirit and the senses, a borderline between two distinct realms that can be crossed.

Yet this movement is not unambiguously sustained by all the articulations of the text. Thus in the line "L'homme y passe à travers des forêts de symboles," "passer à travers" can have two very different spatial meanings. It can be read as "traverser la forêt"; one can *cross* the woods, as Narcissus goes through the looking-glass, or as the acrobat, in Banville's poem that echoes in Mallarmé's "Le Pitre châtié," goes through the roof of the circus tent, or as Vergil, for that matter, takes Dante beyond the woods in which he lost his way. But "passer à travers" can also mean to remain enclosed in the wood, to wander and err around in it as the speaker of "A une passante" wanders around in the crowd. The latter reading in fact suits the represented scene better than the former, although it is incompatible with the transcendental claims usually made for the sonnet. The transcendence of substitutive, analogical tropes linked by the recurrent "comme," a transcendence which occurs in the declarative assurance of the first quatrain, states the totalizing power of metaphor as it moves from analogy to identity, from simile to symbol and to a higher order of truth. Ambivalences such as those noted in "passer à travers," as well as the theoretical ambivalence of anthropomorphism in relation to tropes, complicate this expectation perhaps more forcefully than its outright negation. The complication is forceful enough to contaminate the key word that carries out the substitutions which constitute the main structure of the text: the word "comme."

When it is said that "Les parfums, les couleurs et les sons se répondent . . . *comme* de longs échos," then the preposition of resemblance, "comme," the most frequently counted word in the canon of Baudelaire's poetry, does its work properly and clearly, without upsetting the balance between difference and identity that it is assigned to maintain. It achieves a figure of speech, for it is not actually the case that an answer is an echo; no echo has ever answered a question except by a "delusion" of the signifier[3]—but it is certainly the case that an echo sounds like an answer, and that this similarity is endlessly suggestive. And the catachresis "se répondent" to designate the association between the various senses duly raises the process to the desired higher power. "Des parfums . . . / Doux comme les hautbois, verts comme les prairies" is already somewhat more complex, for although it is possible in referential and semantic terms to think of oboes and of certain scents as primarily "soft," it makes less sense to think of scents as green; "green scents" have less compelling connotations than "green thoughts" or "green shades." The relaying "comme" travels by ways of "hautbois," solidly tied to "parfums" by ways of "doux" and altogether compatible with "vert," through the pastoral association of the reedy sound still reinforced by the "(haut)*bois*, verts" that would be lost in English or German translation. The greenness of the fields can be guided back from color to scent with any "unsweet" connotation carefully filtered out.

All this is playing at metaphor according to the rules of the game. But the same is not true of the final "comme" in the poem: "Il est des parfums frais comme . . . / Doux comme . . . / —Et d'autres . . . / Ayant l'expansion des choses infinies / *Comme* l'ambre, le musc, le benjoin et l'encens." Ce comme n'est pas un comme comme les autres. It does not cross from one sense experience to another, as "frais" crosses from scent to touch or "doux" from scent to sound, nor does it cross from the common sensorium back to the single sense of hearing (as in "Les parfums, les couleurs et les sons se répondent" "Comme de longs échos . . .") or from the sensory to the intellectual realm, as in the double register of "se confondent." In each of these cases, the "comme" is what avoids tautology by linking the subject to a predicate that is not the same: scents are said to be like oboes, or like fields, or like echoes. But here "comme" relates to the subject "parfums" in two different ways or, rather, it has two distinct subjects. If "comme" is related to "l'expansion des choses infinies," which is grammatically as well as tonally possible, then it still functions, like the other "commes," as a comparative simile: a common property ("l'expansion") links the finite senses to an experience of infinity. But "comme" also relates to "parfums": "Il est des parfums frais . . . /—Et d'autres . . . / Comme l'ambre, le musc, le benjoin et l'encens"; the somewhat enigmatic hyphen can be said to mark that hesitation (as well as rule it out). "Comme" then means as much as "such as, for example" and enumerates scents which contrast with "chairs d'enfants" as innocence contrasts with experience or nature with artifice. This working out by exemplification is quite different from the analogical function assigned to the other uses of "comme."

Considered from the perspective of the "thesis" or of the

symbolist ideology of the text, such a use of "comme" is aberrant. For although the burden of totalizing expansion seems to be attributed to these particular scents rather than the others, the logic of "comme" restricts the semantic field of "parfums" and confines it to a tautology: "Il est des parfums . . . / Comme (des parfums)." Instead of analogy, we have enumeration, and an enumeration which never moves beyond the confines of a set of particulars: "forêt" synthesizes but does not enumerate a set of trees, but "ambre," "musc," "benjoin," and "encens," whatever differences or gradations one wishes to establish between them, are refrained by "comme" ever to lead beyond themselves; the enumeration could be continued at will without ceasing to be a repetition, without ceasing to be an obsession rather than a metamorphosis, let alone a rebirth. One wonders if the evil connotations of these corrupt scents do not stem from the syntax rather than from the Turkish bath or black mass atmosphere one would otherwise have to conjure up. For what could be more perverse or corruptive for a metaphor aspiring to transcendental totality than remaining stuck in an enumeration that never goes anywhere? If number can only be conquered by another number, if identity becomes enumeration, then there is no conquest at all, since the stated purpose of the passage to infinity was, like in Pascal, to restore the one, to escape the tyranny of number by dint of infinite multiplication. Enumerative repetition disrupts the chain of tropological substitution at the crucial moment when the poem promises, by way of these very substitutions, to reconcile the pleasures of the mind with those of the senses and to unite aesthetics with epistemology. That the very word on which these substitutions depend would just then lose its syntactical and semantic univocity is too striking a coincidence not to be, like pure chance, beyond the control of author and reader.

It allows, at any rate, for a sobering literalization of the word "transport" in the final line "Qui chantent les transports de l'esprit et des sens." "Transport" here means, of course, to be carried away beyond thought and sensation in a common

transcendental realm; it evokes loss of control and ecstatic un-
reason. But all attentive readers of Baudelaire have always felt
that this claim at self-loss is not easily compatible with a colder,
analytic self-consciousness that moves in a very different direction. In the words of our text, "les transports de l'esprit"
and "Les transports des sens" are not at all the same "transports." We have learned to recognize, of late, in "transports"
the spatial displacement implied by the verbal ending of meta-
phorein. One is reminded that, in the French-speaking cities of
our century, "correspondance" meant, on the trolley-cars, the
equivalence of what is called in English a "transfer"—the priv-
ilege, automatically granted on the Paris Métro, of connecting
from one line to another without having to buy a new ticket.

The prosaic transposition of ecstasy to the economic codes
of public transportation is entirely in the spirit of Baudelaire
and not by itself disruptive with regard to the claim for transcendental unity. For the transfer indeed merges two different
displacements into one single system of motion and circulation, with corresponding economic and metaphysical profits.
The problem is not so much centered on *phorein* as on *meta*
(trans . . .), for does "beyond" here mean a movement beyond some particular place or does it mean a state that is beyond movement entirely? And how can "beyond," which posits
and names movement, ever take us away from what it posits?
The question haunts the text in all its ambiguities, be it "passer à travers" or the discrepancy between the "comme" of
homogeneity and the "comme" of enumeration. The apparent
rest and tranquility of "Correspondances" within the corpus
of *Les Fleurs du mal* lies indeed beyond tension and beyond
motion. If Nature is truly a temple, it is not a means of transportation or a railroad station, Victorian architects who loved
to build railroad stations in the shape of cathedrals notwith-
standing. Nature in this poem is not a road toward a temple,
a sequence of motions that take us there. Its travels, whatever
they are, lie far behind us; there is no striving here, no quest-
ing for an absence or a presence. And if man (l'homme) is at
home among "regards familiers" within that Nature, then his

language of tropes and analogies is of little use to them. In this realm, transfer tickets are of no avail. Within the confines of a system of transportation—or of language as a system of communication—one can transfer from one vehicle to another, but one cannot transfer from being like a vehicle to being like a temple, or a ground.

The epistemological, aesthetic, and poetic language of transports or of tropes, which is the theme though not singly the rhetoric of this poem, can never say nor, for that matter, sing or understand the opening statement: "la Nature est un temple." But the poem offers no explicit alternative to this language which, like the perfumes enumerated by "comme," remains condemned to the repetition of its superfluity. Few poems in *Les Fleurs du mal* state this in a manner that is both so obvious yet, by necessity, so oblique. The poem most remote from stating it is also the one closest to "Correspondances," its "echo" as it were, with which it is indeed very easy to confuse it. Little clarity can be gained from "Correspondances" except for the knowledge that disavows its deeper affinity with "Obsession."

Written presumably in February 1860, at least five years after "Correspondances" (of which the date is uncertain but anterior to 1855), "Obsession" (*O.C.*, 1:73) alludes to many poems in *Les Fleurs du mal*, such as "l'Homme et la mer" (1852) and "De profundis clamavi" (1851). But it more than alludes to "Correspondances"; it can be called a *reading* of the earlier text, with all the complications that are inherent in this term. The relationship between the two poems can indeed be seen as the construction and the undoing of the mirrorlike, specular structure that is always involved in a reading. On both the thematic and the rhetorical level, the reverted symmetries between the two texts establish their correspondence along a positive / negative axis. Here again, our problem is centered on the possibility of reinscribing into the system elements, in either text, that do not belong to this pattern. The same question can be asked in historical or in generic terms but, in so doing, the significance of this terminology risks being unsettled.

One can, for instance, state the obvious difference in theme and in diction between the two poems in terms derived from the canonical history of French nineteenth-century lyric poetry. With its portal of Greek columns, its carefully balanced symmetries, and its decorous absence of any displayed emotion, "Correspondances" has all the characteristics of a Parnassian poem, closer to Heredia than to Hugo. The "romantic" exaltation of "Obsession" 's apostrophes and exclamations, on the other hand, is self-evident. If nature is a "transport" in "Obsession," it is a temple in "Correspondances." However, by putting the two texts side by side in this manner, their complementarity is equally manifest. What is lost in personal expressiveness from the first poem is gained in the symbolic "depth" that has prompted comparisons of "Correspondances" with the poetry of that other neo-classicist, Gérard de Nerval, or supported the claim of its being the forerunner of symbolism. Such a historicizing pattern, a commonplace of aesthetic theory, is a function of the aesthetic ideologization of linguistic structures rather than an empirical historical event. The dialectical interaction of "classical" with "romantic" conceptions, as summarized in the contrastive symmetries between these two sonnets, ultimately reveals the symbolic character of poetic language, the linguistic structure in which it is rooted. "Symbolist" art is considered archaic when it is supposed to be spontaneous, modern when it is self-conscious, and this terminology has a certain crude wisdom about it that is anything but historical, however, in its content. Such a combination of linguistic with pseudo-historical terms, of "symbolic" with "classic" (or *parnassien*) or with "romantic" (or *symboliste*), a combination familiar at least since Hegel's *Lectures on Aesthetics*, is a necessary feature of systems that combine tropes with aesthetic and epistemological norms. In this perspective, the relationship between the neo-classical "Correspondances" and the post-romantic "Obsession" is itself structured like a symbol: the two sonnets complement each other like the two halves of a *symbolon*. Historicizing them into a diachrony or into a valorized qualitative hierarchy is more convenient than it is legitimate. The terminology of traditional literary history, as a succession of periods or literary movements, remains useful only if the terms are seen for what they are: rather crude metaphors for figural patterns rather than historical events or acts.

Stated in generic rather than historical terms, the relationship between "Correspondances" and "Obsession" touches upon the uncertain status of the lyric as a term for poetic discourse in general. The lyric's claim of being song is made explicitly in "Correspondances" ("qui *chantent* les transports. . ."), whereas "Obsession" howls, laughs, and speaks but does not pretend to sing. Yet the *je-tu* structure of the syntax makes it much closer to the representation of a vocal utterance than the engraved, marmorean gnomic wisdom of "Correspondances." The reading however disclosed a discrepancy that affects the verb "chanter" in the concluding line: the suggestive identification of "parfum" with song, based on common resonance and expansion, is possible only within a system of relays and transfers that, in the syntax if not in the stated meaning of the poem, becomes threatened by the stutter, the *piétinement* of aimless enumeration. This eventuality, inherent in the structure of the tropes on which the claim to lyricism depends, conflicts with the monumental stability of a completed entity that exists independently of its principle of constitution and destruction. Song is not compatible with aphasia and a stuttering Amphion is an absurd figure indeed. No lyric can be read lyrically nor can the object of a lyrical reading be itself a lyric—which implies least of all that it is epical or dramatic. Baudelaire's own lyrical reading of "Correspondances," however, produced at least a text, the sonnet entitled "Obsession."

The opening of "Obsession" reads the first quatrain of "Correspondances" as if it were indeed a sylvan scene. It naturalizes the surreal speech of live columns into the frightening, but natural, roar of the wind among the trees:

> Grands bois, vous m'effrayez comme des cathédrales;
> Vous hurlez comme l'orgue;

The benefits of naturalization—as we can call the reversal of anthropomorphism—are at once apparent. None of the uncertainties that obscure the opening lines of "Correspondances" are maintained. No "comme" could be more orthodox than the two "commes" in these two lines. The analogism is so perfect that the implied anthropomorphism becomes fully motivated.

In this case, the unifying element is the wind as it is heard in whistling keyholes, roaring trees, and wind instruments such as church organs. Neither is there any need to invoke hallucination to account for the fear inspired by stormy forests and huge cathedrals: both are versions of the same dizziness of vast spaces. The adjustment of the elements involved (wood, wind, fear, cathedral, and organ) is perfectly self-enclosed, since all the pieces in the structure fit each other: wood and cathedral share a common shape, but wood also fits organ by way of the noise of the roaring wind; organ and cathedral, moreover, are linked by metonymy, etc. Everything can be substituted for everything else without distorting the most natural experience. Except, of course, for the "vous" of address in the apostrophe "Grands bois," which is, of course, absurd from a representational point of view; we are all frightened by windy woods but do not generally make a spectacle of ourselves talking to trees.

Yet the power of the analogy, much more immediately compelling than that of synesthesia in "Correspondances," naturalizes even this most conventional trope of lyric address: when it is said, in line 4, that the terror of the wind corresponds to the subjective fear of death

> et dans nos coeurs maudits,
>
> . . .
>
> Répondent les échos de vos *De profundis,*

then the analogy between outer event and inner feeling is again so close that the figural distance between noise (wind) and speech or even music almost vanishes, all the more so since wind as well as death are designated by associated sounds: the howling of the wind and the penitential prayer, aural metonymy for death. As a result, the final attribution of speech to the woods (*vos* De profundis) appears so natural that it takes an effort to notice that anthropomorphism is involved. The claim to verbality in the equivalent line from "Correspondances," "Les parfums, les couleurs et les sons se répondent" seems fantastic by comparison. The omnipresent metaphor of interiorization, of which this is a striking example, here travels initially by ways of the ear alone.

The gain in pathos is such as to make the depth of *De profundis* the explicit theme of the poem. Instead of being the infinite expanse, the openness of "Vaste comme la nuit et comme la clarté," depth is now the enclosed space that, like the sound chamber of a violin, produces the inner vibration of emotion. We retrieve what was conspicuously absent from "Correspondances," the recurrent image of the subject's presence to itself as a spatial enclosure, room, tomb, or crypt in which the voice echoes as in a cave. The image draws its verisimilitude from its own "mise en abŷme" in the shape of the body as the *container* of the voice (or soul, heart, breath, consciousness, spirit, etc.) that it exhales. At the cost of much represented agony ("Chambres d'éternel deuil où vibrent de vieux râles), "Obsession" asserts its right to say "I" with full authority. The canon of romantic and post-romantic lyric poetry offers innumerable versions and variations of this inside/outside pattern of exchange that founds the metaphor of the lyrical voice as subject. In a parallel movement, reading interiorizes the meaning of the text by its understanding. The union of aesthetic with epistemological properties is carried out by the mediation of the metaphor of the self as consciousness of itself, which implies its negation.

The specular symmetry of the two texts is such that any instance one wishes to select at once involves the entire system with flawless consistency. The hellenic "temple" of "Correspondances," for example, becomes the Christian "cathédrale" of "Obsession," just as the denominative, impersonal third person discourse of the earlier poem becomes the first person discourse of the later one. The law of this figural and chiastic transformation is negation. "Obsession" self-consciously denies and rejects the sensory wealth of "Correspondances." The landscape of denial from "De profundis clamavi":

> C'est un pays plus nu que la terre polaire;
> —Ni bêtes, ni ruisseaux, ni verdure, ni bois!

reappears as the desire of "Obsession":

> Car je cherche le vide, et le noir, et le nu!

in sharp denial of

> Doux comme les hautbois, verts comme les prairies

from "Correspondances." Similar negations pervade the texts, be it in terms of affects, moods, or grammar.

The negation, however, is indeed a figure of chiasmus, for the positive and negative valorizations can be distributed on both sides. We read "Obsession" thematically as an interiorization of "Correspondances," and as a negation of the positivity of an outside reality. But it is just as plausible to consider "Obsession" as the making manifest, as the exteriorization of the subject that remains hidden in "Correspondances." Naturalization, which appears to be a movement from inside to outside, allows for affective verisimilitude which moves in the opposite direction. In terms of figuration also, it can be said that "Correspondances" is the negation of "Obsession": the figural stability of "Obsession" is denied in "Correspondances." Such patterns constantly recur in nineteenth- and twentieth-century lyric poetry and create a great deal of critical confusion, symptomatic of further-reaching complexities.

The recuperative power of the subject metaphor in "Obsession" becomes particularly evident, in all its implications, in the tercets. As soon as the sounds of words are allowed, as in the opening stanza, to enter into analogical combinations with the sounds of nature, they necessarily turn into the light

imagery of representation and of knowledge. If the sounds of
nature are akin to those of speech, then nature also speaks by
ways of light, the light of the senses as well as of the mind.
The philosophical phantasm that has concerned us throughout this reading, the reconciliation of knowledge with phenomenal, aesthetic experience, is summarized in the figure of
speaking light which, as is to be expected in the dialectical mode
of negation, is both denied and asserted:

> Comme tu me plairais, ô nuit! sans ces étoiles
> Dont *la lumière parle* un langage connu!

Light implies space which, in turn, implies the possibility of
spatial differentiation, the play of distance and proximity that
organizes perception as the foreground-background juxtaposition that links it to the aesthetics of painting. Whether the
light emanates from outside us before it is interiorized by the
eye, as is the case here in the perception of a star, or whether
the light emanates from inside and projects the entity, as in
hallucination or in certain dreams, makes little difference in this
context. The metamorphic crossing between perception and
hallucination

> Mais les ténèbres sont elles-mêmes des toiles
> Où vivent, jaillissant de mon oeil par milliers,
> Des êtres disparus aux regards familiers

occurs by means of the paraphernalia of painting, which is also
that of recollection and of re-cognition, as the recovery, to the
senses, of what seemed to be forever beyond experience. In
an earlier outline, Baudelaire had written

> Mais les ténèbres sont elles-mêmes des toiles
> Où [peint] . . . (presumably for "se peignent"; *O.C.*,
>   1:981)

"Peint" confirms the reading of "toiles" as the device by means
of which painters or dramatists project the space or the stage
of representation, by enframing the interiorized expanse of the
skies. The possibility of representation asserts itself at its most
efficacious at the moment when the sensory plenitude of

"Correspondances" is most forcefully denied. The lyric depends entirely for its existence on the denial of phenomenality as the surest means to recover what it denies. This motion is not dependent, in its failure or in its illusion of success, on the good or the bad faith of the subject it constitutes.

The same intelligibility enlightens the text when the enigma of consciousness as eternal mourning ("Chambres d'éternel deuil où vibrent de vieux râles") is understood as the hallucinatory obsession of recollection, certainly easier to comprehend by shared experience than by esoteric *correspondances.* "Obsession" translates "Correspondances" into intelligibility, the least one can hope for in a successful reading. The resulting couple or pair of texts indeed becomes a model for the uneasy combination of funereal monumentality with paranoid fear that characterizes the hermeneutics and the pedagogy of lyric poetry.

Yet, this very title, "Obsession," also suggests a movement that may threaten the far-reaching symmetry between the two texts. For the temporal pattern of obsessive thought is directly reminiscent of the tautological, enumerative stutter we encountered in the double semantic function of "comme," which disrupted the totalizing claim of metaphor in "Correspondances." It suggests a psychological and therefore intelligible equivalent of what there appeared as a purely grammatical distinction, for there is no compelling thematic suggestion, in "comme l'ambre, le musc, le benjoin et l'encens," that allows one to think of this list as compulsively haunting. The title "Obsession," or the last line of the poem, which names the ghostly memory of mourned absences, does therefore not correspond to the tension, deemed essential, between the expansiveness of "des choses infinies" and the restrictive catalogue of certain kinds of scents introduced by "comme." Yet, if the symmetry between the two texts is to be truly recuperative, it is essential that the disarticulation that threatens the first text should find its counterpart in the second: mere naturalization of a grammatical structure, which is how the relationship between enumeration and obsession can be understood, will not suffice, since it is precisely the tension between an experienced and a purely linguistic disruption that is at issue. There ought to be a place, in "Obsession," where a similar contrast between infinite totalization and endless repetition of the same could be pointed out. No such place exists. At the precise point where one would expect it, at the moment when obsession is stressed in terms of number, "Obsession" resorts to synthesis by losing itself in the vagueness of the infinite

> Où vivent, jaillissant de mon oeil *par milliers,*
> Des êtres disparus aux regards familiers.

There could be no more decisive contrast, in *Les Fleurs du mal,* than between the reassuring indeterminacy of these infinite thousands—as one had, in "Correspondances," "des forêts"—and the numerical precision with which, in "Les sept vieillards" (*O.C.,* 1:87–88), it is the passage from one altogether finite to another altogether finite number that produces genuine terror:

> Aurais-je, sans mourir, contemplé le huitième,
> Sosie inexorable, ironique et fatal,
> Dégoûtant Phénix, fils et père de lui-même?
> —Mais je tournai le dos au cortège infernal.
>
> Exaspéré comme un ivrogne qui voit double,
> Je rentrai, je fermai ma porte, épouvanté,
> Malade et morfondu, l'esprit fiévreux et trouble,
> Blessé par le mystère et par l'absurdité!

Unlike "Obsession," "Les sept vieillards" can however in no respect be called a reading of "Correspondances," to which it in no way corresponds.

The conclusion is written into the argument which is itself written into the reading, a process of translation or "transport" that incessantly circulates between the two texts. There always are at least two texts, regardless of whether they are actually written out or not; the relationship between the two sonnets, obligingly provided by Baudelaire for the benefit, no doubt, of future teachers invited to speak on the nature of the lyric, is an inherent characteristic of any text. Any text, as text, compels reading as its understanding. What we call the lyric, the instance of represented voice, conveniently spells out the rhetorical and thematic characteristics that make it the paradigm of a complementary relationship between grammar, trope, and theme. The set of characteristics includes the various structures and moments we encountered along the way: specular symmetry along an axis of assertion and negation (to which correspond the generic mirror-images of the ode, as celebration, and the elegy, as mourning), the grammatical transformation of the declarative into the vocative modes of question, exclamation, address, hypothesis, etc., the tropological transformation of analogy into apostrophe or the equivalent, more general transformation which, with Nietzsche's assistance, we took as our point of departure: the transformation of trope into anthropomorphism. The lyric is not a genre, but one name among several to designate the defensive motion of understanding, the possibility of a future hermeneutics. From this point of view, there is no significant difference between one generic term and another: all have the same apparently intentional and temporal function.

We all perfectly and quickly understand "Obsession," and better still the motion that takes us from the earlier to the later text. But no symmetrical reversal of this lyrical reading-motion is conceivable; if Baudelaire, as is eminently possible, were to have written, in empirical time, "Correspondances" after "Obsession," this would change nothing. "Obsession" derives from "Correspondances" but the reverse is not the case. Neither does it account for it as its origin or cause. "Correspondances" implies and explains "Obsession" but "Obsession" leaves "Correspondances" as thoroughly incomprehensible as it always was. In the paraphernalia of literary terminology, there is no term available to tell us what "Correspondances" might be. All we know is that it is, emphatically, *not* a lyric. Yet it, and it alone, contains, implies, produces, generates, permits (or whatever aberrant verbal metaphor one wishes to choose) the entire possibility of the lyric. Whenever we encounter a text such as "Obsession"— that is, whenever we read—there always is an infra-text, a hypogram like "Correspondances" underneath. Stating this relationship, as we just did, in phenomenal, spatial terms or in phenomenal, temporal terms—"Obsession," a text of recollection and elegiac mourning, *adds* remembrance to the flat surface of time in "Correspondances"—produces at once a hermeneutic, fallacious lyrical reading of the unintelligible. The power that takes one from one text to the other is not just a power of displacement, be it understood as recollection or interiorization or any other "transport," but the sheer blind violence that Nietzsche, concerned with the same enigma, domesticated by calling it, metaphorically, an *army* of tropes.

Generic terms such as "lyric" (or its various sub-species, "ode," "idyll," or "elegy") as well as pseudo-historical period terms such as "romanticism" or "classicism" are always terms of resistance and nostalgia, at the furthest remove from the materiality of actual history. If mourning is called a "chambre d'éternel deuil où vibrent de vieux râles," then this pathos of terror states in fact the desired consciousness of eternity and of temporal harmony as voice and as song. True "mourning" is less deluded. The most *it* can do is to allow for noncomprehension and enumerate non-anthropomorphic, non-elegiac, non-celebratory, non-lyrical, non-poetic, that is to say, prosaic, or, better, *historical* modes of language power.

10
Aesthetic Formalization: Kleist's *Über das Marionettentheater*

IN A letter to Körner dated February 23, 1793, Schiller gave the following description of the perfect aesthetic society:

I know of no better image for the ideal of a beautiful society than a well executed English dance, composed of many complicated figures and turns. A spectator located on the balcony observes an infinite variety of criss-crossing motions which keep decisively but arbitrarily changing directions without ever colliding with each other. Everything has been arranged in such a manner that each dancer has already vacated his position by the time the other arrives. Everything fits so skilfully, yet so spontaneously, that everyone seems to be following his own lead, without ever getting in anyone's way. Such a dance is the perfect· symbol of one's own individually asserted freedom as well as of one's respect for the freedom of the other.[1]

Schiller's English translators and commentators, Elizabeth Wilkinson and L. A. Willoughby, cite the passage as a fitting description of Schiller's main theoretical text, the *Letters on the*

Aesthetic Education of Mankind. It is said to reflect "the philo-
sophic and aesthetic complexity of the [book's] form as a
whole."² What strikes them as particularly suggestive in the
model of the dance is what they call the *tautology* of art, "its
inherent tendency to offer a hundred different treatments of
the same subject, to find a thousand different forms of expression for the thoughts and feelings common to all men. . . .
The perpetually repeated figures—so highly formalized that they
can easily be recorded in notation—admit of only as much in-
dividuality in their successive execution by the different dancers
as can be expressed through the grace of bodily movement."³
The privileged spectacle of the dance, which recurs in many
authors and many texts, is also a particularly fitting figure for
"the second nature of true wisdom which, though indistin-
guishable from the spontaneous play of childhood's innocence, is reached only on the other side of knowledge, sophis-
tication, and awareness of self."⁴

The Schiller text, with its commentary, condenses the
complex ideology of the aesthetic in a suggestive concatena-
tion of concepts that achieve the commonplace, not by their
banality but by the genuine universality of their stated aspirations. The aesthetic, as is clear from Schiller's formulation, is
primarily a social and political model, ethically grounded in an
assumedly Kantian notion of freedom; despite repeated attempts by commentators, alarmed by its possible implications,
to relativise and soften the idea of the aesthetic state (*Aesthe-
tischer Staat*) that figures so prominently at the end of the *Letters on Aesthetic Education,* it should be preserved as the radical
assertion that it is. The "state" that is here being advocated is
not just a state of mind or of soul, but a principle of political
value and authority that has its own claims on the shape and
the limits of our freedom. It would lose all interest if this were
not the case. For it is as a political force that the aesthetic still
concerns us as one of the most powerful ideological drives to
act upon the reality of history. But what is then called, in conscious reference to Kant and to the questionable version of Kant
that is found in Schiller, the *aesthetic,* is not a separate cate-

gory but a principle of articulation between various known faculties, activities, and modes of cognition. What gives the aesthetic its power and hence its practical, political impact, is its intimate link with knowledge, the epistemological implications that are always in play when the aesthetic appears over the horizon of discourse. We hear these claims, somewhat muted in Schiller's letter to Körner (though present in numberless instances throughout his writings) but clearly sounded in the cogent commentary of his interpreters.

It appears in this commentary in two closely interrelated of its aspects. First, and most traditionally, in the paradox of a wisdom that lies somehow beyond cognition and self-knowledge, yet that can only be reached by ways of the process it is said to overcome. Second, and more originally, in the reference to systems of formalization and notation rigorous enough to be patterned on the model of mathematical language. Such a degree of formalization is made possible by what is here called "the tautology of essential art," a term used by Wilkinson and Willoughby to designate the universality of "thoughts and feelings common to all men." As the privileged and infinitely varied mode of expression of this universality, art is in fact what defines humanity in the broadest sense. Mankind, in the last analysis, is human only by ways of art. On the other hand, as a principle of formalization rigorous enough to produce its own codes and systems of inscription, tautology functions as a restrictive coercion that allows only for the reproduction of its own system, at the exclusion of all others. Neither in Schiller's letter nor in the commentary on this letter is any allowance made for the possible tension between these two functions.

In the same literary tradition, other versions of the same theme tell a different tale and reveal some of what is hidden behind Schiller's ideology of the aesthetic. Kleist's *Über das Marionettentheater* is among the furthest-reaching of these texts.[5] It has engendered a tradition of interpretation, primarily but not exclusively in German, rich enough to produce at least one anthology of critical essays,[6] and it has inspired poets and novelists, most prominently Rilke and Thomas Mann, as well as academic critics. Yet for all the attention it has received it has remained curiously unread and enigmatic. It belongs among the texts of the period which our own modernity has not yet been able to confront, perhaps because the Schillerian aesthetic categories, whether we know it or not, are still the taken-for-granted premises of our own pedagogical, historical, and political ideologies.

The reading of Baudelaire's "Correspondances" produced a version of the disruption of the tropological chain by way of a pattern of enumeration no longer accessible to the processes of anthropomorphism and naturalization that guarantee the intelligibility of tropes. The tension, in this poem, occurs indeed between number as trope (the infinitesimal as the underlying principle of totalization) and number as tautology (the stutter of an endless, but not infinitesimal, enumeration that never goes anywhere). "Correspondances," in other words, is structured like the distinction between calculus and arithmetic, with tropes of infinitude reduced to the literal, disfigured status of sheer finite numbers. The Kleist text is, or pretends to be, more overtly mathematical, though along somewhat different lines. Its model is that of analytical geometry, rather than of calculus, as an attempt to articulate the phenomenal particularity of a spatial entity (line or curve) with the formalized computation of number: the curve belongs to the order of the aesthetic or of the word (logos), the formal computation that produces it to the order of number (arithmos). Inevitably, the word that combines both "word" and "number," *logarithm*, makes at least a furtive, and somewhat dubious, appearance in the text.[7]

The articulation between trope and epistemology, in Baudelaire's poem, is carried out by the conceptualization of particulars that travels from individual sensations to such infinite generalities as "l'esprit," "la nature," or "les sens." Numbers are at first wrapped up in the infinity of words until they reappear, like the return of the repressed, in the disruptive quantification of specific instances as conveyed, for instance, by the semantic ambivalence of the word "comme." Number is omnipresent but always already conceptualized in words, in language. Kleist's text is concerned with the same articulation of the aesthetic with the epistemological but by way of formal computation. Whereas aesthetic words turn out to produce material numbers in Baudelaire, aesthetic numbers produce material words in Kleist. If Baudelaire's text is about the disarticulation of entities by words, Kleist's is about the disarticulation of words themselves.

Still, the notion of the infinite appears in *Marionettentheater* as well, and even so conspicuously that it has become the target, the *thesis* of the text, ostensible enough to have mobilized the attention of its interpreters at the exclusion of most anything else. As is fitting in any well-conducted argument, the thesis emerges at the end, as the conclusion of a consistent development. The key term of this conclusion is indeed the concept of infinity:

. . . as one line, when it crosses another, suddenly appears on the other side of the intersecting point, after its passage through infinity; or as the image in a concave mirror, after retreating into infinity, suddenly reappears close before our eyes, so, too, grace will reappear after knowledge *(Erkenntnis)* has gone through infinity. So that we shall find grace at its purest in a body which is entirely devoid of consciousness or which possesses it in an infinite degree; that is, in the marionette or in the god.

The idea of innocence recovered at the far side and by way of experience, of paradise consciously regained after the fall into consciousness, the idea, in other words, of a teleological and apocalyptic history of consciousness is, of course, one of the most seductive, powerful, and deluded topoi of the idealist and romantic period.

Schiller's concept of the naive and the self-conscious which, as Wilkinson's commentary suggests, typifies the trajectory of his aesthetic theory, is a striking example of this ubiquitous model. No wonder that commentators as well as poets and novelists respond so selectively to Kleist's concluding statement. Within the bewildering and mystifying context of *Marionettentheater*, it provides an enclave of familiarity, an anchor of the commonplace in the midst of an uncanny scene of extravagance and paradox. It has been very easy to forget how little this pseudo-conclusion has to do with the rest of the text and how derisively ungermane it is to the implications of what comes before.

For one thing, *Marionettentheater* is not composed as an argument but as a succession of three separate narratives encased in the dialogical frame of a staged scene. And since the very concept of argument is equated, in the body of the text, with mathematical computation and proof, one of the tensions in the text certainly occurs between a statement such as the one on infinity quoted above, and the formal procedures that allow one to reach and understand this statement. In a computation or a mathematical proof, the meaning and the procedure by which it is reached, the hermeneutics, if one wishes, and the poetics (as formal procedure considered independently of its semantic function), entirely codetermine each other. But in another mode of cognition and of exposition, such as narrative, this mutual supportiveness cannot be taken for granted, since it is not the only generative principle of the discourse. And although *Marionettentheater* can be said to be *about* proof, it is not set up as one but as the story or trope of such a demonstration, and a very cagy story at that.

The concluding commonplace on the restorative powers of consciousness, for example, does not reach us as an utterance attributed to an established authority, but as the statement of one of the two protagonists in the staged scene of a dialogue between a first-person "I" and a third person "he," neither of whose credibility goes unchallenged. The function of this scene, which frames the embedded narratives told alternatively by the two characters (stories 1 and 3 told by "he" and story 2 by "I") is itself multiple and of some complexity. It is, on the first level of evidence, a scene of persuasion in which "he" apparently convinces "I" of a paradoxical judgment that the latter initially resisted. At the end of the conversation, K has apparently been convinced and the dialogue seems to end in harmonious agreement. The agreement is reached because K, at first confused, has now, as C puts it, been "put into possession of all that is needed to *understand* (him)" (italics mine). Persuasion is linked to a process of understanding and what is "understood" is that the increased formalization of consciousness, as in a machine, far from destroying aesthetic effect, enhances it; consciousness's loss is aesthetic's gain. What concerns us at this point is not the validity of this assertion but the formal observation that this loss of hermeneutic control is itself staged as a scene of hermeneutic persuasion.

This scene abounds in stage business to the point of achieving the pantomimic liveliness associated with texts such as Diderot's *Neveu de Rameau*. We are told when and how the interlocutors nod and smile, sniff tobacco, express enthusiasm or, on the contrary, manifest their doubts or hesitations; K and C, with the alternating symmetry of a dance figure in a ballet, cast down their gaze to the floor or lift it to eye-level. A second dialogue of gestures doubles the dialogue of words, and the parallelism between both is far from assured. When, at the moment of final agreement, K is said to be "ein wenig zerstreut" (slightly distracted), this signal should at least arouse one's suspicion. This stress on staging, on the mimesis of the diegetic narratives—the text *shows* people engaged in the act of *telling*—emphasizes the self-consciousness of the representational mode within the hermeneutic context of a persuasion and problematizes the relationship between a rhetoric and a hermeneutics of persuasion. When a persuasion has to become a scene of persuasion one is no longer in the same way persuaded of its persuasiveness.

This may well be why the scenes of persuasion are also scenes of instruction. *Über das Marionettentheater* is also a text about teaching, staging all the familiar devices of pedagogy. It appears as the pseudo-conversation or discussion of a "seminar" or a "tutorial" in which the cards are stacked from the beginning. Herr C., who is the successful first dancer of the local opera, has all the authority of the professional on his side in this conversation about his own craft with a sheer amateur; K's apparent objections are there only to set off the mastery of the expert and the outcome of the debate is never in question. C's credentials guarantee from the start that he will have the last word, although the proposition he is made to defend— that mechanical puppets are more graceful than live dancers— is, at first sight, paradoxical to the point of absurdity. Moreover, when K in turn gets *his* chance to tell a story (the story of the young man who lost his gracefulness after seeing himself in a mirror), he acts himself, in the *mise en abŷme* of the story within the story, as the ephebe's teacher whose unquestioned duty implies that he put the young man, for his own good, to the test (". . . um die Sicherheit der Grazie, die ihm beiwohnte, zu *prüfen* . . .") (italics mine). The function as well as the devices or methods of education figure prominently in this latter-day *Emile*.

The education, moreover, is in a very specific discipline, closer to Schiller than to Rousseau: the ephebe, as well as K, are being educated in the art of gracefulness, *Anmut*. Their education is clearly an *aesthetic* education that is to earn them citizenship in Schiller's aesthetic state. This didactic aim, however, can only be reached if the discipline that is to be taught can itself be formalized or schematized to the point of becoming a technique. Teaching becomes possible only when a degree of formalization is built into the subject-matter. The aesthetic can be taught only if the articulation of aesthetic with mathematical (and epistemological) discourse—the burden of Kant's *Critique of Judgment*—can be achieved. This articulation, always according to Kant, is also the only guarantee that theoretical reason can be linked to the practical judgment of the ethical world. The possibility thus arises that the postulate of ethical authority is posited for the sake of maintaining the undisputed authority of teachers in their relationship to their pupils.

The scene of instruction which repeats itself on all narrative levels of discourse also becomes, most clearly in the third anecdote (that of the bear), a scene of *reading*. Whatever the bizarre figure of the bear may represent or symbolize, his relationship to C is marked by his apparent ability to *read* him. "Eye to eye, as if he could *read* my soul, he stood, with threateningly lifted paw—Aug in Auge, als ob er meine Seele darin *lesen* könnte, stand er, die Tatze schlagfertig erhoben . . ." (italics mine). The understanding *(begreifen)* aimed at by C occurs by way of a reading, of which the exemplary version is told in this episode. But this reading is also a combat, a battle of which it is not at all certain that it will remain harmless mock-combat. This element of battle will be present in the other scenes as well. All we wish to retain for the present is that the theatricality of the text is centered on agonistic scenes of persuasion, of instruction, and of reading. And since the scene of reading is the most explicit and the most dangerous test of the three, it follows that the reading of this text, *Über das Marionettentheater* by Heinrich von Kleist, is the testiest of all these juxtaposed tests, especially if the reader also happens to be a teacher.

One cannot avoid the perhaps most dangerous (for oneself, that is) of all observations, namely that academic as well as nonacademic literary readers have collectively flunked this test. *Marionettentheater* has produced fine articles of considerable subtlety, erudition, and wit (next to others of distressing banality) but its interpretation has certainly failed to coalesce into anything resembling a consensus, even on a relatively primitive level of signification.

The spectacle of so much competence and attention producing so little result certainly puts to the test any attempt to add one more reading to those that have already been undertaken. More often than not the diversity that becomes manifest in the successive readings of a text permits one to determine a central crux that works as a particularly productive challenge to interpretation. Not so with *Marionettentheater;* this brief narrative engenders a confusion all the more debilitating because it arises from the cumulative effect produced by the readings. Each of the essays (including the bad ones) is quite

convincing in itself, until one reads the next one, equally persuasive yet entirely incompatible with its predecessors. The
outcome, seen from the perspective of literary scholarship, is
anything but graceful. The collective body of interpreters resembles the harassed fencer of the final story rather than the
self-assured teacher. C and his interlocutor maintain a measure of composure, but the dance performed by the commentators offers only chaos. Far from finding, as in Schiller's description of the aesthetic dance, that the spot toward which
one directs one's step has been vacated, one finds oneself
bumping clumsily into various intruders or getting entangled
in one's own limbs and motions. One is left speculating on what
it is, in this text, that compels one, despite clearly perceived
warnings, to enter upon this unpromising scene. For it would
appear that anyone still willing to engage a bear in a fencing
match after having read *Über das Marionettentheater* should have
his head examined.

Still, the interpretation of the enigmatic little text continues and, under the salutary influence of contemporary meth-
odology, the readings have become increasingly formalized.[8]
They allow one to reach the true aesthetic dimension of the
text, the uneasy mixture of affirmation and denial, of gracefulness and violence, of mystification and lucidity, of hoax and
high seriousness, that characterizes it and accounts for its en-
during fascination. This response, of course, carries out the
program of the narrative which promises increased aesthetic
pleasure as a reward for increased formalization. That this
happens at the expense of stable and determinable meaning is
a fair enough price to pay for the mastery over form. The real
test comes later, after the possibility of assertion has been de-
canonized by means of a systematic poetics and this poetics
threatens to become, in its turn, canonized as exemplary. A
contemporary version of this story is familiar to us in the
pedagogical success of semiotics. The formalization, which
makes genuine teaching possible, is inherent in the linguistic
medium; therefore it is not only legitimate but absolutely indispensable. Its negative impact on semantic certainty, on the

dubious status of referentiality, is equally persuasive. What remains problematic is whether the pedagogical function can remain compatible with aesthetic effect. Formalization inevitably produces aesthetic effects; on the other hand, it just as compulsively engenders pedagogical discourse. It produces education, but can this education still be called *aesthetic* education? It produces a special kind of grace, but can this elegance be taught? Is there such a thing as a graceful teacher or, rather, is a teacher who manages to be graceful still a teacher? And if he is not, what then will he *do* to those who, perhaps under false pretenses, have been put in the position of being his pupils? The problem is not entirely trivial or self-centered, for the political power of the aesthetic, the measure of its impact on reality, necessarily travels by ways of its didactic manifestations. The politics of the aesthetic state are the politics of education.

The problematization of reading conceived as the determination of meaning is signaled, in this text, in a variety of ways. It takes the form, first of all, of a complication of the mimetic function of narrative. In lyric poems, like those of Baudelaire, this was not the primary concern: the claim is that of a voice addressing entities or conceptually generalized expressions of particular entities, and the refinements of narrative strategy are not centrally involved. In the Kleist text, however, we are dealing, from the start, with the compatibility of narrative (which is aesthetic) with epistemological argument or, to be somewhat more specific, with the possibility of a system of formalization that narrative and argument would share in common. The various thematic components of the problem (teaching, combat, consciousness, etc.) occur as necessary components of this system. The problem of mimesis is also bound to assert itself, by ways of the possibility, or the necessity, of narrative formalization. Imitation, to the extent that it pretends to be natural, anthropologically justified to the point of defining the human species and spontaneous, is not formalized in the sense that mathematical language is; it is not entirely independent of the particular content, or substance, of the entity it chooses to represent. One can conceive of certain mimetic constants or even structures but, to the extent that they remain dependent on a reality principle that lies outside them, they resist formalization. It is to be expected, then, that a text like Kleist's, which examines the epistemology of narrative, will engage the themes of mimetic imitation critically. Hence its necessarily theatrical mode, the emphasis on stage and scene; hence, also, the prominence of its critique of mimetic themes and the variety of its narrative stylistics.

For, just as *Jacques le fataliste* is a catalogue of narrative cruxes, *Über das Marionettentheater* condenses, in a very short space, the main stylistic devices by means of which narrative succeeds in both obeying and subverting the mimetic imperative under which it functions. The anecdotes of the ephebe and the bear are told as straightforward diegetic narratives, but the scene that frames them, the dialogue between C and K, is shown as a mimesis and set up, like Rousseau's Preface to *Julie* or like *Le neveu de Rameau*, in the form of a dialogue, with all the possibilities of substitution and exchange this implies. This mimetic model is itself complicated, however, by the constant alternation between direct quotation (pure mimesis, so to speak) and the evasive device of *style indirect libre*. The two modes constantly alternate and intertwine over brief narrative spaces.[9] The result is a deliberate foregrounding of the narrator that reintroduces a diegetic element and weakens the mimesis, exactly in the same way that subjunctive or conditional verb forms weaken the authority of assertions made in the indicative. The resulting narrative pattern is of some complexity: purely diegetic narratives are encased in a mimetic framework which, however, reintroduces its own diegetic components.

The unsettling of mimesis extends to the themes as well as to the style and ironizes the ordinary supports of intelligibility. The first and most obvious of these devices is verisimilitude or plausibility *(Wahrhaftigkeit)* which, in the narrative mode of a dramatized scene of persuasion or instruction, becomes equivalent to the reliability of the narrator. After having told the anything but self-evident story of the fencing bear, C asks:

"Do you believe this story?" "Absolutely, replies K, with enthusiastic approval. Even coming from a stranger, so plausible
it is: and how much more coming from you!" Narrative authority, so it seems, can get away with any degree of absurdity. When K has just completed his almost equally fantastic
tale of the repining ephebe, sentenced to narcissistic paralysis
by critical self-consciousness, he feels compelled to add:
"Someone is still alive today who witnessed this strange and
unfortunate incident and who can confirm it word for word,
just as I told it."

From the moment the narrator appears in the guise of a
witness and recounts the events as a faithful imitation, it takes
another witness to vouchsafe for the reliability of the first and
we are caught at once in an infinite regress. The point is not
that these narratives are devoid of meaning; both are eminently instructive but, like most parables or fables, they are
not likely to occur historically. Yet, to be at all persuasive, they
have to be presented in a historical mode. The mimesis, however, is not historically determined; it is part of an ideal content, of a proof that is not itself in essence historical. The result is an unstable combination of reported and narrated
discourse: the source of trustfulness is not located in the event
(as in an imitation) but in the narrator (as in a diegesis), yet
the narrator can establish his credibility only by way of a mimetic authority that can never be certified. The authentifica-
tion of the diegesis can only proceed mimetically, but this mimesis turns out to be itself diegetically overdetermined.

The problem is a particular version, on the level of narrative, of the necessity and the validity of examples in any
cognitive inquiry, not surprisingly so since narrative itself
functions here as an illustrative example in a demonstration.
When K has finished telling his story, C takes over at once:
"On this occasion, said Herr C in a friendly tone, I must tell
you another story of which you will easily understand how it
belongs here." And he proceeds to tell the story of the bear,
which is not less enigmatic in context than it is by itself. Why
does it belong in this place, after the story of the puppets and

of the ephebe, and how does it relate to the ostensible argument, the superiority of marionettes over real dancers? The answer, if there is one, is certainly not "easily understood." The discrepancy, in fact, is such that one spontaneously reads K's enthusiastic assertion of verisimilitude ironically. Yet every reader will attempt, and probably succeed, in making the anecdote fit the argument, following K's own example when he interprets the figure of the bear as an intermediary stage between the lifeless puppet and an omniscient god.

But can any example ever truly fit a general proposition? Is not its particularity, to which it owes the illusion of its intelligibility, necessarily a betrayal of the general truth it is supposed to support and convey? From the experience of reading abstract philosophical texts, we all know the relief one feels when the argument is interrupted by what we call a "concrete" example. Yet at that very moment, when we think at last that we understand, we are further from comprehension than ever; all we have done is substitute idle talk for serious discourse. Instead of inscribing the particular in the general, which is the purpose of any cognition, one has reversed the process and replaced the understanding of a proposition by the perception of a particular, forgetting that the possibility of such a transaction is precisely the burden of the proposition in the first place. Literary texts by no means take the legitimacy of their considerable illustrative powers for granted. Much rather, like *Über das Marionettentheater*, they will take this problematization for their main concern. In this case, the problematization occurs in the ironic treatment of such devices of narrative persuasion as plausibility and exemplification.

One is left with the three narratives (the puppets, the ephebe, and the bear) as allegories of the wavering status of narrative when compared to the epistemologically sound persuasion of proof. They correspond to three textual models that offer varying degrees of resistance to intelligibility. These models offer different versions of the same theme: aesthetic education as the articulation of history with formally arrived-at truth.

The easiest to understand, least absurd (at least at first sight) of the three stories, despite its hyperbolic assertiveness, is certainly that of the ephebe [the second in order of narration]. One easily enough understands, as K puts it in the general proposition that the story is supposed to illustrate, "what disorders consciousness produces in the natural gracefulness of man." We can all remember personal versions of such a fall from grace, of such loss of innocence. (I for one remember trying to drive down a Swiss street after having just read, in a local newspaper, that for every 100 metres one drives one has at least thirty-six decisions to make. I have never been able to drive gracefully since.) But the moral of K's story does not quite correspond to the conclusion stated by C: whereas the latter speaks of a recovered state of naïveté after an experience of infinite self-consciousness, the young man remains frozen in deadly self-alienation.

The principle of specularity, much in evidence in this story of mirrors (the young man at first catches a fatal glimpse of himself in a mirror and finally pines away, Narcissus-like, staring day after day at his image in a mirror) is not really denounced by this unhappy ending. It might be that the ephebe was not specular enough, that his vanity did not allow him to forget himself to the point of becoming, as it were, his reflection—that he was unable to reach for the infinity of self-consciousness, for the absolute knowledge, that is the necessary condition for a recovered self-presence. Or it might be the narrator-teacher, K himself, who is at fault: after all, he deliberately lies when he breaks the young man's self-assurance by telling him his gracefulness is mere illusion ("I laughed and replied—he must be seeing ghosts!") when, in fact, it is quite genuine.

Both readings lead to sound enough pedagogical conclusions. In the specular model of a text-reader or actor-spectator relationship, the first denounces the reader's unwillingness to become the reflection as well as the object of his own image. As for the lie-detector test applied by the teacher, it would denounce the latter's urge to intervene forcefully in a binary structure that has no room for him. Both are valuable hints but they don't do justice to the complexity of this particular episode. For what K actually tells differs considerably from what he announces, thus supplying another instance of the possible discrepancy between an example and the proposition it is supposed to exemplify.

The scene of the fall from grace is indeed more intricate than the story of self-reflection and self-consciousness. The relationship, in fact, is never simply specular. Since this is an aesthetic education and not a parable of consciousness, what the young man confronts in the mirror is not himself but his resemblance to another. This other, moreover, is not another subject but a work of art, a piece of sculpture susceptible of endless reproduction. It is easy enough for the handsome ephebe to be one more cast, one more *Abguss* in the long series of reproductions of the Spinario figure which, as the text tells us, "are to be found in German collections." If aesthetic education is the imitation of works of art considered as models of beauty or of moral excellence, then it is a rather mechanical process that does not involve a deeper problematization of the self.

This however is not what happens in this case: the young man could have continued his game undisturbed for several years if it had not been for the intervention of a third party, the teacher. Gracefulness was clearly not an end in itself but a device to impress his teacher. When the device fails, he at once loses his talent, not because he has grown self-conscious but because he cannot endure the critical gaze of another in whom his desire for selfhood has been invested. The work of art is only a displaced version of the true model, the judgment of authority. The structure is not specular but triangular. The ensuing clumsiness is the loss of control, the confusion caused by shame. And what the young man is ashamed of is not his lack of grace but the exposure of his desire for self-recognition. As for the teacher's motives in accepting to enter into these displacements of identity, they are even more suspect than those of the younger person, to the precise extent that sadism is morally and socially more suspect than masochism. Socrates (or, for that matter, Winckelmann) certainly had it coming to him.

But is all this bad faith not precisely what the aesthetic, as opposed to the mimetic, specular education, is supposed to avoid? Is its purpose not to fix the attention on the free integrity of the work in order to turn it away from the inevitable lack of integrity in the self? This seems to have been Schiller's entire purpose in substituting the detachment of aesthetic play for the heavy breathing of a self that remains incapable of such disinterestedness. Kleist's story, however, has less to do with self-deluded and self-deluding villains than with the carelessness of classical aestheticians who misread Kant. Their motives are open to the worst of suspicions as well as to the most convincing of excuses, thus making the entire question of intents and motivations a great deal less compelling than the philosophical question from which it derives: the assumed integrity, not of the self, but of the work.

Does K's somewhat cryptic statement of denial (" . . . er sähe wohl Geister!") refer necessarily and exclusively to the young man's vanity in believing that his gracefulness equaled that of the statue? Maybe the delusion was to believe that the model was graceful in the first place. The statue, we are reminded, represents the figure of a young boy who is extracting a splinter from his foot, an action very unlikely to be the least bit graceful or requiring, at the very least, a considerable amount of idealization to be made to appear so. More important still is the fact that the original perfection, the exemplary wholeness of the aesthetic model is itself, however slightly yet unquestionably, impaired. Up till now, we have read the young man's blushing ("er errötete . . .") as mere shame, a wound of the ego, but it now appears that the redness may well be the blood of an injured body. The white, colorless world of statues is suddenly reddened by a flow of blood, however understated. What is not more than the pinprick of a splinter will soon enough grow to a very different order of magnitude.

But, again, is it not the point of aesthetic form that imitates a work of art (ek-phrasis) to substitute the spectacle of pain for the pain itself, and thus sublimate it by drawing away from the pains of experience, focusing instead on the pleasures of imitation? The splinter-extracting ephebe, thus becomes a miniature *Laokoon,* a version of the neo-classical triumph of imitation over suffering, blood, and ugliness. But if this were to be the lesson of the anecdote why then is the wound so carefully hidden from sight that very few commentators, if any, have hinted at the potential ridicule of trying to imitate gracefully someone engaged in minor repairs on his own body. Even if he had been cutting his toenails, it would have been ludicrous, but extracting a splinter . . . !

The point is that the neoclassical trust in the power of imitation to draw sharp and decisive borderlines between reality and imitation, a faculty which, in aesthetic education, becomes the equivalent ability to distinguish clearly between interested and disinterested acts, between desire and play, depends, in the last analysis, on an equally sharp ability to distinguish the work of art from reality. None of the connotations associated with reality can invade art without being neutralized by aesthetic distance. Kleist's story suggests however that this may be a ruse to hide the flaw that marred aesthetic perfection from the start or, in a more perverse reading, to enjoy, under the cover of aesthetic distance, pleasures that have to do with the inflicting of wounds rather than with gracefulness. The scene would be closer to Michel Leiris than to Schiller unless, of course, one is aware of the potentially violent streak in Schiller's own aesthetic theory. If the aesthetic model is itself flawed or, worse, if it covers up this lesion by a self-serving idealization, then the classical concept of aesthetic education is open to suspicion. The theoretical problem, however, has been displaced: from the specular model of the text as imitation, we have moved on to the question of reading as the necessity to decide between signified and referent, between violence on the stage and violence in the streets. The problem is no longer graceful imitation but the ability to

distinguish between actual meaning and the process of signification. This distinction remained concealed in the specular
model in which meaning is taken for granted (the statue *is*
graceful) and in which the semiotics of this meaning, when it
is transposed in the sign-system of dancelike gestures, is made
to correspond unproblematically to its model—although the
crucial difference was signaled in the story: the imitator is
merely drying himself off whereas the original is curing a
wound. The imitation conceals the idealization it performs. The
technique of imitation becomes the hermeneutics of signification. This progression (if it is one) occurs between the stories
of the ephebe and of the bear, between the story of text as a
specular model and text as the locus of transcendental signification.

The third story, narrated by C and enthusiastically decreed to
be *wahrscheinlich* by his interlocutor, is dominated by the figure of a super-reader who reduces the author to near-nothing-
ness. The apparently one-sided balance in favor of reader over
author does not correspond to an actual shift in their respective status. The superiority of reading over writing, as represented by the superiority of the reading bear over the fencing
author, reflects the shift in the concept of text from an imita-
tive to a hermeneutic model. From being openly asserted and
visible in the first case, meaning is concealed in the second and
has to be disclosed by a labor of decoding and interpretation.
This labor then becomes the only raison d'être of a text for
which "reading" is indeed the correct and exhaustive metaphor. This also implies that the relationship between author-
reader and reader-reader now becomes in a very specific sense
antagonistic. For the meaning that has to be revealed is not
just any meaning, but the outcome of a distinction between
intended and stated meaning that it is in the author's interest
to keep hidden. What is at stake is the mastery of the writer
over his text. If the author knows that he produces meaning,
and knows the meaning he produces, his mastery is established. But if this is not the case, if meaning is produced that

he did not intend and if, on the other hand, the intended meaning fails to hit the mark, then he is in difficulty. One consequence of such loss of control over meaning will be that he is no longer able to feign it. For this is indeed the best and perhaps the only proof of his mastery over meaning, that he is free to decree it, at his own will, as genuine or as fake; it takes a stolid realist to believe in the existence of pure, un-feigned fiction. Hence the need to mislead the reader by con-stantly alternating feints with genuine thrusts: the author de-pends on the bewilderment and confusion of his reader to assert his control. Reading is comparable to a battle of wits in which both parties are fighting over the reality or fictionality of their discourse, over the ability to decide whether the text is a fic-tion or an (auto)biography, narrative or history, playful or se-rious.

The status of the reading performance thus remains per-ilously poised between being a simulacrum and being the real thing; fencing is an apt metaphor for this state of affairs. Death is at the center of the action and it is impossible to know at what point the comedy of dying may turn into actual violence, just as it is impossible to know, in a dance, when the display of feigned eroticism may turn into actual copulation. The pos-sibility that this might happen is never entirely absent from spectacles of mock-combat or mock-seduction; it creates the tension between aesthetic contemplation and voyeurism with-out which neither theater nor ballet would be in business.

Kleist puts his own text *en abŷme* in the figure of the super-reader or super-author made invincible by his ability to know feint from what is so aptly called, in German, *Ernstfall;* the words *Ernst* and *ernsthaft* occur prominently at this point in the text. What is at issue is clearly also a matter of economy. The need to assert control by repeatedly testing the ability to tell feint from thrust is eminently wasteful. The entire hermeneu-tic ballet is a display of waste: either we master the text and then we are able but have no need to feint, or we don't and then we are unable to know whether we feint or not. In the first case, interpretation is superfluous and trivial, in the second it is necessary but impossible. Why then indulge in reading (or writing) at all since we are bound to end up looking foolish, like the fencer in the story, or to become the undoer of all pleasure and play, like the bear has become by the end of the story, when he has killed off all possibility for play by scoring whenever he deigns to enter the fray—which he does only out of defensive necessity. No one is hurt, for the bear never attacks, except for the game itself, forever slain in the unequal contest between seriousness and play. Thus Kant would have forever ended the play of philosophy, let alone the play of art, if the project of transcendental philosophy had succeeded in determining once and forever the limits of our faculties and of our freedom. If it were not for the mess of the *Critique of Judgment* and the breakdown of aesthetic theory, we would all be fighting this transcendental bear in vain.

And how about Kleist's own text? By staging the figure of the super-reader, has he himself become like the bear and achieved the infallible discrimination of genuine seriousness—"der Ernst des Bären"—reducing his commentators to a harassed pack of snipers beaten in advance? Can *he* say, for example, with full authority, that his text is or is not autobiographical? The received opinion is that, in this late work, Kleist achieves self-control and recovers "a naive form of heroism"[10] by overcoming a series of crises, victories over "Todeserlebnisse" that can only be compared to as many deaths and resurrections. This is, of course, a very reassuring way to read *Marionettentheater* as a spiritual autobiography and, as we have suggested, it is not entirely compatible with the complications of the tone and the diction.

The only explicit referential mark in the text is the date of the action, given as the winter of 1801. Now 1801 is certainly an ominous moment in a brief life rich in ominous episodes. It is the year when Kleist's self-doubts and hesitations about his vocation culminate in what biographers call his "Kant crisis." It is also the year during which Kleist's engagement to Wilhelmine von Zenge begins to falter and during which he is plagued by doubts similar to those which plagued Kierkegaard in his relationship to Regina and Kafka in his relationship to Felice. Between the two events, the Kant crisis and the forthcoming breach of promise with Wilhelmine (the final break occurred in the spring of 1802), there seems to be a connection which, if only he could understand it, would have relieved Kleist from his never resolved self-desperation. To uncover this link would be the ground of any autobiographical project.

The link actually and concretely existed in the reality of Kleist's history, but it took a somewhat circuitous route. For when Kleist next met his bride-to-be, in 1805 in Königsberg, she was no longer Fräulein Wilhelmine von Zenge but Frau Professor Wilhelmine von Krug. Dr. Wilhelm Traugott Krug was Kant's successor in the latter's chair in philosophy at the University of Königsberg. Kleist, who had wanted to be, in a sense, like Kant and who, one might conjecture, had to give up Wilhelmine in order to achieve this aim, found himself replaced, as husband, by Krug, who also, as teacher philosopher, replaced Kant. What could Kleist do but finish writing, in the same year 1805, a play to be called—what else could it have been—*Der zerbrochene Krug?*

All this, and much more, may have been retained, five more years later, in 1810, when he wrote *Über das Marionettentheater*, in the innocuous-looking notation: winter of 1801. But he may just as well have selected this date at random, as he wrote city of M———, like Mainz, although he was to go to Mainz only in 1803. Who is to say that this notation is random while the other isn't? Who can tell what terrible secrets may be hidden behind this harmless looking letter M? Kleist himself is probably the one least able to tell us and, if he did, we would be well-advised not to take his word for it. To decide whether or not Kleist knew his text to be autobiographical or pure fiction is like deciding whether or not Kleist's destiny, as a person and as a writer, was sealed by the fact that a certain doctor of philosophy happened to bear the ridiculous name of Krug. A story that has so many K's in it (Kant, Kleist, Krug, Kierkegaard, Kafka, K) is bound to be suspicious no matter how one interprets it. Not even Kleist could have dominated such randomly overdetermined confusion. The only place where infallible bears like this one can exist is in stories written by Heinrich von Kleist.

Why did Herr C, once he had discovered, as we can assume he had, that the bear could tell feint from thrust, persist in trying to feint? Could he not have matched the bear's economy of gestures by making all his attacks genuine, forcing the bear to take them seriously? Granted it would have been tiresome, but not more so than the actual situation, and the fatigue would have been shared. Both would have sweated instead of C alone—and, for all we know, he might have scored. Such a commonsensical solution however is logically possible only if one concedes that C is free to choose between a direct and an oblique attack. But this is precisely what has to be proven. It is only a hypothesis, and as long as it has not been verified, C can never unambiguously attack. From the point of view of the bear, who knows everything, he always feints and, as seems indeed to be the case, the bear hardly ever has to make a move at all. From C's own point of view, which is deluded, no thrust ever goes where it is supposed to go. His blows are always off the mark, displaced, deviant, in error, off-target. Such is language: it always thrusts but never scores. It always refers but never to the right referent. The next textual model—actually the first in the order of narration—will have to be that of the text as a system of turns and deviations, as a system of tropes.

The puppets have no motion by themselves but only in relation to the motions of the puppeteer, to whom they are connected by a system of lines and threads. All their aesthetic charm stems from the transformations undergone by the linear motion of the puppeteer as it becomes a dazzling display of curves and arabesques. By itself, the motion is devoid of any aesthetic interest or effect. The aesthetic power is located neither in the puppet nor in the puppeteer but in the text that spins itself between them. This text is the transformational system, the anamorphosis of the line as it twists and turns into the tropes of ellipses, parabola, and hyperbole. Tropes are quantified systems of motion. The indeterminations of imitation and of hermeneutics have at last been formalized into a mathematics that no longer depends on role models or on semantic intentions.

The benefits of this formalization are considerable. They guarantee, among other things, the continuity and the balance that are a necessary condition for beautiful lines and shapes. This is possible because they are once and for all cleansed from the pathos of self-consciousness as well as from the disruptions and ironies of imitation. Unlike drama, the dance is truly aesthetic because it is not expressive: the laws of its motion are not determined by desire but by numerical and geometric laws or topoi that never threaten the balance of grace. For the dancing puppets, there is no risk of affectation (*Ziererei*), of letting the aesthetic effect be determined by the dynamics of the represented passion or emotion rather than by the formal laws of tropes. No two art forms are in this respect more radically opposed than drama and dance.

Balanced motion compellingly leads to the privileged metaphor of a center of gravity; from the moment we have, as the aesthetic implies, a measure of phenomenality, the metaphor of gravity is as unavoidable, in sequential art forms such as narration or dance, as is the metaphor of light in synchronic arts such as, presumably, painting or lyric poetry. The great merit of the puppets, "the outstanding quality one looks for in vain in the large majority of our dancers" is that they follow "the pure law of gravity (das blosse Gesetz der Schwere)."[28] Their motion exists only for the sake of the trope, not the reverse, and this guarantees the consistency and predictability of truly graceful patterns of motion.

On the other hand, it is said of the same puppets, almost in the same breath, that they are *antigrav*, that they can rise and leap, like Nijinsky, as if no such thing as gravity existed for them. The contradiction is far-reaching: if one gallicizes *antigrav* by hearing the French "grave" in "grav," then one can hear in *antigrav* a rejection of the seriousness connoted by *Ge-*

setz der Schwere, in which *Schwere* has all the implications of *Schwermut* and heavy-heartedness. The undecidability between seriousness and play, theme of the story of the bear, would then be resolved in a very Rilkean synthesis of rising and falling. By falling (in all the senses of the term, including the theological Fall) gracefully, one prepares the ascent, the turn from parabola to hyperbole, which is also a rebirth. Caught in the power of gravity, the articulated puppets can rightly be said to be dead, hanging and suspended like dead bodies: gracefulness is directly associated with dead, albeit a dead cleansed of pathos. But it is also equated with a levity, an un-seriousness which is itself based on the impossibility of distinguishing between dead and play. Rather than speaking of a synthesis of rising and falling one should speak of a continuity of the aesthetic form that does not allow itself to be disrupted by the borderlines that separate life from death, pathos from levity, rising from falling. More than Rilke's angel, the puppet inhabits both sides of these borders at the same time.

The text indeed evokes the puppet's dance as a *continuous* motion. A nonformalized, still self-reflexive consciousness—a human dancer as opposed to a puppet—constantly has to interrupt its motions by brief periods of repose that are not part of the dance itself. They are like the parabases of the ironic consciousness which has to recover its energy after each failure by reinscribing the failure into the ongoing process of a dialectic. But a dialectic, segmented by repeated negations, can never be a dance; at the very most, it can be a funeral march. And although a march can resemble a minuet in its structure—theme, trio, theme da capo—it can never come near it in the gracefulness which, in this text, is the necessary condition for aesthetic form. By freeing the tropes of their semantic function, one eliminates the discontinuities of dialectical irony and the teleology of a meaning grounded in the weightiness of conceptual understanding. The aesthetic form "needs the ground only . . . in order to skirt it, to recharge the elasticity of the limbs by momentary friction; we [dancers, that is, that are not puppets] need it in order to *rest* on it." The puppet's ground is not the ground of a stable cognition, but another anamorphosis of the line as it becomes the asymptote of a hyperbolic trope.

Thus conceived, tropes certainly acquire a machinelike, mechanical predictability. They animate the forms like the crank turned by an organ-grinder. This does not prevent the creation of a dialogue between the puppet and the crank-turning puppeteer. Such a dialogue occurs as the visible motions of the puppets are linked to the inner, mental imaginings of the puppeteer by what Kleist calls "the way of the dancer's soul— der Weg der Seele des Tänzers." The "soul" results from the substitution of the machinist's consciousness for the movement of the marionettes, one more substitution added to the transformations that keep the system going. As an affective exchange between subjects, dialogism is the most mechanical of figures; nothing is more mechanical than the overpowering romantic figure of interiorization and self-consciousness. Hegel will say the same thing in a crucial passage from the *Encyclopedia* when he defines thought *(Denken)* as the substitution of *Gedächtnis* (the learning by rote of a conventional code) for *Erinnerung* (interiorization, represented in Kleist's text as the affective response of a consciousness to a mechanically formalized motion).

We have traveled some way from the original Schiller quotation to this mechanical dance, which is also a dance of death and mutilation. The violence which existed as a latent background in the stories of the ephebe and of the bear now moves into full sight. One must already have felt some resistance to the unproblematic reintegration of the puppet's limbs and articulations, suspended in dead passivity, into the continuity of the dance: "all its other members (are) what they should be, dead, mere pendula, and they follow the law of pure gravity."

The passage is all the harder to assimilate since it has been preceded by the briskly told story of an English technician able to build such perfect mechanical legs that a mutilated man will be able to dance with them in Schiller-like perfection. "The circle of his motions may be restricted, but as for those available to them, he accomplishes them with an ease, elegance and gracefulness which fills any thinking mind with amazement." One is reminded of the protest of the eyeless philosopher Saunderson in Diderot's *Lettre sur les aveugles* when, to the deistic optimism of the Reverend Holmes, disciple of Newton, Leibniz, and Clarke, he opposes the sheer monstrosity of his own being, made all the more intolerable by the mathematical perfection of his highly formalized intellect: "Look at me well, Mr. Holmes, I have no eyes. . . . The order (of the universe) is not so perfect that it does not allow, from time to time, for the production of monsters."[11] The dancing invalid in Kleist's story is one more victim in a long series of mutilated bodies that attend on the progress of enlightened self-knowledge, a series that includes Wordsworth's mute country-dwellers and blind city-beggars. The point is not that the dance fails and that Schiller's idyllic description of a graceful but confined freedom is aberrant. Aesthetic education by no means fails; it succeeds all too well, to the point of hiding the violence that makes it possible.

But one should avoid the pathos of an imagery of bodily mutilation and not forget that we are dealing with textual models, not with the historical and political systems that are their correlate. The disarticulation produced by tropes is primarily a disarticulation of meaning; it attacks semantic units such as words and sentences. When, in the concluding lines of Kleist's text, K is said to be "ein wenig zerstreut," then we are to read, on the strength of all that goes before, *zerstreut* not only as distracted but also as dispersed, scattered, and dismembered. The ambiguity of the word then disrupts the fluid continuity of each of the preceding narratives. And when, by the end of the tale, the word *Fall* has been overdetermined in a manner that stretches it from the theological Fall to the dead pendulum of the puppet's limbs to the grammatical declension of nouns and pronouns (what we call, in English, the grammatical *case*), then any composite word that includes *Fall* (*Beifall, Sündenfall, Rückfall* (§46) or *Einfall*) acquires a disjunctive plurality of meanings.

C's story of the puppets, for instance, is said to be more

than a random improvisation: "die Äeusserung schien mir, durch die Art, wie er sie vorbrachte, mehr als ein blosser *Einfall . . ."* As we know from another narrative text of Kleist,[12] the memorable tropes that have the most success *(Beifall)* occur as mere random improvisation *(Einfall)* at the moment when the author has completely relinquished any control over his meaning and has relapsed *(Zurückfall)* into the extreme formalization, the mechanical predictability of grammatical declensions *(Fälle)*.

But *Fälle*, of course, also means in German "trap," the trap which is the ultimate textual model of this and of all texts, the trap of an aesthetic education which inevitably confuses dismemberment of language by the power of the letter with the gracefulness of a dance. This dance, regardless of whether it occurs as mirror, as imitation, as history, as the fencing match of interpretation, or as the anamorphic transformations of tropes, is the ultimate trap, as unavoidable as it is deadly.

Notes

Preface

1. Theodor W. Adorno, *Aesthetische Theorie* in *Gesammelte Schriften*, (Frankfurt am Main, 1970), vol. 7. See also "Parataxis: Zur späten Lyrik Hölderlins," in *Noten zur Literatur* (Frankfurt am Main, 1965), 3:156–209.

2. Erich Auerbach, *Mimesis: The Representation of Reality in Western Literature* (Princeton: Princeton University Press, 1953).

1. Intentional Structure of the Romantic Image

1. The line is ambiguous, depending on whether one gives the verb "entstehn" a single or a double subject. It can mean: words will originate that are like flowers ("Worte, die wie Blumen sind, müssen dafür entstehn"). But the meaning is much richer if one reads it: words will have to originate in the same way that flowers originate ("Worte müssen dafür entstehn wie Blumen entstehn"). Syntax and punctuation allow for both readings.

2. The Image of Rousseau in the Poetry of Hölderlin

1. "[Die] Beziehungen [zwischen Rousseau und Hölderlin] klarzulegen, ist eine der, auch für die allgemeine Kulturgeschichte, für die historische Grundlage des Begriffes Romantik, wichtigsten unter den anzustellenden Einzeluntersuchungen." Hölderlin, *Sämtliche Werke*, Propyläen-Ausgabe (Berlin, 1923), 4:327.

2. In his commentary on the ode "Rousseau," Friedrich Beissner gives some bibliographical information. Hölderlin, *Sämtliche Werke: Grosse Stuttgarter Ausgabe*, Friedrich Beissner, ed. (Stuttgart: W. Kohlhammer, 1943ff.), henceforth cited as *St. A.* A good example of the way Rousseau is treated in German studies is Ernst Müller, *Hölderlin. Studien zur Geschichte seines Geistes* (Stuttgart, 1944), pp. 100ff. The French works on Hölderlin by Pierre Bertaux and E. Tonnelat are hardly more explicit. There are some indications, relating mostly to the work of Hölderlin's youth, in G. Bianquis, "Hölderlin et la Révolution française," *Études germaniques* (1952), 7:105–116, T. Claverie, *La Jeunesse de Hölderlin* (Paris, 1921) and Maurice Delorme, *Hölderlin et la Révolution française* (Monaco: Ed. du Rocher, 1959). There are some very valuable sugges-

tions in Jean Starobinski, *Jean-Jacques Rousseau. La transparence et l'obstacle* (Paris: Plon, 1957), pp. 327–332, and elsewhere.

3. A passage from the *Social Contract* (Book 3, ch. 12), which serves as the epigraph to the "Hymn to Humanity" (1791), the ode entitled "Rousseau" (1799), and strophes 10-11-12 of the hymn "Der Rhein."

4. Heinz Otto Burger, "Die Hölderlin-Forschung der Jahre 1940–1955," *Deutsche Vierteljahrschrift* (1956), 30:185–222, or, in the former pagination of the journal, pp. 329–366. Bernhard Böschenstein, in *Hölderlins Rheinhymne* (Zürich: Atlantis, 1959), is of the same opinion (p. 150). Since then the most important treatment is, to my knowledge, that of Kurt Wais, "Rousseau et Hölderlin," *Annales de la Société Jean-Jacques Rousseau* (1959–1962), 35:287–308. Nevertheless, this study falls short of H. O. Burger's.

5. One must distinguish between the German literary studies and the philosophical studies. Following their master, the neo-Kantian philosophers have always treated Rousseau with the greatest respect, but they have primarily been concerned with the political part of his work. See, for example, the excellent article by Ernst Cassirer on the Second Discourse, "Das Problem J.-J. Rousseau," in *Archiv für Geschichte der Philosophie*, 1932.

6. The same thing is even more true in England and in America, where Rousseau is often little appreciated. A work as completely negative as that of Irving Babbitt, *Rousseau and Romanticism* (Boston, 1919), could not have had a comparable influence in Germany.

7. Hence I will not treat—except for some brief allusions—the very important implicit presence of Rousseau in *Hyperion* and in the versions of *Empedokles*; in both cases the similarity to the problematic described in the present essay is striking.

8. Schiller, *Werke*, Nationalausgabe (Weimar, 1962), 20:469.

9. ". . . in dem Ideale, das er von der Menschheit aufstellt (ist) auf die Schranken derselben zuviel, auf ihr Vermögen zu wenig Rücksicht genommen, und überall (ist) mehr ein Bedürfniß nach physischer Ruhe als nach moralischer Übereinstimmung darin sichtbar." Schiller, 20:451–452.

10. One example among many is the following passage by a specialist in German idealist philosophy: Johannes Hoffmeister. Speaking of Rousseau, he writes: "Aber dies beides, die Kulturkritik und das Naturrechtdenken, die Rückkehr zur Natur und der Fortschritt zur Freiheit, das steht bei ihm fast beziehungslos nebeneinander." *Die Heimkehr des Geistes, Studien zur Dichtung und Philosophie der Goethezeit* (Hameln, 1946), p. 224. Böschenstein's judgment seems to me to be also completely determined by Schiller's critique of Rousseau.

11. With the exception of H. O. Burger, "Die Hölderlin-Forschung," who nevertheless does not develop his point of view.

12. Norbert von Hellingrath, *Hölderlin-Vermächtnis*, 2. Auflage (München, 1944), p. 135.

13. "Der Kern von Hölderlins Rousseaubild im 'Rhein' [ist] der Verzicht auf Aktivität, um reines Gefäß der größeren Naturkräfte zu sein . . . Rousseau löscht allen Eindrang seines Innern aus, auch das Denken, um nur noch den gleichmäßigen Puls der Schöpfung zu vernehmen." Bernhard Böschenstein, *Hölderlins Rheinhymne*, p. 91.

14. Kurt Wais, "Rousseau et Hölderlin," pp. 304–306, and 307–308.

15. First noted, I believe, by H. O. Burger, "Die Hölderlin-Forschung," pp. 219/363. Friedrich Beissner, in "Hölderlins letzte Hymne," *Hölderlin-Jahrbuch* (1948/49), pp. 66–102, did not point out the parallel with the Fifth Rêverie.

16. French criticism devoted to Rousseau is far from arriving at agreement on this question, even in the most recent works. The work of Jean Starobinski (*Jean-Jacques Rousseau*) has contributed much to clarify this problem, but he often still insists on the unhistorical character of Rousseau's thought. See, for example, ch. 3, "La Solitude," and also the discussion following the lecture of Kurt Wais, *Annales*, 35:309. This is a point on which an in-depth study of the relation between Hölderlin and Rousseau could be useful, especially if one also takes Hegel into consideration. At the time of writing, the announced volume of the political writings in the Pléiade edition had not yet appeared.

17. "Oh come! in the depths of the mountain world the secret of our hearts will rest like the precious stone in the mine; in the bosom of woods that tower to the sky we shall be as among the pillars of the inmost temple, where the godless draw not near; and we shall sit by the spring, and behold our world in it—sky and house and garden and ourselves. On a clear night we shall often wander in our orchard's shade and listen for the loving god in us, while the plant raises its bowed head from its midday sleep, and the still life of your flowers is refreshed when they bathe their tender arms in the dew and the night air breathes its penetrating coolness around them, and above us the meadow of the sky blooms with all its twinkling flowers, and to one side the moon behind westerly clouds shyly imitates the setting of the youthful sun as if for love of him—. . ." Friedrich Hölderlin, *Hyperion*, Willard R. Trask, tr. (New York: Frederick Ungar, 1965), p. 144.

18. We know that Hölderlin intended to contribute an article on "Rousseau as author of the Héloïse" (among other literary essays) to the journal *Iduna* that he tried, in vain, to found. See the letter to Neuffer of June 4, 1799, *St. A.*, 6(1):323. Kurt Wais (p. 297) makes some pertinent remarks about Rousseau's influence in *Hyperion*, but without beginning to exhaust the subject.

19. See *St. A.*, 1(2):392. Comparing this poem to "The Rhine," Friedrich Beissner notes quite correctly the subtle sliding movement that leads, already in the work of youth, to the identification of Hölderlin with Rousseau. His remarks on the relation between action and reverie in "An die Stille" are discussed below.

20. "An die Ruhe" is much closer to the later poems on Rousseau; as in "Rousseau" and in "The Rhine" sleep is here an awaiting (ll. 27–28) in the anticipation of an ideally projected future (ll. 14ff.; cf. "Rousseau," strophes 9–10). The heroic element is present only in the background, in the Virgilian simile of the second strophe; the "I" who becomes "he" before becoming Rousseau awakes from repose not in order to enter into combat but in order to isolate himself in his hut (ll. 21–22) and there to worship tranquillity. The explicit presence of Rousseau seems always to entail a deepening of the notion of repose.

21. ". . . die Anspannung und Sammlung aller Kräfte zu der desto wirksameren Leistung." *St. A.*, 1(2):392.

22. "Bei ihr [die Poesie] sammelt sich der Mensch, und sie giebt ihm Ruhe, . . . wo alle Kräfte regsam sind, und nur wegen ihrer innigen Harmonie nicht als thätig erkannt werden." *St. A.*, 6(1):305. This text is also a direct echo of Schiller.

23. In the "cool shroud" of "An die Stille" and in the allusion to Rousseau's tomb at the end of "An die Ruhe" which is put on the same level as the regenerative activity of repose. One would be wrong, in my view, to interpret these passages as opening, in some sense, to death, to a non-being that would constitute one of the poles of Hölderlin's poetic world. In that case, the antinomy of life and death (to which, on

another level, the antinomy of good and evil corresponds) would never be leveled in his work; this is the conclusion of, for example, Walter Rehm in "Tiefe und Abgrund in Hölderlins Dichtung," *Hölderlin-Gedenkschrift* (Tübingen, 1943), pp. 70–133; see also *Orpheus. Der Dichter und die Toten*, p. 195. He sees Hölderlin as torn, until the end, between two irreconcilable conceptions of depth, one benevolent and creative ("*gnadenvoll schaffend*") and the other maleficent and ruinous ("*dämonisch verwirrend*") ("Tiefe und Abgrund," p. 117). Without any polemical intention, the thesis of the present essay disagrees on many points with that of Rehm. In contrast to what happens in many Romantic and post-Romantic poets, death for Hölderlin—and for Rousseau—is not at all an absolute, but a moment in the dialectic of existence. This dialectic is for him not the dialectic of being and non-being but of immediate presence and mediation. See also n. 33 below on Hölderlin's non-satanism. An extended study of the question would have to base itself on the thematics of death and evil in the work of Hölderlin.

24. Where the action is no longer directed toward Greece but toward contemporary Germany.

25. *St. A.*, 2(2):403 and 677.

26. That the identification of Hölderlin with Rousseau is particularly strong is corroborated by the close link, already indicated by Hellingrath, between the autobiographical poem "An die Deutschen" and the fragment "Rousseau."

27. ". . . das Unendliche / . . . er faßt es nie. / Doch lebts *in ihm* und gegenwärtig, / . . ." "Rousseau," ll. 21–23.

28. This fulfillment is distinguished very precisely from the eternal harmony of the "Hymne an die Menschheit." Soon after it is compared to storms ("*Gewittern*") in the plural; this *Vollendung* signifies the moments, the articulations, of consciously understood historical becoming (and not the "end of history" in a Hegelian sense).

29. This premonition ("*Ahnen*") linked to the notion of interpretation amounts to a poetic definition of what Heidegger, since *Sein und Zeit*, 1(5):§32, calls the hermeneutic circle. His own commentaries on Hölderlin are nothing but a demonstration of this notion. On this subject see the helpful article by Alexander Gelley, "Staiger, Heidegger, and the Task of Criticism," *Modern Language Quarterly* (September 1962), 23(3):195–216.

30. Bernhard Böschenstein, *Hölderlins Rheinhymne*. The method that proceeds by establishing the meaning of certain key terms on the basis of their recurrence appears incontestably to be most fruitful in the case of Hölderlin, especially when Böschenstein applies it tactfully, for instance in making the rate of recurrence itself an expressive factor. All the same, it is regrettable that he chose arbitrarily to limit the field of his inquiry to the texts after 1800; it is true that before this date Hölderlin's vocabulary is no doubt less stable than in the later works, but it is no less true that the explanatory value of certain terms when they appear in the work of youth goes beyond that which they have later (and an example of this can be found in n. 52 below). The simple synchronic cross-section of this method should be replaced by the history of the genesis of principal terms. These general remarks do not at all lessen the value of the result obtained for the first section of the poem, the one that deals with the Rhine strictly speaking. The many other interpretations of "The Rhine" (Allemann, Hof, Mittner, etc.) are further from our point of view than Böschenstein.

31. One should reiterate that this contact is not necessarily the act of a consciousness. It takes place for the Rhine, which is not at all to be taken as a metaphor or an

analogical symbol, as well as for Rousseau, in the behavior of the former as well as in the knowledge of the latter. There is no trace of anthropomorphism in Hölderlin, but, insofar as earthly destiny is concerned, a perfect equality between the inanimate object that is the river and a human consciousness. His poetry passes from one to the other with utter ease, without considering these transitions in the least strange or in any way related to the baroque *concetto*. The distinctions between the Rhine and Rousseau come later.

32. Böschenstein, *Hölderlins Rheinhymne*, pp. 67–68.

33. This neo-Hellenic Prometheus, then, has nothing of Milton's Satan, whom contemporary sensibility interprets as the hero whose *mal* is self-consciousness. Hölderlin's pietistic heritage prevents him at all times from losing himself in this kind of existential Manichaeism which is already present in Blake and which is called upon to take such an important place in Romantic and post-Romantic poetry and thought. Whatever certain interpreters may think, for Hölderlin the problem of evil is not central; the real danger comes rather from an excess of abandon to the sacred (see also n. 23).

34. A first version of this passage is particularly clear in this regard. See *St. A.*, "Lesarten," 2(2):726, Müller, *Hölderlin*, p. 123ff. and also Böschenstein, p. 78.

35. See the letter to Hegel of January 26, 1795, *St. A.*, 6(1):155.

36. The reasons why "fühlen" should be translated by "sentiment" rather than by "sensation" are developed below.

37. Hellingrath, *Hölderlin-Vermächtnis*, 4:347, wrongly opposes "Söhne der Erde" (l. 150) to "sterblicher Mann" (l. 154). But in doing so he is no more and no less in error than Böschenstein when he interprets "Drum überraschet es auch / Und schrökt den sterblichen Mann," as a defeat.

38. Böschenstein's remarks on the cosmology of the elements in Hölderlin are excellent (p. 139 and others). See also Martin Heidegger, "Hölderlins Erde und Himmel," *Hölderlin-Jahrbuch* (1958–1960), 11:17–39.

39. On account of his restrictive interpretation of Rousseau in this passage, Böschenstein is forced to devalue the importance of the "Brautfest" in order to make a too hasty and unfounded comparison to the celebration of "Friedensfeier." The importance that Hölderlin himself attaches to this metaphor in his description of the poem's structure would suffice to contradict this interpretation. It is not false to see a gradation leading from Rousseau to Socrates in the last section of the poem, but certainly not, as Böschenstein thinks, at the expense of Rousseau.

40. J.-J. Rousseau, *Oeuvres complètes*, Gagnebin and Raymond, ed. (Paris: Bibliothèque de la Pléiade, 1962), p. 1,045.

41. See Marcel Raymond, notes to the *Rêveries*, *Œuvres complètes*, p. 1,798, and *Jean-Jacques Rousseau. La quête de soi et la Rêverie* (Paris: Corti, 1962), pp. 215ff., and Georges Poulet, *Études sur le temps humain*, 1re série (Paris: Plon, 1949), pp. 158ff. After more than a century of erroneous interpretations, Raymond and Poulet have made some definitive observations about these pages. For both critics it is still a question of a "conjunction of two original elements: inner feeling and pure sense perception [*sentiment intime et pure sensation*]" (Poulet, p. 193). The movement in Rousseau's text seems to me nevertheless to go dialectically from "pure sensation" to "sentiment intime," so that it is a matter of going beyond mere sense perception in a Hegelian sense (*Aufhebung*) here. This is certainly the movement in the Fifth *Rêverie*, where Rousseau speaks at first of a joint action of sense perception ("le bruit continu [de l'eau] frap-

pant sans relâche mon oreille et mes yeux") and the internal movements of reverie. But the more the text develops, the more clearly it indicates that what reveals itself in this way is precisely not the object, the cause of sense perception, but "nothing that is outside itself *(rien d'extérieur à soi)"* (p. 1,047). It seems, then, that the expression "to fix my senses" ought to be read as a going beyond sense perception, a lifting of that superficial eyelid Nerval speaks of: "Et comme un œil naissant couvert par ses paupières / Un pur esprit s'accroit sous l'écorce des pierres!" ("Vers dorés"). The present essay is trying to demonstrate that Hölderlin at least reads Rousseau in this way. In fact, when one looks more closely, Georges Poulet's study describes this dialectic with admirable precision, culminating in the conclusion that in Rousseau sense perception "is only the passive element that binds being to matter, whereas [the inner sentiment] is the active element par excellence, the side of spirit, the true I" (p. 192).

42. Müller, *Hölderlin*, p. 21. Hölderlin also owned an *Allgemeines Repertorium für empirische Psychologie* from 1792.

43. When in reality it is founded on the priority of heroic action over inner thought, an "error" to be distinguished from the ontic-ontological confusion that is in question here. The Greeks were destroyed, but they did not lose contact with the source.

44. In Starobinski's sense of "transparent." I can only indicate in passing that in Wordsworth's central passages on imagination (especially in the *Prelude*), the sound of water has exactly the same poetic function. Wordsworth's "Imagination" is quite similar to the "sentiment of existence" in Rousseau and to Hölderlin's "sweet talent to hear"—but of course this cannot be demonstrated quickly.

45. Dedicated to Heinse (and then altered after his death), the first version of the final strophe of "The Rhine" says it very clearly: "Du aber . . . schauest die Erde / Und das Licht an, ungleich scheinet das Paar, denkst du / Doch göttlich beide . . ." *St. A.*, 2(2):729.

46. A superiority which manifests itself in an act of protective love. In "The Rhine," the earth is characterized by this theme of love (". . . wie die Mutter, / Alliebend . . ."). The theme of love, which we will not develop here, is closely linked to the fundamental theme of consciousness.

47. This is so obvious for Hölderlin that he has no difficulty in fusing the figures of Rousseau and Bonaparte. Like his friends Hegel and Schelling, he sees Bonaparte (in any case until the peace of Lunéville) as the culmination of the French Revolution. He is like the practical side of Rousseauist ideality. With this aspect of his thought, which he shares with a number of his contemporaries, Hölderlin appears as one of the founders of the ideological conception of history, which, since Romanticism, holds sway in the world.

48. As is known, it is in this universality of consciousness that Hölderlin finds the Dionysian character of Rousseau, a Dionysus who has nothing in common with the Dionysian spirit of the *Birth of Tragedy* (rather Hölderlin's "earth" would be the Apollinian spirit of Nietzsche, while his Apollo—the fire from heaven—resembles in a number of traits Nietzsche's Dionysus). This relation between Dionysus ("Gemeingeist") and Rousseau's "volonté générale," which gains its final expression in the collective festival, has been well depicted by Böschenstein, paralleling Starobinski (Böschenstein, pp. 86 and 148). See also Kurt Wais, p. 306, n. 1. The thematics that leads from Rousseau to Dionysus takes in a number of other poems and therefore goes outside the bounds of this article.

49. As several interpreters have pointed out, Herakles is present throughout the

poem, but only in the background. Since I am not at all presenting an exegesis of the poem in its entirety, it is not necessary to develop this theme. All the same, in Hölderlin the presence of Dionysus and Herakles signifies almost necessarily the presence of Christ. The relationship between Rousseau and Christ can be approached only on the basis of the hymns "Der Einzige" and "Patmos" and is therefore far beyond our present objective.

50. Following Böschenstein, one should read "vergessen" as an active verb, not as passive. Thus translated literally: "The best seems to him / To be almost completely forgetting / There where the ray does not burn . . ." and not "almost completely forgotten."

51. "Der 'sterbliche Mann' der sich in sein Unvermögen zurückzieht." Böschenstein, p. 107.

52. The symbol of this rebirth is the nightingale (l. 165) which already appeared at the end of *Hyperion* in a passage that is a striking parallel to this strophe of "The Rhine": "Bellarmin! Ich hatt' es nie so ganz erfahren, jenes alte feste Schiksaalswort, daß eine neue Seeligkeit dem Herzen aufgeht, wenn es aushält, und die Mitternacht des Grams durchduldet, und daß, wie Nachtigallgesang im Dunkeln, göttlich erst in tiefem Laid das Lebenslied der Welt uns tönt. Denn, wie mit Genien, lebt' ich izt mit den blühenden Bäumen, und die klaren Bäche, die darunter flossen, säußelten, wie Götterstimmen, mir den Kummer aus dem Busen . . . etc." *St. A.*, 3:157. One should quote almost the entire final letter of the novel.

53. These lines have been the occasion for a polemic in which the main interpreters of Hölderlin have taken part. See H. O. Burger, "Die Hölderlin-Forschung," pp. 363–364. Our interpretation quite clearly sets itself apart from that of Beissner (still followed by Böschenstein and Wais) for whom the passage marks a momentary error that Hölderlin immediately corrects (in which case, one may ask, what would be the function of such a self-critique in the very tight structure of the last hymns?). But our interpretation also sets itself apart from that of K. Kerenyi, "Hölderlins Vollendung," in *Hölderlin-Jahrbuch* (1954), pp. 25–45, for whom this moment represents a direct contact with the divine—we see it rather as a retreat before the threat of this contact. We also separate ourselves from Rehm ("Tiefe und Abgrund in Hölderlins Dichtung," p. 120) for whom the passage marks some sort of self-abandonment, eyes closed, to the depth of the divine. None of these interpretations can be dismissed on the basis of the local detail of syntax or meaning; the divergencies therefore spring from the interpreters' total conceptions of Hölderlin's poetic project. I would simply indicate that the verb "sich wiegen lassen" maintains, in a somewhat muted form, the movement of oscillation in the preceding line between the past and the future. Hence it designates precisely the internalization of the temporal "ec-stasis" in the reverie: the rhythm causes a "forgetting" of time, without nevertheless effacing it. "*Fast* vergessen . . ." says Hölderlin in "The Rhine" and in his great poem on memory: "Es nehmet aber / Und giebt Gedächtniß die See, . . ." ("Andenken," ll. 55–56). Historical memory is also a dialectic of mediation and immediacy.

3. *Wordsworth and Hölderlin*

1. Wordsworth, *The Prelude*, Ernest de Selincourt, ed.; rev. ed., Helen Darbishire, ed. (Oxford: Clarendon, 1959). All citations are from the 1805 manuscript un-

less otherwise indicated, and are henceforth cited in the text by volume and line nos. only.

2. Wordsworth and Coleridge, *Lyrical Ballads 1798*, W. J. B. Owen, ed., 2d ed. (Oxford: Oxford University Press, 1969), p. 167.

3. *The Prose Works of William Wordsworth*, W. J. B. Owen and Jane Worthington Smyser, eds. (Oxford: Clarendon, 1974), 3:32.

4. Friedrich Hölderlin, *Sämtliche Werke—Grosse Stuttgarter Ausgabe*, Friedrich Beissner, ed. (Stuttgart: W. Kohlhammer, 1943ff.), 2(1):195, ll. 14–15. All citations are from this volume, and are henceforth cited in the text by page and line numbers only.

4. Autobiography As De-Facement

1. Gérard Genette, *Figures III* (Paris: Editions du Seuil, 1972), p. 50.

2. For a critical edition of these essays, see W. J. B. Owen and Jane Worthington Smyser, eds., *The Prose Works of William Wordsworth* (Oxford: Clarendon, 1974). Page numbers cited in text refer to Owen, ed., *Wordsworth's Literary Criticism* (London: Routledge & Kegan Paul, 1974).

5. Wordsworth and the Victorians

1. Frederick W. H. Myers, *Wordsworth* (London, 1881). Myers, who taught at Cambridge University, was a friend and associate of Henry Sidgwick, the founder of an influential group interested in the phenomena of Spiritualism. Myers wrote his book on Wordsworth in his later, more sedate years. On Frederick Myers' rather tempestuous life and career see Alan Gauld, *The Founders of Psychical Research* (New York: Schocken, 1968).

2. Myers, p. 123.

3. In G. M. Harper, *William Wordsworth, His Life, Works and Influence*, 2 vols. (London, 1916). Harper was the first to have access to documents which were not available to the main earlier biographer Emile Legouis, *La Jeunesse de William Wordsworth—1770–1798* (Paris, 1896, translated into English in 1897). Legouis later devoted an entire book, *William Wordsworth and Annette Vallon* (London, 1922), to the episode in the poet's life.

4. F. W. Bateson, *Wordsworth, A Re-Interpretation* (London: Longmans, 1954).

5. Geoffrey Hartman, "Words, Wish, Worth: Wordsworth," in Harold Bloom et al., *Deconstruction and Criticism* (New York: Continuum, 1979), p. 205.

6. Leslie Stephen, "Wordsworth's Ethics," *Cornhill Magazine* (1876), 34:206. Reprinted in *Hours in a Library*, 3d (London, 1879).

7. Matthew Arnold, ed., *Poems of Wordsworth* (London, 1879).

8. The line from "Resolution and Independence" describing the leech gatherer as "The oldest man he seemed that ever wore grey hairs" can serve as one good example among many.

9. As becomes quite apparent in the parallelism of the "two roads" which Meyer Abrams finds in twentieth-century Wordsworth interpretation. See the introduction to *Wordsworth: A Collection of Critical Essays*, M. H. Abrams, ed. (Englewood Cliffs, N.J.: Prentice-Hall, 1972).

10. Now in William Empson, *The Structure of Complex Words* (Totowa, N.J.: Rowman, 1979), pp. 289–305.

11. "Preface of 1815" (to the *Lyrical Ballads*) in *The Prose Works of William Wordsworth*, W. J. B. Owen and Jane Worthington Smyser, eds. (Oxford: Clarendon, 1974), 3:31.

12. Quotations from *The Prelude* are all from the 1805 version unless otherwise indicated.

13. The fact that "the face of earth and heaven" is that of a "prime teacher" adds complexities that cannot here be dealt with.

14. The reading of "eye" as displacing "breast" resurfaces in the 1850 version

> who, with his soul
> *Drinks* in the feelings of his Mother's eye!
>
> (II.237, my emphasis)

6. Shelley Disfigured

1. All the quotations from *The Triumph of Life* are from the critical edition established by Donald H. Reiman, *Shelley's "The Triumph of Life," A Critical Study* (Urbana: University of Illinois Press, 1965). Together with G. M. Matthews' edition, " 'The Triumph of Life': A New Text" in *Studia Neophilologica* (1960), 32:271–309, this edition is authoritative. On the complex history of the text's composition and publication, see Reiman, pp. 119–28.

2. The passage appears in Appendix C in Reiman, p. 241:

> Nor mid the many shapes around him [Napoleon] chained
> Pale with the toil of lifting their proud clay
>
> Or those gross dregs of it which yet remained
> Out of the grave to which they tend, should I
> Have sought to *mark* any who may *have* stained
>
> Or have adorned the doubtful progeny
> Of the new birth of this new tide of time
> In which our fathers lived and we shall die
>
> Whilst others tell our sons in prose or rhyme
> The manhood of the child; unless my guide
> Had said, "Behold Voltaire—We two would climb
>
> "Where Plato and his pupil, side by side,
> Reigned from the *center to the circumference*
> Of thought; till Bacon, great as either, spied
>
> "The spot on which they met and said, 'From hence
> I soar into a loftier throne.'—But I—
> O World, who from full urns dost still dispense,
>
> "Blind as thy fortune, fame and infamy—
> I who sought both, prize neither *now*; I find
> What names have died within thy memory,
>
> "Which ones still live; I know the place assigned
> To such as sweep the threshold of the fane
> Where truth and its inventors sit enshrined.—
>
> "And if I sought those joys which now are pain,
> If he is captive to the car of life,
> *'Twas that we feared our labour would be vain.*"

3. One can confront, for example, the following statements: "The bleak facts, however, are narrated with the verve of a poet who has tapped new sources of creative strength, and Shelley's dream-vision is set in the frame of a joyous morning in spring. The poem leaps into being, at once adducing a simile which is far from despairing." Meyer H. Abrams, *Natural Supernaturalism*, 1971, p. 441. And "I find the

attempts of some critics [of *The Triumph*] to envision its potential climax as joyous and optimistic and its title as indicative of such a conclusion to be very mistaken." Harold Bloom, *Shelley's Mythmaking*, 1959, p. 223.

4. There is considerable disagreement, among the critics of *The Triumph*, on the importance and the valorization of this passage, as there is much disagreement about the importance of Rousseau as a source of the poem—next to Dante, Spenser, Milton (*Comus*), Wordsworth, etc. Generally speaking, the interpreters who dismiss the importance of Rousseau also tend to interpret the figure of the "shape all light" as unambiguously nefarious; see, for instance, H. Bloom, pp. 267–70 or J. Rieger, *The Mutiny Within: The Heresies of P. B. Shelley* (New York: 1967) and, on the obverse side of the question and among several others, Carlos Baker, *Shelley's Major Poetry* (Princeton: Princeton University Press, 1948), pp. 264–68 or, in a different vein, Kenneth Neill Cameron, *Shelley, The Golden Years* (Cambridge: Harvard University Press, 1974). Cameron sees the scene of the shape's trampling Rousseau's thought into dust as "not destruction, but rebirth" (p. 467). Reiman, who stresses and documents the importance of Rousseau more than other readers, and whose conviction that the shape is Julie is so strong that he even finds her name inscribed in the manuscript, reads the figure as a figure of love and includes her in his claim that "Everywhere, in *The Triumph*, the dark side of human experience is balanced by positive alternatives" (p. 84). It is perhaps naive to decide on a clear valorization on this level of rhetorical complexity; one would have to determine for what function of language the shape is a figure before asking whether an alternative to its function is even conceivable.

5. Reiman (p. 67) correctly refers to a "sandy beach" but his commitment to a positive interpretation leads to irrelevant considerations on assumedly alternating movements of good and evil. The suggestion of a desert (rather than the "desert shore" of l. 164) is implicit in all commentators who quote l. 400 ("And suddenly my brain became as sand . . .") without the ensuing context of shore and waves.

6. Compare the landscape of aging in *Alastor*:

> And nought but gnarled roots of ancient pines
> Branchless and blasted, clenched with grasping roots
> The unwilling soil. A gradual change was here,
> Yet ghastly. For, as fast years flow away,
> The smooth brow gathers, and the hair grows thin
> And white, and where irradiate dewy eyes
> Had shone, gleam stony orbs. . . .

(ll. 530–36)

7. Shelley's consistently very high opinion of Rousseau is supported by the references to Rousseau in his writings and correspondence. For a brief summary of this question, see for example K. N. Cameron, p. 648. The Rousseau text Shelley most admired is *Julie*.

8. On Shelley's Platonism, see James A. Notopoulos, *The Platonism of Shelley* (Durham, N.C.: Duke University Press, 1949) which abundantly documents Shelley's extensive involvement with the Platonic tradition but fails to throw light on the most difficult passages of *The Triumph of Life*. The ambivalent treatment of Plato in *The Triumph* is read by Notopoulos as a denunciation of homosexuality.

9. "In the April prime / . . . . . / I found myself asleep / Under a mountain. . . ." The condition of being alive is also referred to as "that hour of rest" (l. 320) and Shelley refers to "a sleeping mother . . ." (l. 321) and "no other sleep" that will quell the ills of existence.

10. One may wish to read, against common usage, the verb to glimmer with full transitive force: the veil of light *glimmers* the hills. . . .

11. The same construction recurs later on, this time with reversed emphasis, measure insisting against the melodies of the "sweet tune":

> And still her feet, no less than the sweet tune
> To which they moved, seemed as they moved, to blot
> The thoughts of him who gazed on them. . . .

(ll. 382–84)

12. See also, in the *Hymn of Apollo*:

> I am the eye with which the Universe
> Beholds itself and knows itself divine. . . .

(ll. 31–32)

The sunrise of *The Triumph* and that of the *Hymn* (1820) differ to the precise extent that the identification sun/eye is no longer absolute in the later poem.

13. As in an otherwise similar scene in Mallarmé's *Hérodiade*, where the emphasis falls on the hardness of the mirror as frozen water:

> O miroir!
> Eau froide par l'ennui dans ton cadre gelée. . . .

14. When the shape's hair sweeping the river is said to be "As one enamoured is upborne in dream / O'er the lily-paven lakes mid silver mist / To wondrous music . . ." (ll. 367–69).

15. "Swift as a spirit . . ." is reminiscent of the *Spirit of Plato (From the Greek)*: "I am the image of swift Plato's spirit, / Ascending heaven; Athens doth inherit / His corpse below," which implies the identification of the sun with a non-natural, in this case spiritual, element. The dichotomy between a natural, historical world and the world of the spirit, though still at work in the poem and allowing for readings such as Bloom's or Rieger's, is here superseded by a different dimension of language. The thematic assertion of this no longer Platonic conception of language occurs in the similarity between Rousseau's and Plato's hierarchical situation in history. This is hardly a condemnation of Plato (or of Rousseau) but a more evolved understanding of the figural powers of language.

16. Lines 33–39.

8. Image and Emblem in Yeats

(For full details, see bibliography for this essay beginning page 315.)

1. *The Autobiographies of W. B. Yeats*, "The Trembling of the Veil," Book V, ii.

2. A possible exception is T. Parkinson, *W. B. Yeats, Self-Critic*, but this study is confined to one single, early revision.

3. Edmund Wilson, *Axel's Castle*, L. MacNeice, *The Poetry of Yeats*, R. Ellmann, *Yeats, the Man and the Mask*, later much qualified in *The Identity of Yeats*, N. Jeffares, *W. B. Yeats, Man and Poet*.

4. A. Mizener, in *Southern Review* (1942), 7(3):601–23, now in Hall and Steinmann, eds., *The Permanence of Yeats*, p. 142.

5. Especially Edmund Wilson, Jeffares, and MacNeice.

6. F. A. C. Wilson, *W. B. Yeats and the Tradition*, and more implicitly T. R. Henn, *The Lonely Tower*.

7. Graham Hough, *The Last Romantics*, and Frank Kermode, *Romantic Image*.

8. Allen Tate, "Yeats's Romanticism: Notes and Suggestions," in *Southern Review* (1942), 7(3):591–600, now in Hall and Steinmann.

9. See Parkinson, pp. 32ff. for examples.

10. Studied by Parkinson, pp. 25ff.

11. Foundation of the Rhymer's Club dates from early 1891. Yeats had been in London since the early spring of 1887, but the poems included with *The Wanderings of Oisin* go back to before 1885. During previous stays in London, between 1867 and 1880, W. B. Yeats is only from two to fifteen years old.

12. Richard Ellmann in *The Identity of Yeats*, chapter on Style and Rhetoric.

13. See S. Ullmann, *Style in the French Novel* (Cambridge: Cambridge University Press, 1957) on the use of inversion in French prose style with the same "distancing" effect (pp. 173ff.). Mr. Ullmann's remarks could apply to English poetic diction as well as to French prose style.

14. Quotations from Yeats's poetry, unless otherwise specified, are taken from *The Variorum Edition of the Poems of W. B. Yeats*, Peter Allt and Russell K. Alspach, eds., hereafter referred to as *Var*.

15. The passage was originally as follows:

> We rode on murmuring. Many a shell
> That in immortal silence sleeps
> And dreams of her own melting hues,
> Her golds, her azures, and her blues,
> Pierced with soft light the shallowing deeps. . . .
>
> *(The Wanderings of Oisin and Other Poems)*

16. Some examples among many follow:

> I'd drive thy woolly sheep,
> If so I might, along a dewy vale,
> Where all night long the heavens weep and weep,
> Dreaming in their soft odour-laden sleep;
> Where all night long the lonely moon, the white
> Sad Lady of the deep, pours down her light;
> And 'mong the stunted ash-trees' drooping rings,
> All flame-like gushing from the hollow stones,
> By day and night a lonely fountain sings,
> And there to its own heart for ever moans.
>
> *(The Island of Statues, Var., pp. 649–50)*

> Yon wind goes sadly, and the grass and trees
> Reply like moaning of imprisoned elf:
> The whole world's sadly talking to itself.
> The waves in yonder lake where points my hand
> Beat out their lives lamenting o'er the sand;
> The birds that nestle in the leaves are sad, . . .
>
> *(Var., p. 652)*

> Go gather by the humming sea
> Some twisted, echo-harbouring shell,
> And to its lips thy story tell,

> And they thy comforters will be,
> Rewording in melodious guile
> Thy fretful words a little while, . . .
> ("The Song of the Happy Shepherd," *Var.*, p. 66)

> The sea swept on and cried her old cry still,
> Rolling along in dreams from hill to hill.
> ("The Sad Shepherd," *Var.*, p. 68)

> But naught they heard, for they are always listening,
> The dewdrops, for the sound of their own dropping.
> (*Var.*, p. 68)

> See how the sacred old flamingoes come,
> Painting with shadow all the marble steps . . .
> ("Anashuya and Vijaya," *Var.*, p. 72, ll. 29–30)

> The island dreams under the dawn
> The great boughs drop tranquility . . .
> ("The Indian to his Love," *Var.*, p. 77)

17. These examples all date from before 1885 and have not been substantially altered by later revision. "The Indian to His Love" went through innumerable changes, but the parrot image appears in this form in the first printed version (*Dublin University Review*, Dec. 1880):

> A parrot swaying on a tree
> Rages at his own image in the dim enamelled sea.

18. Yeats lived in Dublin between 1880 and 1887.

19. Letter to Villiers, *Correspondence 1862–1871*, p. 258.

20. In his youth, Yeats was much less receptive to Wordsworth, partly, no doubt, because Matthew Arnold was anathema to J. B. Yeats.

21. The Yeats-Ellis edition of the *Prophetic Books* was begun in 1889.

22. The poems are so placed as a result of editing, since "The Song of the Happy Shepherd" was originally conceived as the epilogue to the two early verse plays *The Island of Statues* and *The Seeker* (*Var.*, pp. 644ff. and 681ff.). But Yeats grouped the poems together, in obvious and willed contrast, ever since the 1895 edition of *Poems*, and there can be little doubt that "The Sad Shepherd," although originally entitled "Miserrimus" (parallel titles from 1895 on) was written as a deliberate counterpart to the other, somewhat like *L'Allegro* and *Il Penseroso*. The poems are in *Var.*, pp. 64 and 67.

23. "The Song of the Happy Shepherd," l. 54.

24. This poem appears at the beginning of the collected editions from the 1906 edition of *The Poetical Works of W. B. Yeats* on (after a dedication poem). Previous editions had the poems now grouped under the title "The Rose" before those now called "Crossways."

25. *The Letters of W. B. Yeats*, Allen Wade, ed. (London: Rupert Hart-Davis, 1954), hereafter referred to as *Letters*, p. 88.

26. The image reappears in the later work; see, for instance, "The Hero, the Girl, and the Fool" (*Var.*, p. 447).

27. See N. Jeffares, *W. B. Yeats, Man and Poet*, p. 68.

28. *Ideas of Good and Evil* (hereafter referred to as *IoGE*), "Symbolism in Painting," p. 227.

29. For instance, in D. G. Rossetti's "The Blesséd Damozel":

The blesséd damozel leaned out
From the gold bar of heaven;
Her eyes were deeper than the depth
Of waters stilled at even;
She had three lilies in her hand,
And the stars in her hair were seven.

Her robe, ungirt from clasp to hem,
No wrought flowers did adorn,
But a white rose of Mary's gift,
For service meetly worn;
Her hair that lay along her back
Was yellow like ripe corn.

30. His later judgment of Shelley is much more negative: "Shelley was not a mystic, his system of thought was constructed by his logical facility to satisfy desire, not a symbolical revelation received after the suspension of all desire" (*Essays, 1931–36*, p. 58).

31. Yeats alludes to Nerval in "The Symbolism of Poetry" (*IoGE*, p. 252), but this allusion seems to be founded only on a passage in Symons.

32. My italics.

33. Interesting and very Yeatsian contradictions and ambivalences are already apparent in this youthful poem: like Oisin, the heroes are somewhat reluctantly leaving their world for dubious rewards that do not quite seem worth the cost, lured away by an enchantment which resembles love, but makes love impossible.

34. See also *Var.*, p. 670, ll. 101ff.; p. 672, l. 150.

35. See, for instance, "Anashuya and Vijaya" (*Var.*, p. 71, ll. 1ff.), "The Indian to His Love" (*Var.*, p. 77, ll. 2 and 11ff.), "The Lake Isle of Innisfree" (*Var.*, p. 117), etc.

36. *Letters*, p. 110.

37. Russell K. Alspach, "Some Sources of Yeats's *The Wanderings of Oisin*," in *PMLA* (September 1943), 57(3):849–66.

38. *Letters*, p. 87.

39. See G. Hartman, *The Unmediated Vision* (New Haven: Yale University Press, 1954).

40. Notes to the first edition of *The Wind among the Reeds* (1899), *Var.*, p. 810.

41. In the last stanza of the poem "Ephemera," later suppressed, *Var.*, p. 81, ll. 24eff.

42. *Where There is Nothing*, vol. 1 of *Plays for an Irish Theater* (London: Bullen, 1903), p. 122.

43. The expression occurs for the first time in the Prologue to *The Shadowy Waters* (*Var.*, p. 218, ll. 25–26) and recurs in late poems such as "Vacillation" and "A Dialogue of Self and Soul" (*Var.*, p. 502, l. 75, and p. 478, l. 40).

44. *Essays 1931–1936*.

45. *In the Seven Woods, being Poems Chiefly of the Irish Heroic Age* (Dundrum: Dun Emer Press, 1903).

46. Letter to Frank Fay, January 1904 (*Letters*, p. 424). The earlier poem on Cuchulain, in *The Rose*, is conventional.

47. *In the Seven Woods*, p. 25.

48. Mario Praz, *The Romantic Agony* (New York: Oxford University Press, 1952), p. 365.

49. Both Ellmann (in his first book on Yeats, *Yeats, the Man and the Mask*) and Jeffares have helped to popularize the oversimplification of the young Yeats as an irresponsible dreamer, in contrast to the active and socially committed man who, after 1900, undertook the foundation and the direction of the Abbey Theater. This mixture of indolence with an almost feverish public activity is characteristic of Yeats throughout his life, and is never influenced by ethical considerations. The young Yeats, in his twenties, is just as active and public-minded as the middle-aged man, more so, in fact, never tiring of the business and intrigue of literary and theosophical societies. As for the title *Responsibilities*, it suffices to read the first poem in this volume, entitled "The Grey Rock," to see that the "responsibility" is toward the divine, as opposed to the responsibility toward men and country—although the poem is often misread and made to state the opposite of what it states. (See, for instance, G. Brandon Saul, *Prolegomena to the Study of Yeats's Poems*, p. 90, and P. Ure, *Towards a Mythology*.)

50. *The Wild Swans at Coole*, published in 1919, can be considered as the first instance of a volume of poems that is masterly as a whole, although there certainly are examples of perfect poems during the more barren period from 1903 until 1916.

51. See, for instance, *Au.*, p. 371; also preface to *God and Fighting Men* by Lady Gregory (1905), section VII (XIX, XXI).

52. *The Only Jealousy of Emer* and *The Unicorn of the Stars* are other instances of obvious self-dramatization.

53. Players and painted stage took all my love,
And not those things that they were emblems of.
("The Circus Animals' Desertion," *Var.*, p. 630)

54. Identification of Conchubar with the blind man and Cuchulain with the fool is clear from the stage business in the play (the blind man sitting on Conchubar's throne, for instance) as well as from the letter to Frank Fay (*Letters*, p. 424) and a passage in *Wheels and Butterflies* (pp. 102ff.).

55. April 1904, *Letters*, pp. 433ff.

56. Yeats adds, with excessive politeness, "and yours [AE's] nearly always rises" . . .

57. The distinction between joy and ecstasy comes from Nietzsche's *Birth of Tragedy*, where the Apollonian mood of the later drama is characterized as joy *(Heiterkeit)*, achieved by means of a triumph of the will over Dionysian ecstasy *(Rausch)* and the tragic consequences to which this ecstasy leads. (See Schlecta, ed., 1:98, and also p. 184 of this essay.)

58. The introductory poem to *The Shadowy Waters* (*Var.*, p. 217) dated September 1900, and which gives its title to *In the Seven Woods* (in which it does not appear), is probably the first instance of Yeats's "new" style.

59. Other examples of poems starting with a natural setting, by no means a complete catalogue: "A Prayer for my Daughter" (*Var.*, p. 403), "Sailing to Byzantium" (407), "Meditations in Time of Civil War" poem II ("My House"), (419) and VI ("The Stare's Nest by my Window") (424), "In Memory of Eva Gore-Booth and Con Markiewicz" (475), "Blood and the Moon" part IV (482), "Coole Park, 1929" (488), "Coole Park and Ballylee, 1931" (490), "Vacillation" part V, (501) and VI (502), etc.

60. Examples of poems starting with a concrete situation: "Vacillation," part IV

(501), "Meditations in Time of Civil War," part V ("The Road at my Door") (423), "The Municipal Gallery Revisited" (601), "A Bronze Head" (618), etc.

61. A memory from Shelley's "On Life": "The caverns of the mind are obscure and shadowy; or pervaded with a lustre, beautiful and bright indeed, but shining not beyond their portals." See *IoGE*, p. 123.

62. Ellmann, *The Man and the Mask.*

63. Ellmann, *The Identity of W. B. Yeats.*

64. Hough, *The Last Romantics*, p. 259.

65. Kermode, *Romantic Image*, for instance, on p. 89.

66. *Ibid.*, pp. 163–64.

67. Wilson, *W. B. Yeats and the Tradition*, p. 212. Mr. Wilson then goes on to interpret the honey-bees as "the souls of the just," of all details in the Porphyry text perhaps the one least relevant to this poem.

68. Helen Gardner, "Symbolic Equations," in *New Statesman* (February 1, 1958), 55:141, singles out, among others, the line "O honey-bees . . ." for a severe criticism of F. A. C. Wilson and his method; a lively controversy ensued, started off by a reply from Kathleen Raine, coming to the defense of Mr. Wilson (*NS*, February 8, 1958, p. 170). Final replies by Mr. Wilson himself (*NS*, March 1, 1958, p. 273) and Helen Gardner (*NS*, March 8, 1958, p. 305) show the opponents holding firm to their respective positions.

69. The note on "honey of generation," for instance, is at least half helpful and reveals a real source, which would otherwise only be apparent to a reader of Yeats's essay on Shelley, where the same symbol is mentioned and interpreted (*IoGE*, p. 121). But Yeats has a genius for deliberate confusion and loves to parody scholarly precision: the more precise he appears, the less reliable he often is—even quite gratuitously (as when, in a private letter to Sturge Moore, he mentions an article in the *Times Literary Supplement* and gives a detailed but totally false reference. See *W. B. Yeats and T. Sturge Moore: Their Correspondence*, pp. 67 and 194).

70. *IoGE*, p. 121.

71. See, for instance, "The Tower," part III (*Var.*, p. 415, ll. 166ff.) and the story of John Bond in *A Vision* (1937), pp. 44ff.

72. For another, naively explicit statement describing Homer as the first poet to have destroyed, in fact, the genuine tradition because of his "preoccupation with things," see "The Autumn of the Body" in *IoGE*, pp. 301ff. "Homer" is an ambiguous emblem, and Yeats plays on the prestigious authority of the name to mask some of his most destructive statements under a false appearance of positivity. On the relationship between Homer and Christianity in "Vacillation," see pp. 192ff. of this essay.

73. Another, much more obviously emblematic use of the river-cave image appears in a now suppressed early stanza of "Meditations . . ." (*Var.*, p. 420).

74. The theme of "labor" appears clearly in a poem from *The Wind among the Reeds*, which is almost like an early version of "Adam's Curse":

> O cloud-pale eyelids, dream-dimmed eyes,
> The poets labouring all their days
> To build a perfect beauty in rhyme
> Are overthrown by a woman's gaze
> And by the unlabouring brood of the skies: . . .
>
> ("He tells of the Perfect Beauty," *Var.*, p. 164)

75. Joseph Hone, *W. B. Yeats, 1865–1939*, pp. 164–65.

76. Of a similar pattern, with the same value emphasis in *On Baile's Strand*, is Cuchulain's resigned acceptance of mild, domestic women "of threshold and hearth-stone" instead of the wild creatures "none can kiss and thrive, / For they are but whirling wind" (*Plays*, p. 262). See also the poem, "The Arrow," from the same period:

> This beauty's kinder, yet for a reason
> I could weep that the old is out of season.
>
> (*Var.*, p. 199)

77. Kermode, *Romantic Image*, chapters 4 and 5.

78. The title and the general thesis of *Matière et mémoire*, by the philosopher who has rightly been called the theoretician of symbolism, is very revealing here. Bergson was concerned with showing, by what is fundamentally a phenomenological method, that in any given consciousness memory and perception are simultaneously present, while insisting, on the other hand, that they are separated by an essential difference, not of degree but of kind. His theory of memory and perception contains the implicit promise of a reconciliation between the extreme forms of idealism and realism, because it conceives of consciousness as composite, as an entity in which forms of pure materiality and of pure spirituality can exist side by side. The same hope animates the natural image in the romantic tradition. See H. Bergson, *Matière et mémoire* (Paris, 1900). Also V. Jankélévitch, *Bergson* (Paris, 1931), pp. 128ff. and E. Fiser, *Le Symbole littéraire: essai sur la signification du symbole chez Mallarmé, Bergson et Marcel Proust* (Paris, 1941).

79. The specifically Mallarméan attitude being, of course, that the poet should *not* glorify memory, but "know" the exile exactly for what it is: "Pour n'avoir *pas* chanté la région où vivre." The poem is the reverse of Baudelaire's "L'invitation au voyage," but the fundamental pattern of the summer-winter imagery nevertheless remains.

80. "Communiquer substantiellement avec ce qu'il y a de substantiel dans les choses," Jean Wahl, *Traité de métaphysique* (Paris, 1953), p. 73.

81. F. A. C. Wilson (pp. 68ff.) has traced Yeats's source and gives the original text of the myth used by him in full detail.

82. "The Celtic Element in Literature," *IoGE*, p. 279. I omit the part of the quotation that says: "They (those men) worshipped nature and the abundance of nature . . ." because it may create the false impression of a kind of pantheistic pagan rite. In the sequel of the essay, Yeats makes a radical distinction between the "Greek way" to look at nature, as in Homeric pantheism and its romantic imitators, and *his* way, which belongs to a fictional, pre-Homeric world and which is the way of the emblem.

83. This dance recurs frequently, in various forms. One finds it, to take three very different examples, as early as Part I of *The Wanderings of Oisin* (from the 1895 version):

> And in a wild and sudden dance
> We mocked at Time and Fate and Chance . . .
>
> (*Var.*, p. 20)

or in the fin-de-siècle version of a Masonic initiation ritual in the story *Rosa Alchemica* (*Early Poems and Stories*, London: Macmillan, 1925, pp. 494ff.), or, with a strong emphasis on the important god-beast theme, in *The Player Queen* (*Plays*, pp. 415ff.).

84. Cf.:

> An aged man is but a paltry thing,
> A tattered coat upon a stick, unless
> Soul clap its hands and sing, and louder sing
> For every tatter in its mortal dress, . . .
>   ("Sailing to Byzantium," *Var.*, p. 407)

85. Yeats has his own, occult version of the Platonic myth of recollection, and he expounds it in great detail in a long note, later suppressed, on the poem "An Image from Past Life." The note throws a great deal of light on the nature of the reminiscence of Maud Gonne in "Among School Children": "(Robartes distinguishes) between the memory of concrete images and the abstract memory, and affirm[s] that no concrete dream-image is ever from our memory. . . . 'No lover, no husband has ever met in dreams the true image of wife or mistress. She who has perhaps filled his whole life with joy or disquiet cannot enter there. Her image can fill every moment of his waking life but only its counterfeit comes to him in sleep; and he who classifies these counterfeits will find that just in so far as they become concrete, sensuous, they are distinct individuals; never types but individuals. They are forms of those whom he has loved in some past earthly life, chosen from *Spiritus Mundi* by the subconscious will, and through them, for they are not always hollow shades, the dead at whiles outface a living rival' . . ." From the Cuala edition of *Michael Robartes and the Dancer* (Dundrum, 1921), now also in *Var.*, pp. 821–22.

86. Kermode's reference to the poem "The Living Beauty" (p. 84) suggests this interpretation for the difficult passage in stanza 7 ("Both nuns and mothers worship images" till "And yet they too break hearts").

87. See, for instance, the essay on Baudelaire by a disciple of Bachelard, J. P. Richard, *Poésie et profondeur* (Paris, 1955).

88. See note 43 above. An early example, already with the same connotations, appears in *Oisin*, *Var.*, p. 53, l. 96.

89. See her lament at having to abandon Oisin to the world, *Var.*, p. 56, ll. 129ff.

90. It does not follow, however, that because Yeats uses emblems associated with a certain doctrine, he necessarily adheres to this doctrine, especially since his general attitude toward emblems is so equivocal.

91. An overwhelming majority of Yeats's interpreters consider his treatment of the erotic to be positive, and the opinion here expressed appears as a lone dissension—with one notable exception: Margaret Rudd's study of Yeats and Blake, *Divided Image*. Avowedly written from the point of view of a religious conviction most alien to Yeats (Catholicism), it contains a very poor and sketchy summary of the work but, in the concluding chapter, has the great virtue of stressing the fundamental point that Yeats is hostile to the idea of incarnation. However unconvincing the argument that leads up to this conclusion, and although one may not share the author's value judgments derived from it, this reaches closer to the center of Yeats's problem than many overpositive interpretations.

92. A similar confusion between imagery and statement, for the same reasons, occurs in Keats's *Endymion*, although the difference between the theme of love in the two poems helps to clarify Yeats's attitude: the sensual emphasis is distracting in *Endymion*, but it is not totally incompatible with the general development, for erotic love undoubtedly has a place in the hero's progression toward his ideal state; one could say that his (or rather, Keats's) transcendence of the world of the senses is still incom-

plete but not, as in *Oisin*, that the sexual imagery of fulfillment contradicts the renunciation which is explicitly demanded. Keats's intuitive Platonism (if one wishes to call it so) is much more orthodox than Yeats's.

93. Another example is Murrough in the poem "The Grey Rock" (*Var.*, p. 275), who, like Oisin, returns to earth because "He claimed his country's need was most" (l. 101) and scorns the love of the goddess Aoife. However, Yeats contrasts himself and his Rhymer friends to Murrough: *they*, to the contrary, remained faithful to the gods. Cuchulain, in a sense, betrays his divine calling, both in *On Baile's Strand* and in *The Only Jealousy of Emer*, but many other heroes (Red Hanrahan, John Sherman, Forgael, Martin in *The Unicorn from the Stars*, the swineherd and the stroller from the late plays *The King of the Great Clock Tower* and *A Full Moon in March*, etc.) all choose the way of the gods.

94. See, in "Under Ben Bulben"

> Michael Angelo left a proof
> On the Sistine Chapel roof,
> Where but half-awakened Adam
> Can disturb globe-trotting Madam
> Till her bowels are in heat,
> Proof that there's a purpose set
> Before the secret working mind:
> Profane perfection of mankind.

> (*Var.*, pp. 638–39)

95. See Jean Pommier, *La Mystique de Baudelaire* (Paris, 1932), p. 39 and note 97.

96. See also, from "The Song of Wandering Aengus":

> And pluck till time and times are done
> The silver apples of the moon,
> The golden apples of the sun.

> (*Var.*, p. 150)

97. The word has the same meaning in "Among School Children": "Honey of generation had *betrayed* . . ." (*Var.*, p. 444).

98. The autobiographical allusion is, in all likelihood, to Yeats's betrayal of his "divine" love for Maud Gonne.

99. Cf. *Paradise Lost* IV.456ff.

100. We are told that she followed the hound for exactly nine years, possibly a biographical allusion (*Var.*, p. 761, l. 268). Dectora, in all likelihood, is not Maud Gonne but a heterogeneous creation, mostly patterned on Florence Farr, to whom the play is dedicated.

101. See, for instance, "The Lover's Song," "The Chambermaid's First and Second Song," *Var.*, pp. 574–75; "Chosen," p. 535, ll. 10ff.; "Lullaby," p. 522; *A Vision* (1937), p. 52; notice also the recurring oath of the prime minister in *The Player Queen*: "Sleep of Adam!"

102. The later version of the play labors to make this episode more convincing; Dectora remains much more obviously under the magical spell of Forgael's song, even when he develops scruples and doubts, not about his own task but about his right to drag others with him on the road to what he knows to be oblivion. His final decision is attributed to a direct summons, a sign from the gods (*Var.*, p. 247, ll. 524ff., also ll. 564–65). There is a suggestion, too, that Dectora remains closer to a human state of mind, but this is now treated as a virtue rather than a weakness (*Var.*, p. 250, ll.

574–76, 578–81, 583); Aerbrick, too, is given more importance, and his references to the "broken" tree of life and the "scattered" birds may possibly imply a critical attitude toward Forgael's dogged determination (although Yeats's description of the character in a letter to Florence Farr—*Letters*, p. 455—suggest that he is more than ever the villain).

103. *A Vision*, p. 37. All quotations from *A Vision* are from the 1937 edition.

104. *A Vision*, pp. 279–80.

105. See p. 159 above.

106. "Opinion" in this sense ("Opinion is not worth a rush . . .," p. 385) helps to clarify the lines from "The Double Vision of Michael Robartes": "So she had outdanced thought. / Body perfection brought, / For what but eye and ear silence the mind / With the minute particulars of mankind?" To outdance thought is to rid oneself of worldly opinions. Eye and ear, as organs that can grasp pure form, are opposed to mind which, in the sense of "opinion," implies material ties. The reference to Blake is at least half ironic.

107. The exact opposite is the case for Valéry, for whom the shadow is nothingness and whose eyes, instead of being turned toward the reflection, face the sun, affirming the equality of divine and natural light.

> L'âme exposée aux torches du solstice,
> Je te soutiens, admirable justice
> De la lumière aux armes sans pitié!
> Je te rends pure à ta place première:
> Regarde-toi! . . . Mais rendre la lumière
> Suppose d'ombre une morne moitié.

("Le Cimetière marin")

The sun as Eros (in "La Jeune Parque") is the highest divinity in his mythology, while for Yeats the solar fire cleanses man of all erotic sentiment.

108. The poem, as is well known, is addressed to Iseult Gonne who, by forcing genealogy a little (for she was only Maud Gonne's niece), rates as the granddaughter of Zeus and Leda and who, to judge by a drawing that appears in Henn's *The Lonely Tower*, was also exceedingly pretty.

109. F. A. C. Wilson's *W. B. Yeats and the Tradition* provides ample evidence of the manner in which Yeats seems to belong to the Platonic tradition, in opposition to those (certainly easier to refute) who think of him as an affirmative realist. The author had access to Yeats's library and provides highly valuable information on Yeats's knowledge of Platonic and related sources. His conclusion, Yeats's classification with what he calls heterodox mysticism or the "subjective" tradition (as in Yeats's "subjective," antithetical man), seems to be founded on a false distinction. The split in the Western tradition, as Yeats sees it, is not so much caused by the difference between an "outward" and an "inward" God, the former associated with orthodox Christianity, the latter with the hermetic tradition that includes Platonism, as it is caused by the distinction between an incarnated and a totally supernatural God, regardless of whether the incarnation occurs in the object (matter) or in the consciousness of the object (mind). Christianity and Platonism contain elements of both, but, on the whole, the West tends toward an incarnate divinity. Yeats at times considers that Platonism is even more "Western" than Christianity in this respect (while F. A. C. Wilson makes Platonism "tend towards the religions of the East") because it conceives of incarnation as mere copy. When the true element in Christianity emerges, in the revelation

that Christ possesses no human attributes whatever, it occurs in Byzantium, at the closing of Plato's Academy (*A Vision*, p. 279). The *Sophia* of divine wisdom can never have passed through the degradation of the human mind or of matter, and never could God be identified with an extension of the I, no matter how transcendental. The passage from the subjective I to the otherness of the divine always involves, for Yeats, the murder of the I.

110. *A Vision*, p. 40. Yeats has this said by Michael Robartes after he has gone to the East and cured himself of the illusions of his "alchemical" period.

In the poem "The Tower," the rejection of Plato and Plotinus is founded on the belief that the incarnate world (life and death) has no being of its own, because it is a product of the immaterial "soul"; Plato is rejected because of his belief in the reality of the incarnate world:

> I mock Plotinus' thought
> And cry in Plato's teeth,
> Death and life were not
> Till man made up the whole,
> Made lock, stock and barrel
> Out of his bitter soul, . . .
>
> (*Var.*, p. 415)

Memories of Berkeley are of Berkeley the spiritualist, not of modern idealism. To complicate matters, Yeats gives a note where he reveals his source as being Plotinus himself, thus indicating his awareness of the dual nature of Neoplatonism.

111. Cf. the passage from *A Vision* (p. 281) quoted above (". . . all the rest is bird and beast . . .").

112. F. A. C. Wilson thinks Yeats may have found it in Mme. Blavatsky's *Isis Unveiled* (Wilson, p. 266, n. 14).

113. Yeats is also playing ironically on the popular belief that Saint Patrick rid Ireland of the snakes, and thus ridiculing the orthodox Catholic notion of contrition, the possibility of overcoming evil while remaining within the altogether natural process of penance and momentary abstinence. See also, on the same theme, "Crazy Jane Talks with the Bishop" (*Var.*, p. 513). True asceticism is only of value when it accepts full annihilation, like the Stylites willing to "wither to a bag of bones" ("Demon and Beast," *Var.*, p. 401).

114. F. A. C. Wilson gives a very useful set of references for the emblematic sources of this poem (see Wilson, pp. 205ff.), but by isolating the poem out of the dramatic sequence of the series "A Woman Young and Old," he presents as a reconciliation what turns out to be a murder.

115. To the point of a kind of matricidal indifference:

> What matter if the knave
> That the most could pleasure you,
> The children that he gave,
> Are somewhere sleeping like a top
> Under a marble flag?
>
> (Those Dancing Days are Gone," *Var.*, p. 525)

116. A full study tracing the evolution of the emblem "wine" through Yeats's work would be very rewarding.

117. From *Oedipus at Colonus:*

Stranger: . . . Get up from that seat before you ask it. You are in a place where no
             man is permitted to set his foot.
Oedipus: What place? And to what God sacred?
Stranger: A place where none may set his foot, for it belongs to the Dreadful God-
             desses, daughters of the earth and of darkness.
Oedipus: I will pray for them if you tell me their names.
Stranger: We natives call them the Furies, but there are pleasanter names.

                                                                    (*Plays*, p. 522)

       also:

                 Come praise Colonus' horses, and come praise
                 The wine-dark of the wood's intricacies,
                 The nightingale that deafens daylight there,
                 If daylight ever visit where,
                 Unvisited by tempest or by sun,
                 Immortal ladies tread the ground
                 Dizzy with harmonious sound,
                 Semele's lad a gay companion.

                                             (*Plays*, p. 544, also *Var.*, p. 446)

       118. And, of course, Homer, who is linked to Oedipus in Yeats's mind, Oedipus'
death being "an image from Homer's age" (*A Vision*, p. 28).

       119. The same setting, with the same wine emblem, appears in the epilogue poem
to *A Vision*, "All Souls' Night," except that the "sacred wood" of Athens has become
Oxford:

                 Midnight has come and the great Christ Church Bell
                 And many a lesser bell sound through the room;
                 And it is All Souls' Night.
                 And two long glasses brimmed with muscatel
                 Bubble upon the table. A ghost may come . . .

       In this case, too, the revelation contained in *A Vision* is not "for sober ear." Yeats's
Dionysus worship was, at times, fairly literal, and he took great delight in Burgundy.
Had he not already written, in an earlier poem

                 Far-off, most secret, and inviolate Rose,
                 Enfold me in my hour of hours; where those
                 Who sought thee in the Holy Sepulchre,
                 Or in the wine-vat, dwell beyond the stir
                 And tumult of defeated dreams; . . .

                                             ("The Secret Rose," *Var.*, p. 164)

       The allusion is to the Rhymers, Lionel Johnson and Dowson, both converts, wor-
shippers of the Virgin, and notorious drunkards. Dowson's "Vilanelle of the Poet's
Road" (from which Yeats quotes in *Au*, p. 311) is highly relevant to "Her Vision in
the Wood."

       120. Yeats probably has Mithraic rites in mind in his description of Dionysian
orgies in *The Resurrection*, at the death of Christ (*Plays*, pp. 585ff.), where he calls the
worshippers "Asiatic Greeks." Mithraic religion is all male, but, in the same passage
from this play, it is said that "they imitate women that they may attain in worship a
woman's self-abandonment" (*Plays*, p. 586).

121.

> "For she had fiery blood
> When I was young,
> And trod so sweetly proud
> As 'twere upon a cloud,
> A woman Homer sung . . ."
>
> (*Var.*, p. 255)

122. *Var.*, p. 809.

123. In his *Prolegomena to the Study of Yeats's Poems* George Brandon Saul asks: "Lacking Greek, was Yeats likely to insist on the strictly literal meaning of Eumenides?" He apparently did, in spite of his lack of knowledge of Greek, since in his *Oedipus at Colonus* he alludes to the etymology of the term: ". . . Remind them (the Furies) to be good to suppliants, seeing that they are called the Good People, and then pray for whatever you most need . . ." (*Plays*, p. 536). Yeats's Furies, who reappear in the late poem "To Dorothy Wellesley," are not so much the avenging spirits of the *Oresteia* as the divine powers under whose protection Oedipus chooses to die, the carriers of the will of the gods to man.

124. The Christian equivalent would be the "staring virgin" from "Two Songs from a Play" (*Var.*, p. 437), a poem that deals with the emblematic continuity of the Christ-Dionysus myth and is thus very closely related to this poem.

9. Anthropomorphism and Trope in the Lyric

1. Friedrich Nietzsche, "Über Wahrheit und Lüge im aussermoralischen Sinn," *Werke*, Karl Schlechta, ed. (Munich: Carl Hanser, 1966), 3:314.

2. Charles Baudelaire, *Oeuvres complètes*, Pléiade ed. (Paris: Gallimard, 1974), 1.11. Further citations will be made from this edition, identified as *O.C.*

3. See Ovid's version of the Narcissus story, *Metamorphoses*, III, 341ff.

10. Aesthetic Formalization: Kleist's Über das Marionettentheater

1. Friedrich Schiller, *On the Aesthetic Education of Man, in a Series of Letters*, ed. and transl. by Elizabeth M. Wilkinson and L. A. Willoughby (Oxford, Clarendon Press: 1967), p. 300; translation modified.

2. *Ibid.*, p. cxxxi.

3. *Ibid.*

4. *Ibid.*, p. cxxxii.

5. Heinrich von Kleist, "Über das Marionettentheater" in *Sämtliche Werke und Briefe*, Helmut Sembdner, ed. (Munich: Hanser, 1961), 2:338–345. Translations of *Marionettentheater* are available in English, often dispersed in periodical publications; I have consulted several but often found it necessary to stay closer to the original in order to make specific points.

6. *Kleists Aufsatz über das Marionettentheater, Studien und Interpretationen*, ed. Helmut Sembdner, ed. (Berlin: Erich Schmidt, 1967). For a recent critical overview of articles on *Marionettentheater* see William Ray, "Suspended in the Mirror: Language and the Self in Kleist's 'Über das Marionettentheater,' " *Studies in Romanticism* (Winter 1979), 18(4):521–546.

7. Kleist's mathematical references are not always correct and make mistakes unworthy of a gymnasium student. For example, a curved (as opposed to a straight) line could hardly be "of the first degree" (§14). Helmut Sembdner is certainly right in saying that the analogy between logarithms and asymptotes, in §17, is "nicht ganz treffend" (p. 930). The errors may be deliberate, with mystifying or parodic intent. Incorrect details in the mathematical language do not imply however that Kleist's notion of "the mathematical" as a model for aesthetic formalization is arbitrary or aberrant.

8. See, for example, Hélène Cixous, "Les Marionettes," *Prénoms de personne* (Paris: Editions du Seuil, 1974), pp. 127–152, or H. M. Brown, "Kleist's 'Über das Marionettentheater':'Schlüssel zum Werk,' or 'Feuilleton'?" *Oxford German Studies* (1968), 3:114–125.

9. For example:

> "Haben Sie, fragte er . . . haben Sie von jenen mechanischen
> Beinen gehört . . ."
> Ich sagte, nein: dergleichen wäre mir nie vor Augen gekommen.
> Es tut mir leid, erwiderte er; . . .

The lines spoken by C are direct speech, but "Ich sagte, nein" is free indirect speech as is clear from the subjunctive "wäre." Alternations between the two modes of discourse occur continuously throughout the dialogue.

10. *Sämtliche Werke*, 2:1032.

11. "Lettre sur les aveugles," in Denis Diderot, *Oeuvres complètes*, R. Lewinter, ed. (Paris: Club français du livre, 1969), 2:157–233.

12. "Über die allmähliche Verfertigung der Gedanken beim Reden," *Sämtliche Werke*, pp. 319–324.

Bibliography
for Essay 8

A very thorough bibliography of Yeats's works has been compiled by Allan Wade, *A Bibliography of the Writings of W. B. Yeats*, rev. ed. (London: Rupert Hart-Davis, 1958). Numbers listed with the primary source material refer to the corresponding entry in the Wade bibliography.

Primary Sources

In the absence of a comprehensive collected edition, it remains a rather laborious task to read the whole of W. B. Yeats's work. The following list is intended as a selective guide toward a reasonably thorough coverage of Yeats's writings.

Poetry
The Variorum Edition of the Poems of W. B. Yeats. Peter Allt and Russell K. Alspach, eds. New York: Macmillan, 1957 (Wade 211 W). Contains all the published poems, narrative poems (including "The Shadowy Waters"), variants, prefaces to editions of poems, etc. This long-awaited edition has facilitated the study of Yeats's poetry to an immeasurable degree. See also, under secondary works, the entry on George Brandon Saul. American editions generally follow the English ones in Wade's bibliography.

It is useful to consult some of Yeats's books of poetry in their original edition, to observe the "style" of presentation, binding, etc.

Plays

The Collected Plays of W. B. Yeats. New York: Macmillan, 1953 (Wade 211 R).
No variorum edition of the plays is in existence. To obtain an idea of
the changes that may occur in a given play, one can compare, for instance, the version of *The Countess Kathleen* in *Collected Plays* with the
versions of the same play in *The Countess Kathleen and Various Legends
and Lyrics* (London: Fisher Unwin, 1892) (Wade 6); in *Poems* (London:
Fisher Unwin, 1895) (Wade 15); in vol. 3 of *The Collected Works in Verse
and Prose of W. B. Yeats* (Stratford on Avon: Shakespeare Head Press,
1908) (Wade 77); in *The Countess Kathleen* (London: Fisher Unwin, 1912)
(Wade 93); and in *Plays and Controversies* (London: Macmillan, 1933) (Wade
139).

    Aside from the *Collected Plays*, one should consult: *Plays and Contro-
versies.* London: Macmillan, 1923 (Wade 139). Contains some of the articles published by Yeats in *Samhain* (originally *Beltaine*, later *The Arrow*),
the organ of the Abbey Theatre. Important prose-texts on Yeats's conception of the theater.

Wheels and Butterflies. London: Macmillan, 1934 (Wade 175). With important
commentaries.

The King of the Great Clock Tower. London: Macmillan, 1935 (Wade 179A). With
important commentaries.

A Full Moon in March. London: Macmillan, 1935 (Wade 182). With important
commentaries.

Essays

"The Poetry of Sir Samuel Ferguson." In *Dublin University Review* (October
and November 1886).

Letters to the New Island. Horace Reynolds, ed. Cambridge: Harvard University Press, 1934 (Wade 173). Examples of early Yeats articles, written
around 1890.

Is the Order of R. R. & A. C. to Remain a Magical Order? (April 1901) (Wade
33).

A Postscript to Essay Called "Is the Order . . . ." (May 4, 1901) (Wade 34).
    Both last items are extremely rare. Houghton Library has a copy of
the first (Wade 33).

Ideas of Good and Evil. London: Bullen, 1903 (Wade 46).

Discoveries. Dundrum: Dun Emer Press, 1907 (Wade 72).

Vol. 8 of *Collected Works in Verse and Prose of W. B. Yeats.* Stratford on Avon:
Shakespeare Head Press (Wade 82). Contains several essays, including
"The Pathway," not found elsewhere.

The Cutting of an Agate. New York: Macmillan, 1912 (Wade 102). Combines
some of the contents of the two previous items. English edition (London: Macmillan, 1919) (Wade 126) contains "Certain Noble Plays of Japan."

Per Amica Silentia Lunae. London: Macmillan, 1918 (Wade 120). Now also available in a hybrid volume entitled *Mythologies* (New York: Macmillan, 1959).

Essays. London: Macmillan, 1924 (Wade 141). Most comprehensive collection of Yeats essays up to 1924, now superseded by *Essays and Introductions* (London: Macmillan, 1961).

A Vision. London: Werner Laurie, 1925 (Wade 149).

A Vision. London: Macmillan, 1937 (Wade 191).

Essays 1931–1936. Dublin: Cuala Press, 1937 (Wade 191).

On the Boiler. Dublin: Cuala Press, 1938 (Wade 201).

If I Were Four-and-Twenty. Dublin: Cuala Press, 1940 (Wade 205).

Pages from a Diary Written in Nineteen Hundred Thirty-Nine. Dublin: Cuala Press (Wade 207).

Tribute to Thomas Davis. Oxford: Blackwell, 1947 (Wade 208).

Narrative Prose

John Sherman and Dhoya by Ganconagh. London: Fisher Unwin, 1891 (Wade 4).

The Celtic Twilight. London: Lawrence and Bullen, 1893 (Wade 8).

The Secret Rose. London: Lawrence and Bullen, 1897 (Wade 21).

The Tables of the Law and The Adoration of the Magi. London: Elkin Matthews, 1904 (Wade 25).

Stories of Red Hanrahan. Dundrum: Dun Emer Press, 1904 (Wade 59). Stories first published in *The Secret Rose,* considerably altered with the "assistance" of Lady Gregory; later editions of this title follow the present version.

Early Poems and Stories. London: Macmillan, 1925 (Wade 147). The most easily available edition with some of the previously listed stories.

Letters

The Letters of W. B. Yeats. Allan Wade, ed. London: Rupert Hart-Davis, 1954 (Wade 211J).

W. B. Yeats Letters to Katherine Tynan. Roger McHugh, ed. New York: McMullen, 1953.

Letters on Poetry from W. B. Yeats to Dorothy Wellesley. London: Oxford University Press, 1940 (Wade 325).

Florence Farr, Bernard Shaw, and W. B. Yeats. Clifford May, ed. New York: Dodd, Mead, 1942.

J. B. Yeats: Letters to his Son W. B. Yeats. Joseph Hone, ed. London: Faber and Faber, 1946.

W. B. Yeats and T. Sturge Moore: Their Correspondence. Ursula Bridge, ed. London: Routledge and Kegan Paul, 1953.

Important Prefaces and Contributions
Not Included Under Essays
Irish Fairy and Folk Tales. W. B. Yeats, ed. New York: Boni and Liveright (no. 44 of Modern Library).
The Works of William Blake. 3 vols. E. J. Ellis and W. B. Yeats, eds. London: Quaritch, 1893 (Wade 218). Especially the section in vol. 1, "The Symbolic System."
Poems of William Blake. W. B. Yeats, ed. London: Routledge, 1905 (Wade 221).
Literary Ideals in Ireland. London: Fisher Unwin, 1899 (Wade 297).
Ideals in Ireland. Lady Gregory, ed. London: Unicorn, 1901 (Wade 300).
Gods and Fighting Men, by Lady Gregory. New York: Scribner, 1904.
Certain Noble Plays of Japan, by E. Fenollosa and Ezra Pound. Dundrum: Cuala Press, 1916.
Bishop Berkeley: His Life, Writings, and Philosophy, by Joseph Hone and M. M. Rossi. London: Faber and Faber, 1931.
The Oxford Book of Modern Verse. Oxford: Clarendon Press, 1936.
Seanad Eireann (Parliamentary Debates). Vols. 1–10. Dublin: The Stationery Office. Especially Yeats's speech on divorce in vol. 5 (April–November 1925).

Secondary Works: A Selection

Adams, Hazard. *Blake and Yeats: The Contrary Vision.* Ithaca: Cornell University Press, 1955.
Bjersby, Birgit. *The Interpretation of the Cuchulain Legend in the Works of W. B. Yeats.* Cambridge: Harvard University Press, 1951.
Bowra, Sir Maurice. *The Heritage of Symbolism.* London: Macmillan, 1943.
Ellmann, Richard. *Yeats: The Man and the Mask.* New York: Macmillan, 1948.
—— *The Identity of Yeats.* New York: Macmillan, 1954.
Frye, Northrop. "Yeats and the Language of Symbolism." *University of Toronto Quarterly,* 17:1–17.
Hall, James and M. Steinemman, eds. *The Permanence of Yeats.* New York: Macmillan, 1950.
Henn, T. R. *The Lonely Tower.* London: Methuen, 1950.
Hoare, Agnes D. M. *The Works of Morris and Yeats in Relation to Early Saga Literature.* Cambridge: Cambridge University Press, 1937.
Hone, Joseph. *W. B. Yeats.* London: Macmillan, 1942.
—— *W. B. Yeats: The Poet in Contemporary Ireland.* Dublin: Maunsel, 1919.
Hough, Graham. *The Last Romantics.* London: Duckworth, 1949.
Irish Writing, special issue on W. B. Yeats (1955), vol. 31.
Jeffares, Norman. *W. B. Yeats: Man and Poet.* London: Kegan Paul, 1949.
Kelleher, John. "Matthew Arnold and the Celtic Revival." In Harry T. Levin, ed., *Perspectives of Criticism.* Cambridge: Harvard University Press, 1950.

Kermode, Frank. *Romantic Image*. London: Routledge and Kegan Paul, 1957.
Koch, Vivienne. *W. B. Yeats: The Tragic Phase*. London: Routledge and Kegan Paul, 1951.
MacNeice, Louis. *The Poetry of W. B. Yeats*. London: Oxford University Press, 1941.
Moore, Virginia. *The Unicorn: W. B. Yeats's Search for Reality*. New York: Macmillan, 1954.
Parkinson, Thomas. *W. B. Yeats, Self-Critic*. Berkeley: University of California Press, 1951.
Rudd, Margaret. *Divided Image: A Study of William Blake and W. B. Yeats*. London: Kegan Paul, 1953.
Saul, George Brandon. *Prolegomena to the Study of Yeats's Poems*. Philadelphia: University of Pennsylvania Press, 1957. Contains a bibliography and a very thorough list of American (and some British) articles on Yeats, up to 1956.
The Southern Review. W. B. Yeats memorial issue (Winter 1941), vol. 7, no. 3.
Stauffer, Donald. *The Golden Nightingale*. New York: Macmillan, 1949.
Ure, Peter. *Towards a Mythology: Studies in the Poetry of W. B. Yeats*. Liverpool: University Press of Liverpool, 1946.
Ussher, Arland. *Three Great Irishmen: Shaw, Yeats, Joyce*. London: Gollancz, 1952.
Wilson, Edmund. *Axel's Castle*. New York: Scribner, 1931.
Wilson, F. A. C. *Yeats and the Tradition*. London: Gollancz, 1958.

Notes on Permissions

Essay 1 was first printed, in a slightly different French version, as "Structure intentionnelle de l'image romantique," in *Revue internationale de philosophie* (1960), no. 51, pp. 68–84. The translation is the author's, copyright © 1968 by Paul de Man, and first appeared in Harold Bloom, ed., *Romanticism and Consciousness* (New York: Norton, 1970), pp. 65–77. Reprinted by permission.

Essay 2 was first printed, in French, as "L'Image de Rousseau dans la poésie de Hölderlin," in *Deutsche Beiträge zur geistigen Überlieferung* (1965), 5:157–83. The translation, by Andrzej Warminski, was prepared for this volume by permission of the French publisher.

Essay 3 was first presented, in German, as the inaugural lecture for the chair of Comparative Literature at the University of Zürich on January 22, 1966, and was first printed, as "Wordsworth und Hölderlin," in *Schweizer Monatshefte* (March 1966), 45(12):1141–1155. The translation, by Timothy Bahti, was prepared for this volume by permission of the French publisher.

Essay 4 was first printed in *MLN* (December 1979) 94(5):919–30. Reprinted by permission of Johns Hopkins University Press.

Essay 6 was first printed in Harold Bloom et al., eds., *Deconstruction and Criticism* (New York: Seabury, 1979), pp. 39–73. Reprinted by permission of the Continuum Publishing Corporation.

Essay 7 was first printed in Reuben A. Brower and Richard Poirier, eds., *In Defense of Reading* (New York: Dutton, 1962), pp. 22–37. Reprinted by permission.

Essay 8 is excerpted by the author from his Ph.D. dissertation, "Mallarmé, Yeats, and the Post-Romantic Predicament" (Harvard University, 1960).

Essays 9 and 10 were written for this volume but did not receive final correction by the author.

Index

Abrams, M. H., 47
Alspach, Russell K., 174
Aristophanes, 104
Aristotle, 95, 96-97, 102-3
Arnold, Matthew, 83-84, 86
Astrée, L', 101
Auerbach, Erich, 47
Augustine, 10, 101, 102; *Confessions*, 68

Bachelard, Gaston, 2, 7, 14, 37, 205
Bacon, Francis, 95, 96-97
Balzac, Honoré de, *Louis Lambert*, 169, 207
Banville, Théodore de, 247
Barrès, Maurice, 180
Bateson, F. W., 84
Baudelaire, Charles, 7, 155, 162, 168, 172, 200, 204, 205, 207, 208, 214, 225, 273; "Correspondances," 59, 153, 157, 160, 243-52, 253-62, 266-67; "L'Irrémédiable," 160; "L'Homme et la mer," 160-61, 252; "Le Cygne," 198-99; "Rêve parisien," 212; *Les fleurs du mal*, 243, 247, 251, 252, 260; "Elévation," 247; "Obsession," 247, 252-62; "De profundis clamavi," 252; "Les sept vieillards," 260
Béguin, Albert, 48
Beissner, Friedrich, 27, 29, 60
Bergson, Henri, 7
Blake, William, 126, 165, 166, 171, 177, 188, 204; *Prophetic Books*, 155
Boileau, 2
Bonaparte, Napoléon, 23, 101

Böschenstein, Bernhard, 22, 31, 33, 34, 36, 42-43, 44
Botticelli, Sandro, 224, 236
Byron, George Gordon, Lord, 87

Carroll, Lewis, 87
Chateaubriand, Vicomte Francois-René de, 246
Clarke, Samuel, 289
Claudel, Paul, 8, 162
Coleridge, Samuel Taylor, 50, 85
Comyn, Michael, *The Lay of Oisin*, 174
Curtius, Ernst Robert, 47

D'Annunzio, Gabriele, 180
Dante, 103, 247
Delvaux, Paul, 246
De Quincey, Thomas, 79, 83, 86
Descartes, René, 102
Diderot, Denis, 2; *Le neveu de Rameau*, 269, 274; *Jacques le fataliste*, 274; *Lettre sur les aveugles*, 289
Dowson, Ernest, 150, 153

Ellmann, Richard, 188
Empson, William, 2, 88-89, 92

Farr, Florence, 218
Fichte, Johann Gottlieb, 36
Frederick the Great, 97
Frost, Robert, 88
Frye, Northrop, 2

Gautier, Théophile, *Emaux et camées*, 212
Genette, Gérard, 69-71, 240
George, Stefan, 3, 162
Gide, André, 110
Goethe, Johann Wolfgang von, 7; "Grenzen der Menschheit," 37; *Wilhelm Meister*, 145; *Faust*, 206
Gonne, Maud, 163, 164, 181, 196, 197, 203, 223
Gray, Thomas, 72, 77
Gregory, Lady Augusta, 133, 135-37, 141, 143, 181

Hardy, Thomas, 88, 95; "Barbara of the House of Grebe," 93, 100
Hartley, David, 91
Hazard, Paul, 47
Hazlitt, William, 86
Hegel, G. W. F., 244-45; *Phenomenology of Spirit*, 45; *Lectures on Aesthetics*, 253; *Encyclopedia of the Philosophical Sciences*, 288
Heidegger, Martin, 40
Heinse, Johann Jakob Wilhelm, 24
Hellingrath, Norbert von, 19-20, 22
Heredia, José-Maria de, 253
Hermes Trismegistus, 227
Hofmannsthal, Hugo von, 162
Hölderlin, Friedrich, 19-21, 50, 59, 84, 118, 157, 168, 172; "Brot and Wein," 2-7, 15; "Heimkunft," 12-17, 59; "The Rhine," 22-23, 31-44, 61, 63; "Mnemosyne," 23, 45, 59, 60-65; "Hymn to Humanity," 23-24, 25, 30, 34, 41; *Hyperion*, 24-28, 35-36, 43, 206; "An die Ruhe," 25, 27; "An die Stille," 25-26, 27, 29, 45; *Empedocles*, 28, 30; "Das Werden im Vergehen," 28; "Über der Verfahrungsweise des poetischen Geistes," 28; "Über den Unterschied der Dichtarten," 28; "Rousseau," 29-30, 34, 40; "An die Deutschen," 30; "Ermunterung," 59; "Chiron," 59; "Andenken," 198-99
Homer, 97, 102, 134, 136-37; "The Cave of the Nymphs," 139, 142, 190-93
Hone, Joseph, 196
Hough, Graham, 188
Hugo, Victor, 156, 246, 253

Hume, David, *Treatise on Human Understanding*, 38
Huysmans, J.-K., *A rebours*, 180

Johnson, Lionel, 150
Joyce, James, *Ulysses*, 136
Jung, Carl, 166, 192

Kafka, Franz, 284
Kant, Immanuel, 97, 239-40, 264, 279, 284; *Critique of Judgment*, 270, 283
Keats, John, 83, 86, 141, 155, 166, 204, 208, 223; "Hyperion," 117, 125, 175; "I stood tip-toe," 173; "Sleep and Poetry," 173; "Ode on a Grecian Urn," 174, 239; "Ode to a Nightingale," 174; "Endymion," 174-75, 206
Kermode, Frank, 188-89, 197-98
Kierkegaard, Søren, 283-84
Kleist, Heinrich von, "Über das Marionettentheater," 265-90; *Der zerbrochene Krug*, 284
Körner, Christian Gottfried, 263, 265
Krug, Wilhelm Traugott von, 284

Leibniz, Gottfried Wilhelm, 289
Leiris, Michel, 280
Lejeune, Philippe, 71-72
Leonardo da Vinci, 224, 225, 236
Lessing, Gotthold Ephraim, *Laokoon*, 280
Lovejoy, Arthur O., 49

Mabinogion, 200
MacCaffrey, Isabel, 78
Machiavelli, Niccolò, 101
Malebranche, Nicolas, 102
Mallarmé, Stéphane, 3, 57, 145-46, 147, 148, 155, 162, 168, 176, 200, 225; "Un Coup de Dés," 8-9, 15, 176; *Igitur*, 114, 175; "Bucolique," 159; "Le Tombeau d'Edgar Poe," 168; "Hérodiade," 189, 212, 231-32; "Le vierge, le vivace et le bel aujourd'hui," 199; "Autres Poëmes et Sonnets," 207; "Le Pitre châtié," 247
Mann, Thomas, 266
Mantegna, Andrea, 235, 236
Michelangelo, 224, 236

Milton, John, 52, 87, 88, 130, 169; *Paradise Lost*, 64, 117, 215; "On Shakespeare," 75-78
Müller, Ernst, 36
Myers, Frederick, 83

Nerval, Gérard de; 168, 246, 253; *Aurélia*, 207-8
Newton, Isaac, 289
Nietzsche, Friedrich, 20, 183, 239-45, 247, 261, 262; *Genealogy of Morals*, 74; *On Truth and Lie*, 240, 242, 243
Nijinsky, Vaslav, 286
Novalis, *Hymnen an die Nacht*, 207

Ossian, 20
Ovid, 103, 240, 241

Parnassiens, Les, 212, 253
Pascal, Blaise, 250
Pater, Walter, 84, 207, 224, 225
Petrarch, Francesco, 10, 101
Pindar, 31
Plato, 9, 32, 95, 96-97, 102-3, 107, 139, 142, 206, 207, 225-26, 227, 229; *Phaedo*, 104, 136, 137, 140, 203; *Symposium*, 104, 203, 210; *Meno*, 203
Poe, Edgar Allan, 207, 214
Pope, Alexander, 1, 2, 72, 76, 79
Porphyry, 139, 190-92, 194, 195
Praz, Mario, 180
Pre-Raphaelites, 152, 155, 165, 169, 170, 224
Proust, Marcel, *A la recherche du temps perdu*, 69-70

Racine, Jean, 169
Reiman, Donald, 95-96
Revelation, 212
Rilke, Rainer Maria, 162, 204, 266, 287
Rimbaud, Arthur, 7
Robespierre, Maximilien, 23
Roman de la Rose, 110
Ronsard, Pierre de, 169
Rousseau, Jean-Jacques, 19-21, 22-23, 29, 31, 34-35, 37, 40, 44-45, 62, 84, 95-107, 111, 115-16, 118-20, 123; *Julie ou la Nouvelle Héloïse*, 10-17, 22, 25, 27, 28, 41, 44,

69, 101, 120, 206, 274; *Les Rêveries du promeneur solitaire*, 16, 25, 27, 34-40, 42-43, 45; *The Social Contract*, 23, 41, 101, 120; *Confessions*, 68, 102; *Émile*, 270
Russell, George (AE), 219; *New Songs*, 178, 183

Sade, Marquis de, 207
Schelling, Friedrich Wilhelm Joseph von, 52
Schiller, Friedrich, 20, 24, 25, 26, 43, 101, 263, 266, 267, 270, 272, 279, 280, 288, 289; *On Naive and Sentimental Poetry*, 21-22, 23; *Letters on the Aesthetic Education of Mankind*, 263-65
Shakespeare, William, 75-78
Shelley, Percy Bysshe, 126, 155, 165-67, 223; *The Triumph of Life*, 93-123; *Adonais*, 98, 108; "Alastor," 98; "Epipsychidion," 98; *Prometheus Unbound*, 98; "Mont Blanc," 107; "The Cloud," 165
Sinclair, Isaak von, 44
Socrates, 33, 44, 97, 103, 279
Sophocles, *Trachiniae*, 80
Spenser, Edmund, 87, 110, 155, 169; *The Faerie Queene*, 140
Starobinski, Jean, 26
Stephen, Leslie, 85, 86, 87
Stevens, Wallace, 88
Swedenborg, Emanuel, 155-56, 212
Swinburne, Algernon Charles, 150, 155, 180
Symons, Arthur, 150, 153

Tennyson, Alfred Lord, 84, 150, 155
Tynan, Kathleen, 174

Valéry, Paul, 8, 110, 160, 162; "Fragment du Narcisse," 159
Vallon, Annette, 84
Verlaine, Paul, 150
Veronese, Paolo, 186, 209, 224
Villiers de l'Isle-Adam, Philippe-Auguste, Comte de, 207; *Axël*, 196
Virgil, 52, 88, 102, 247
Voltaire, 95, 96-97, 102, 240
Vossler, Karl, 47

Wagner, Richard, *Tristan und Isolde*, 207, 214

Wais, Kurt, 22-23

Weever, John, *Ancient Funerall Monuments*, 72

Wellek, René, 47

Wilde, Oscar, 180; *Salomé*, 189

Wilkinson, Elizabeth, 263, 265, 267

Willoughby, L. A., 263, 265

Wilson, F. A. C., 189-90, 193

Winckelmann, Johann Joachim, 279

Wordsworth, Dorothy, 84

Wordsworth, William, 1, 7, 61, 62, 64-65, 70, 83-89, 92, 95, 96-97, 100, 107, 135, 137, 141, 143, 175-76, 289; *The Prelude*, 11-17, 51-59, 60, 68, 73, 74, 83, 89-92, 121, 125; "Lines Composed a Few Miles Above Tintern Abbey," 41; *Lyrical Ballads*, 50, 52, 127, 151; *Essays upon Epitaphs*, 72-80, 89; *The Excursion*, 72, 73, 80, 83; "The Ruined Cottage," 86; "Ode: Intimations of Immortality," 104; "Composed by the Side of Grasmere Lake," 126-33, 138; Lucy Gray sonnets, 207, 234

Yeats, J. E., 154

Yeats, William Butler, 88, 104, 107, 126, 129, 145-238; "The Statues," 95, 228; "Coole Park and Ballylee, 1931," 133-43, 194-95; "The Wild Swans at Coole," 136, 185, 204; "Blood and the Moon," 137; "Among School Children," 139, 185, 186, 188-89, 197-203, 210, 229; *Ideas of Good and Evil*, 139, 142, 156, 165-67, 170, 171, 195, 200, 205; "Meditations in Time of Civil War," 139, 189-94, 195, 197; *A Vision*, 139, 146, 166, 220-22, 224-25, 226, 233; "Vacillation," 141, 200-1; *Last Poems*, 142, 187, 209; "The Autumn of the Body," 142; *The Autobiographies of W. B. Yeats*, 145; *Poems* (London, 1895), 149, 150; *The Wanderings of Oisin and Other Poems*, 149, 150; *The Wind Among the Reeds*, 150, 162, 166, 167, 169, 170, 172, 176-79, 181, 183, 184-85, 187, 205, 208, 210, 213, 219, 230, 235; *The Countess Kathleen and Various Legends and Lyrics*,

150, 162, 168, 172, 223; *In the Seven Woods*, 150, 179, 181, 184, 196; "The Indian to His Love," 150, 154, 161, 223; *The Shadowy Waters*, 150, 169, 183, 205, 206, 208, 209, 212, 213, 215-18, 222, 224, 230; *The Wanderings of Oisin*, 151-53, 158, 168, 174, 184-85, 187, 197, 206, 209-12, 214, 230; "The Sad Shepherd," 154, 158-59; "The Symbolism of Poetry," 156, 170; "At Algeciras—A Meditation upon Death," 157, 187; "The Song of the Happy Shepherd," 158-59, 161; "Anashuya and Vijaya," 161; *The Island of Statues*, 161, 173, 176, 206; "Ephemera," 162-63, 164; "The White Birds," 162-65, 183, 184, 2203; "The Philosophy of Shelley's Poetry," 165-67; *The Rose*, 168, 179; "Symbolism in Painting," 171; "She Who Dwelt Among the Sycamores," 173-74; "The Man Who Dreamed of Faeryland," 178-79; *On Baile's Strand*, 179, 181-83, 196; "In the Seven Woods," 180; "The Arrow," 180; *Responsibilities*, 180; *The Land of Heart's Desire*, 183; "Adam's Curse," 184, 185, 196-97; "Byzantium," 185, 211, 214, 236; "Supernatural Songs," 186, 226-28; "Michael Robartes and the Dancer," 186, 209, 219, 222, 224, 230, 236; "News for the Delphic Oracle," 186; "A Prayer for Old Age," 187; "Those Images," 187; "The Double Vision of Michael Robartes," 187, 219, 224, 230, 236; "The Celtic Element in Literature," 200; *John Sherman*, 206; *Stories of Red Hanrahan*, 206; "He Hears the Cry of the Sedge," 208; "He Remembers Forgotten Beauty," 208, 219; "He Tells of a Valley Full of Lovers," 208; "He Wishes His Beloved Were Dead," 208, 214; "The Three Bushes," 209; "The Phases of the Moon," 209, 219, 236; *Words for Music Perhaps*, 209; "The Circus Animals' Desertion," 209, 238; *Baile and Aillinn*, 212-13; "The Grey Rock," 213; "He Mourns for the Change That Has Come Upon Him and His Beloved, and Longs for the End of the World," 214; *The Player*

Queen, 218; *The Wild Swans at Coole*, 218; *Michael Robartes and the Dancer*, 218; "Rosa Alchemica," 219-20; "The Hero, the Girl, and the Fool," 223, 230; *Oxford Book of English Modern Verse*, 225; *A Woman Young and Old*, 229, 230; "Her Vision in the Wood," 229-30, 232-37; "Before the World Was Made," 230; "The Chambermaid's First Song," 231; "Chosen," 231; *Oedipus at Colonus*, 232-33; "Crazy Jane and Jack the Journeyman," 233; "A Woman Homer Sung," 234; "Under the Moon," 234;, "All Souls' Night," 236; "Colonus' Praise," 236; *The King of the Great Clock Tower*, 238; *The Herne's Egg*, 238

Zenge, Wilhelmine von, 283-84